The She-Apostle

THE EXTRAORDINARY LIFE AND DEATH OF

LUISA DE CARVAJAL

Glyn Redworth

OXFORD

UNIVERSITY PRESS

OXFORD

UNIVERSITY PRESS

Great Clarendon Street, Oxford OX2 6DP

Oxford University Press is a department of the University of Oxford.
It furthers the University's objective of excellence in research, scholarship,
and education by publishing worldwide in

Oxford New York

Auckland Cape Town Dar es Salaam Hong Kong Karachi
Kuala Lumpur Madrid Melbourne Mexico City Nairobi
New Delhi Shanghai Taipei Toronto

With offices in

Argentina Austria Brazil Chile Czech Republic France Greece
Guatemala Hungary Italy Japan Poland Portugal Singapore
South Korea Switzerland Thailand Turkey Ukraine Vietnam

Oxford is a registered trade mark of Oxford University Press
in the UK and in certain other countries

Published in the United States
by Oxford University Press Inc., New York

British Library Cataloguing in Publication Data

Data available

Library of Congress Cataloging in Publication Data

Data available

Typeset by SPI Publisher Services, Pondicherry, India
Printed in Great Britain
on acid-free paper by
CPI Antony Rowe, Chippenham, Wiltshire

ISBN 978-0-19-953353-4

1 3 5 7 9 10 8 6 4 2

L. E. J.-P.

Acknowledgements

IN telling the story of the extraordinary life and death of Luisa de Carvajal y Mendoza, I have been marvellously assisted by a variety of institutions and individuals, and one example of collegial help stands out vividly in my mind. At a very late stage in the writing of this book, Elizabeth Rhodes amicably challenged me as to why I always called Luisa by her first name, pointing out that men are not normally addressed this way in books written about them. She powerfully brought home the point with a rhetorical question. Who refers to Shakespeare as William? I confess this had never occurred to me, and in my hasty post hoc defence I scuttled to suggest that religious figures, whether male or female, are often called by their first names. Only later did a more authoritative justification come to mind: discarding her illustrious surnames of Carvajal y Mendoza, the subject of this biography herself wanted to be known simply as *Luisa*.

Other debts need to be acknowledged, and I must single out the help of the English College in Valladolid, the University of Manchester, the Catholic Historical Society, the British Academy, and the Arts and Humanities Research Council. Regarding all the individuals who helped during my researches in Belgium, Italy, Spain, as well as closer to home, it has been impossible to thank each one, such is the extent of my indebtedness, but many will find their names in the notes to this book. A singular word of thanks is due to the president of the Patrimonio Nacional in Madrid, don Yago Pico de Coaña de Valcourt, who arranged for Luisa's papers from the Convent of the Incarnation to be made available to me in the Archive of the Royal Palace, where doña Margarita González Cristóbal and her staff showed exemplary friendliness, professionalism, and patience. Two

Peters, Harris and Lake require special mention, as does my enormous debt to the scholarship of four women, Anne J. Cruz, M. Ann Rees, María Nieves Pinillos Iglesias, and, of course, Elizabeth Rhodes.

G.R.

Contents

List of Plates

Picture Acknowledgements

Acknowledgement is made to the following for permission to reproduce illustrations: Archivo Oronoz, Fig. 17; Descalzas Reales-Colección/Archivo Oronoz, Fig. 15; Museo de Bellas Artes Bilbao/ Archivo Oronoz, Fig 11; the Board of Trustees of the Armouries, Fig. 9; Gianni Dagli Orti/Musée du Château de Versailles/The Art Archive, Fig. 16; the British Library Board (all rights reserved 2008, G. 6103 and Sloane 2596), Figs. 5 and 26; Ramon Manent/Corbis, Fig. 29; Guildhall Library, City of London, Fig. 7; José Luis Hoyas, Figs. 20, 21, 22, and 25; Museum of London, Fig. 6; Museum of London Archaeology Service, Figs. 27 and 28; National Portrait Gallery, London, Figs. 14, 18 and 19; Ciaran O'Scea, Fig. 13; Österreichische Nationalbibliothek, Fig. 23; Paisajes Españoles, SA, Fig. 24; Patrimonio Nacional, Figs. 2 and 10; Real Monasterio del Salvador, Madres Brígidas, and Javier Burrieza Sánchez, Figs. 3 and 4; the Rector of the Royal English College, Valladolid, Figs. 1 and 8; Santuario Nacional de la Gran Promesa and Javier Burrieza Sánchez, Fig. 12.

Introduction

The Last House in London

BEFORE dawn one morning in June 1612, an elderly Frenchman took charge of a carriage near Tyburn Field, London's notorious place of execution. Inside was a precious cargo, incongruously wrapped in old sheets. Hired for 10 shillings by his mistress, the carriage skirted the medieval city wall roughly in the direction of the Tower of London. When it reached Finsbury it cut across the fields, heading north for Spitalfields, then a semi-rural community that lay some way from the city proper, out beyond Bishopsgate. At five or six in the morning the Frenchman reached his final destination, a small brick dwelling, the last in London, 'just where the countryside ends'.

A wizened 47-year-old Spanish woman with an aquiline nose was waiting for the carriage. Agitated because it was already light, she hid from view inside the specially installed double doors which gave the house added protection. In attendance were six plainly dressed Englishwomen, each carrying two candles. When everything was ready, and with a cross leading the way, they formed a procession which filed into a tiny chapel. There, with a companion's help, the Frenchman placed his cherished bundles before the altar. What he deposited—and what everyone was risking their lives for—were the freshly mutilated remains of two Catholic priests who had been hung, drawn, and quartered, and then buried three days earlier. No heads were to be found in the jumble of body parts. They were already displayed on pikes at London Bridge.

The architect of this sophisticated operation was doña Luisa de Carvajal y Mendoza. Three days earlier she had instructed the Frenchman to attend the execution and take note of where the dismembered bodies were buried. Drawing upon a large circle of friends and acquaintances, she cajoled a dozen stout fellows into turning up at the dead of night in Tyburn. Only those capable of digging deep down would do as the sheriff's men had intentionally buried the priests' remains below sixteen or more common criminals in compliance with strict orders to prevent the remains from becoming objects of veneration.

Given the complexity of this undertaking, it is astonishing that Luisa had arrived in England only seven years before, at Easter 1605, overflowing with religious zeal, not speaking a word of English.

She had been secretly brought over by a group of English Jesuits who, a few months after her arrival, were to be innocently caught up—or so they claimed—in the Gunpowder Plot. Over the next nine years, Luisa so successfully immersed herself in London's half-hidden community of Catholics that she was able, even as a female, to minister to their spiritual needs and offer practical help. In times of heightened persecution by England's Protestant government, she doled out money to the deserving, distributed banned books, and excavated, preserved, and exported saintly relics. Most of all she provided a secure house for members of the clergy hiding from James I's priest-catchers.

When the new king came down from Scotland to claim the English throne after the first Elizabeth's death in 1603, he inherited a state which was legally empowered to persecute or kill Catholic priests and their lay collaborators. If in theory followers of the old religion were hounded not for their beliefs but for their deeds, this distinction was always blurred in practice. They lived under continuous threat of fine or imprisonment should they attempt to hear mass or in any way practise their religion openly, especially with priests who had been ordained outside of the country. The hopes of English Catholics that the king might be more lenient were speedily dashed. Despite his fine words about love among Christians, James was forced to spend prodigious sums to buy the friendship of the influential men of his new kingdom. The need for easy money soon got the better of him, and, at least for the first half of his reign, sporadic but intense persecution was used to raise money much as it had been under the old queen. Catholics who refused to attend services in the state church were labelled recusants for their refusal to acknowledge the state's religion, being forced to inhabit a community within a community. By acting with discretion they were able to build up a social network out of informal links and friendships. They found doctors who were prepared to visit them when they were sick as well as artisans and builders who were prepared to work for them. As long as they worshipped at the edges of the state's authority—outside city walls or near Catholic embassies—recusants were for the most part able to meet and support each other. They could find like-minded marriage partners and the means to baptize their children according to the rites of the old religion, just as they were able to receive and distribute much needed financial support from their co-religionists on the Continent. Luisa became a capstone of that community. What follows is the story of one of the most remarkable women of James I's England.

Her adventures open up a broader picture of women's lives in Jacobean London and Golden Age Spain, two countries which found themselves on opposing sides after the Reformation had split Europe's states into rival Protestant and Catholic camps. Despite a long-standing resolve to be sent to England, her story raises uncomfortable questions about how far she was in charge of her own destiny. Women at the time had to struggle to make their own decisions, and for all her aristocratic feistiness—and an apparent powerlessness to take no for an answer—her desire to risk death by becoming a missionary in a foreign and hostile land was undoubtedly influenced by men of the cloth. Behind her coming to England was a huddle of priests, usually Jesuits, who had little desire to see mutual toleration take root among the Protestant and Catholic countries of Europe. What lay at the back of their minds was an unspoken expectation that the public persecution of a great Spanish lady might help stymie the attempts by the Calvinist King James to build an enduring peace with Catholic Spain.

More uncomfortable still, Luisa's eagerness to suffer for her beliefs to the point of martyrdom may not be the selfless abnegation of the human will called for by all the world's great religions. Orphaned at the age of 5, she eventually came to live with her uncle, the marquis of Almazán, who subjected her, when still highly impressionable, to grotesque practices involving flagellation and other types of mortification of the flesh. Her story confronts us with the awkward relationship between her abusive childhood and a willingness to risk all in the name of religion.

Of course, lack of information normally makes it unprofitable to do more than raise such repellent issues but Luisa, as will often be the case, is an exception to the rule. By the standards of the early modern world she left behind an astonishing quantity of biographical writing, with almost 180 personal letters surviving, two-thirds of which inform friends in Spain or the Low Countries about why she came to London and what it was like to live there. Because they were written by someone practising poverty, they are full of detailed comments about the practicalities of life in the capital, such as the high cost of housing or the fact that English meat and vegetables looked good but rarely tasted of anything. We even know a lot about Luisa's childhood thanks to the spiritual memoirs she wrote at the behest of her confessors. They probably wanted to know that she was morally strong enough to take on the role of a missionary, something which, before Luisa, had been almost exclusively the preserve of men. They were keen to assure themselves that Luisa was not the sort of woman who would contest male supremacy over the Church. Her fifty surviving poems reveal much about her early years, offering us something of a sideways glimpse into the physical immediacy of her beliefs as their main theme is of a pain which can only be assuaged by martyrdom, a willingness to suffer or even die for her religion. In general, the twists and turns of her life remind us, often in a most disagreeable manner, of the visceral nature of early modern religions and the all-too-human cruelty it spawned.

There is a lighter side too. Never one to miss out on a good argument, the preternaturally cheerful Luisa did not shy away from the company of heretics, and few things gave her as much satisfaction as writing a mischievous pen-portrait of a Protestant whom she has outwitted or who has come to a sticky end. In fact, she positively relished dialogue with those who did not share her beliefs, as one day she found out to her cost in an ugly altercation with the dyed-in-the-wool Protestant shopkeepers of London's busiest shopping street, Cheapside, who were only too willing to drag her off to the local magistrate.

Luisa lived through exciting times, and I shall try to recapture something of what it was like to grow up during an earlier clash of religions, when King Philip II of Spain was fighting a sacred war against the Protestant Dutch and launching a series of *Invincible Armadas* against England. The two countries were soon to be divided when the Pope sanctioned a new calendar (and, in defiance of Luisa, I will use the English calendar after she moved to London). She was an avid reader of lurid tales concerning the first Elizabeth's persecution of her Catholic subjects at precisely the time that reports were rolling in of raids by English sailors on Spanish settlements in the Americas or in the Canaries and the coastal cities of Spain and Portugal. This hothouse world of fanaticism, with its news of calamitous events from all around the globe, along with the intrigue, the flagellation—as well as a desire to offer up her life which just maybe owes a tad too much to the darker side of her childhood—is what shaped Luisa to lead the extraordinary life she did.

I

A Carvajal *and* a Mendoza

LUISA was born on Wednesday, 2 January 1566, in the small hill town of Jaraicejo in the Spanish region of Extremadura near the border with Portugal. Extremadura's broad plains made it suitable for planting wheat but also for grazing cattle and sheep which, in the winter, were brought down from higher ground in the north, near to the province of Ávila. Despite some natural resources, Extremadura was one of Spain's poorest areas but it boasted a petty aristocracy of dons whose ancestors, so they liked to claim, had taken part in the Christian reconquest of territory lost to the Moors after the Islamic invasion of Spain in 711.

Just as with the imaginary character of don Quixote from the neighbouring region of La Mancha, the impoverished nobles of Extremadura saw themselves as Catholic knights, and the European discovery of the New World had provided them with fresh opportunities to conquer and escape their relative poverty. They could satiate a greed for American gold and silver at the same time as parading their valour for the faith. Only a couple of dozen kilometres to the south of Luisa's birthplace lay the town of Trujillo, which was already celebrated for being the hometown of the Pizarro brothers, the conquerors of the Inca Empire in Peru, and further south still was Medellín, birthplace of the greatest conquistador of them all, Hernán Cortés, the vanquisher of the last Aztec emperor, Moctezuma, whose capital of Tenochtitlán he turned into today's Mexico City.

Luisa's highly aristocratic family was markedly superior to the massed ranks of hidalgos, whose sole privilege—apart from an exaggerated sense of their own worth and the right to put *don* before their Christian name—was to leave the paying of income tax to commoners. Her forebears were drawn from members of the titled nobility, including princes of the Church. In Spain, children inherit the surnames of their mothers as well as their fathers, and Luisa was a Mendoza—then among the most prominent of all Spanish aristocratic names—through her mother, María de Mendoza y Chacón, or Pacheco, as she preferred to be called, and who was the daughter of Juan Hurtado de Mendoza y Mendoza, the third count of Monteagudo and the ninth lord of Almazán. Luisa's paternal grandmother was Luisa de Chacón y Fajardo, herself from an illustrious family.[1] Taken together, the various branches of the Mendozas comprised what was easily the most important noble clan in Spain. Among her relatives, Luisa could count the dukes of Infantado, whose renaissance palace in their city of Guadalajara remains one of Spain's architectural jewels, as well as innumerable other dukes, marquises, and other titled nobles.

Her paternal background was barely less prestigious. Born in 1523, her father, Francisco de Carvajal, was the illegitimate son of Gutierre Vargas de Carvajal, a colourful character who was already an abbot three times over when—as it was euphemistically put at the time—he 'stumbled' after developing an intense passion for a great lady from Toledo, herself linked to the Mendoza clan and who was later to marry into the renowned family of the dukes of Alba. The year after Luisa's father's shocking and sinful birth, her grandfather was named bishop of Plasencia, and he owed his rapid promotion in the Church to a mixture of maternal contacts and paternal wealth. On his mother's side, the bishop's uncle was a cardinal as well as being the administrator of the bishopric of Plasencia, whereas his father came from one of Madrid's richest families. At the start of the sixteenth century, Luisa's paternal great-grandfather had sold the Emperor Charles V the Casa de Campo, the great park to the east of Madrid's present-day royal palace. It was, perhaps, from her father's side of the family that Luisa inherited her strong commanding streak. In 1536 her grandfather the bishop had equipped three ships under his brother's command, giving the crew instructions to reach the Pacific by the newly discovered Magellan Straits, which resulted in their becoming the first Spaniards to set foot on the Falkland Islands where they rested for a few days.

Her episcopal grandfather eventually found his vocation, thanks to the future King Philip II, who, as regent on behalf of his absentee father, the Emperor Charles V, appointed him to the Spanish delegation at the Council of Trent, where bishops and theologians were ordered by the Pope to discuss the reforms needed to face down the challenge of Protestantism (and which, as we shall see, were to restrict the types of religious life available to spirited women like Luisa). Bishop Gutierre was overwhelmed by the spiritual energy of the members of the newly formed Society of Jesus whom he encountered at Trent, and coming home from Italy he was fired up with the wish to found a Jesuit college. In 1555 he met St Francis de Borja, Ignatius Loyola's sucessor as head of the Jesuits, and together they agreed he would found a school in his favourite episcopal residence, the town of Jaraicejo.

It was about this time that the bishop was moved to consider his obligations towards Luisa's father, whom so far he had been reluctant to acknowledge. Despite his hesitation, he had nonetheless arranged for him to receive a solid education, which led Luisa to fancy that her father had been 'very learned and distinguished in Latin and Greek'.[2] Though he was legitimized by the crown in 1546, it took the bishop several years before he was prepared publicly to recognize his son, which he did only a few weeks before his death in 1559. In his will he left Luisa's father a large quantity of gold and silver objects as well as clothes and tapestries, but most important of all he left him with a steady income deriving from the rights to the *alcabalas* or local taxes of Jaraicejo. Though not his father's principal heir, Francisco was a wealthy man, capable of making a dynastically enviable marriage with the Mendozas, and apparently he was also left a house. Since the bishop was immensely proud of all he had built in Jaraicejo, there is every reason to believe the local tradition that the dignified house a short walk from his church in the calle de Talavera de la Reina was indeed Luisa's first and only real home.

When Luisa was born it was 'to the great and communal rejoicing of the household'. Her mother had already given birth to five sons but one only had survived, yet her desire for a daughter had been so great that she prayed to a local saint, Peter of Alcántara, for his help in granting her wish. Luisa had an older brother called Alonso, and after she was born four more brothers appeared, Gutierre, Francisco, Enrique, and Juan. Because infant death was so common, it was standard practice to christen children as soon as possible in order to avoid their being cast into the limbo between heaven and hell which was then believed to be the fate of all children who died before being formally admitted into the Church through baptism. High up in Jaraicejo, the winter in 1566 was so cold that Luisa had to wait for what she described as 'fourteen very unhappy days' before she could be taken the short distance to the imposing parish church her grand-father had built, where she was christened Antonia Luysa. The parish register confirms that her baptism took place on 15 January, just as she had been told. Her father selected her first name but it was always by her mother's choice of her maternal grandmother's name that she was invariably known—except when she needed to slip into England unrecognized almost forty years later.[3]

Devoted to her mother, Luisa remembered her as being very beautiful. Later in life she was shown a lock of her mother's hair that presumably had been preserved as a keepsake and which only confirmed what everyone had told her, that her mother's hair had been like fine strands of gold. A precocious child, when her mother was closeted with her most trusted servant, attending to the business of running a substantial household, her daughter would ignore all suggestions that she go out to play with the other children, thereby earning the playful rebuke that here comes little Luisa to give us her opinion and put her little oar in—or spoon, as she put it in Spanish. She copied her mother's generosity to the poor but admitted that she could not be sure whether she did this out of childlike imitation or from the less noble desire to gratify her mother. She was given a money box in the form of a chest which came with its own key and which she always removed, putting it safely to one side. When it was full, she would divide up the coins so as to distribute them among the poor, apparently paying special attention to those in jail. Playfully or not the family's servants would take the key and help themselves to what was in the chest, before watching the old-before-her-time Luisa ponder at how little money there was left inside.

She liked dressing up but not as other children, who are usually attracted to fine or extravagant clothes. Her fascination was with her mother's devotion to the Discalced Franciscan friars, who, as their name suggests, liked to travel around barefooted or in the flimsiest of footwear. The Franciscan house nearby was where her mother liked to hear mass, and when the friars paid her a return visit Luisa would kiss their feet, much to the annoyance of one of her own relatives, a friar of a different order. Why, wondered this Augustinian relative, do you not kiss my feet as you kiss those of the Franciscans? Their feet were of gold and his were not, was her tart reply. In imitation of her favourite friars, she would place a pebble in her shoe so that she would be allowed to walk barefooted, and when she was obliged to dress elegantly she always tried to wear underneath an embroidered Franciscan-style habit—even if it was of the finest brown silk!

Luisa's descriptions of her little games of charity reveal her strength of character but they also make plain how privileged her position in society was, something she could never quite shake off even when she later tried to immerse herself in apostolic poverty. At the age of 4 or 5, her father moved to the ancient city of Léon, the imposing former capital of one of north-eastern Spain's medieval kingdoms. Here she insisted that the poor children from the neighbouring streets be brought to her in their ragged clothes, after which she would ostentatiously place herself in the middle of the recipients of her largesse and dole out the sweet things to eat that she had put to one side from her own meals. When the imperious young Luisa was left alone with her new-found subjects, she would go to a large writing desk of green velvet that housed her trinkets as well as her much-prized dolls—a speciality of the city of Ciudad Rodrigo—and hand them round before the servants could stop her. What gave her most pleasure was to be seated on top of a high table from where she would summon 'all the pages of the household and anyone else that I could muster and have them call me their queen, with all due bowing and scraping, while I distributed amongst them apples, pears, walnuts and chestnuts taken from a basket or a big towel'.[4]

Can we trust what Luisa tells us in her autobiographical writings? There is no hiding the fact that they were composed at a relatively late stage in her life and at the behest of the spiritual confessors who needed to be convinced that the women in their charge were spiritually strong but, more important, knew their place within the male-dominated hierarchy of the Church. It is easy to dismiss spiritual autobiography as 'a highly ritualized rite of passage more than spontaneous self-expression'. The suggestion is that they are an accretion of hand-me-down clichés designed to depict the subject as an example of model, archetypal, and certainly unreal piety.[5] Of course, many similar examples of female religiosity are to be found in women's spiritual autobiographies but this may only be because saints' lives were so avidly read at the time. When Luisa was growing up, they were a staple of the publishing industry in much the same way as celebrity lives are popular today—though with the difference that the lives of the saints were meant to serve as practical models for a wholesome life. A story similar to Luisa's imperious summoning of poor children can certainly be found in a contemporary best-seller, the 1558 edition of the life of the medieval royal saint, Queen Elizabeth of Hungary. But does this degree of similarity mean that we must dismiss Luisa's childhood memories out of hand? Given the circles in which Luisa was brought up, it would be surprising only if she did *not* model her behaviour on the edifying stories which would certainly have been read aloud on numerous occasions by her mother and the women who later brought her up. The essential thing is that in religious autobiographies, individual character still manages to shine out, and it is Luisa's temperament that is recognizable in her memoirs, not the queen of Hungary's. There is a world of difference between the gentle St Elizabeth's wanting to be called mother and Luisa's high-handed desire to be fêted as a queen. Similarly Luisa's memoirs precisely locate her own social milieu in the Spain of the Golden Age, as it can be taken as read that St Elizabeth would not have had the expensive dolls that came only from the city of Ciudad Rodrigo. The same applies to Luisa's admission that she copied her mother's practice of avoiding being seen at windows or in doorways. The story crops up in the lives of many female saints, but to suggest that this is merely a literary convention obscures the fact that her mother probably *did* act out what was universally accepted as the appropriate way for a woman, especially a devout one, to behave.

Strangely, to deny the uniqueness of spiritual autobiographies is a subtle means of playing down the ability of early modern women to achieve a degree of independence. It can too easily be used to make a political statement for our day, where the reiteration of how females were oppressed in earlier times is transformed into a tool for reminding us to continue the struggle in the present. Laudable though these sentiments are, this is a misuse of the past as it diminishes the real achievements of early modern women. No reasonable person can doubt that patriarchy held sway, but Luisa and Elizabeth of Hungary (along with Luisa's near contemporary, Teresa of Ávila) are very different and admittedly highly individualistic examples of how females, if they were rich or fortunate enough, could from time to time subvert patriarchy's rules and lead active and distinctive lives, which is precisely why Luisa's story is important.

Judging by her own writings, her early life was exceptionally happy. Being the only girl among four or five boys, she was probably spoilt by her parents if not by her siblings as well. The death at the age of 4 of a younger brother, Francisco, seems to have troubled her, as she remembered him in the will she drew up just before setting out for England thirty-five years later. She was, however, prone to repeated bouts of illness, prompting her fretful mother to say that, if Luisa ever made it to 10, she would see to it that she joined a nunnery. The decision to move to the colder and more extreme climate of León played havoc with her health, inducing a series of fevers that caused her to be placed on a cot in her mother's room. During one of the occasions when her daughter was ill, doña María was visiting a poor man in the grip of typhoid fever, and although she eventually buried him this was not before she had contracted the disease herself.

Luisa recalled that her father had far less time for religion than her mother, and, given his own father's reluctance to recognize him, it is no surprise that he made a point of dressing in such a way as to stand out as a man of quality. Luisa made a point of insisting that he was not so shallow as to veer towards undue extravagance in the way he dressed, and he cared enough for her mother that when he heard of his wife's illness he rushed to her bedside, only to find her lapsing in and out of consciousness. She died on 1 January 1572, the day before Luisa's sixth birthday, and her father, despite turning to the Church for consolation, followed her twelve days later, dying from the same typhoid as his wife. Forty years later Luisa counselled her eldest brother to put his trust in the Society of Jesus, reminding him of how much its members had done to ensure their father's salvation.[6]

Despite his premature death, Don Francisco de Carvajal had seen to it that generous provision was made for his children, with his only daughter being no exception. She was to receive the very generous sum of 12,000 ducats if she married but only 2,000 ducats if she became a formally professed nun. Simple though these arrangements may seem, they were later to cause a protracted estrangement from her eldest brother when he tried to withhold payment. Her father had also stipulated that before she was 12 years of age she was to go to a nunnery while she deliberated over whether or not to marry.[7] Till then, she was to live with doña Petronila Pacheco, the marchioness of Ladrada, a relative on her mother's side, someone whom, judging by the few references to her, Luisa barely knew. Instead another of her mother's relatives came to the rescue.

The Carvajal orphans—'the oldest of all five was 10 going on 11 years old' being Luisa's tight-lipped remark[8]—were despatched to Philip II's new capital of Madrid, where one of her father's executors lived and where her great-aunt, María Chacón, resided. A formidable character, her great-aunt occupied a place at the very heart of Castilian society. Her son, Bernardo de Rojas, was about to start his dazzling advance through the ranks of the Spanish ecclesiastical hierarchy, as after being made a canon of Seville Cathedral, he was to go on to be inquisitor general, and cardinal-archbishop of Toledo, finally becoming the cherished benefactor of Miguel de Cervantes, the author of *Don Quixote*. María Chacón was in a position to offer her great-niece a home because she was governess to Philip II's brood of young children, and, in particular, to the infant crown prince, Fernando. Luisa was to live a pampered life in the heart of Madrid, at the Royal Convent of Discalced Nuns.[9]

Spanish culture delights in paradoxes. The Descalzas Reales, was, like the Escorial, a religious house as well as a royal palace. Relatively unchanged to this day, it is from the outside an undistinguished building with high walls made of earth-coloured brick and a terracotta roof. Inside are cloisters for the nuns and an ornate chapel that opens onto the street. This convent-palace was established by Philip II's formidable sister and sometime regent of Spain, Princess Juana, the only woman in history ever to have been admitted to the Society of Jesus, although this was too closely guarded a secret for Luisa ever to have known. The princess-regent had proven too influential for the Jesuits to brush aside her request to affiliate to their order, and in 1554, under the pseudonym of 'Mateo Sánchez' and in circumstances of the most absolute confidentiality, she was grudgingly permitted to take the vows of a probationary member of the Society. It is unlikely that Luisa ever saw the royal Jesuitess in the nunnery she founded, as the princess was being nursed in the Escorial for the illness which eventually killed her just a year after Luisa had been orphaned.[10]

A more significant royal figure was the Infanta Isabel Clara Eugenia, who would be regent of the Netherlands throughout the time Luisa lived in England. Three girls all of virtually the same age were now living next door to the nunnery. Isabel was born eight months after Luisa, on 25 August 1566, and her sister, Catalina Micaela, appeared a little over a year later.[11] The heir to the throne, the Infante Fernando, was 1 year old when Luisa came to live with his sisters and he developed a particular fondness for the new arrival, apparently developing a need for her to be present before he would settle down. The princesses' room led directly into the convent, where Luisa recalled having plenty of 'aunties and other relatives' but family links did not prevent her from making a great deal of noise as she raced around in the cloisters with the infantas. In their more sedate moments they would play at dolls or just dress up. Although her years in the Descalzas were to number among the happier times of her life, Luisa still acutely felt the loss of her parents. When she had completely recovered from the fevers she had caught in León, she would find a secret part of the monastery-palace where 'all alone I mourned and wept over their early deaths'. She was also subjected to a religious discipline which set her apart from her royal playmates.[12]

Her father had stipulated that she remain in the day-to-day care of a trusted family servant, Isabel de Ayllón. Luisa adored her. On one occasion, when she was ill again, she told the servant that she would be sorry to die because she was too young to leave her anything. Though Ayllón thought her young charge confessed far too much for someone of her age, she began to teach her to pray in the new Jesuit-inspired fashion for mental or imaginative prayer. In return Luisa protected her from the dark rumours which were circulating in the palace that she was unnecessarily severe and would reach for the rod every time there was a minor infraction. Luisa suffered her beatings in silence for Ayllón's sake, though looking back on her time in the palace she did not think she had been a particularly naughty child. She claimed she could recall no more than a dozen or so sins. Sermons might be missed or meat eaten on a day when the Church decreed that only fish should be consumed, though once she stole some coloured pictures which had caught her eye. These were probably from a work of religious edification, as she liked to pretend she never cared much for romances of chivalry, those books telling of deeds of derring-do populated with heroic knights errant who rejoiced in such romantic sobriquets as Amadís of Gaul or Primaleon of Greece.

After four relatively happy years, life in the palace came to an abrupt end. In 1576, while Philip II's new queen, Ana of Austria, and the rest of the royal family went to the Escorial, María Chacón was ordered to take Prince Fernando on his first royal engagement, a public entry into the city of Toledo, some 40 kilometres south of Madrid.[13] He sat on her lap as they were carried in a litter but tragically she developed a chill and died. It must have felt to Luisa as if she had been orphaned all over again. Now there was no one to prevent her from being placed in the care of her mother's brother, the marquis of Almazán.

It did not occur to anyone to ask the 10-year-old Luisa her opinion about her future. Had they done so, they would have found that, entirely predictably, she wanted to cling on to the life she had become accustomed to in Madrid, though later she would pretend this was really because Ayllón relished life in a palace. Her father's executor made his decision without consulting anyone apart from María Chacón's son, Bernardo de Rojas, and certainly without waiting to ask the little princesses about what should happen to their playmate.[14] Following her great-aunt's death, Luisa was temporarily handed over to an elderly great-uncle while he arranged for her to go to live in the household of her mother's brother, the marquis of Almazán, and soon she set out for the sparsely populated province of Soria, to the north-east of the Madrid. She went to the town of Almazán, where she remained for the next few years, apart from a brief interlude in the isolated village and castle of Monteagudo.

It was to be some time before the marquis took daily charge of Luisa. Along with his wife, he was in residence at the court of the Holy Roman Emperor as ambassador to Philip II's Austrian cousins. In her uncle and aunt's absence, Luisa was sent to live with the marquis's younger daughters, who had been left behind in Spain. A semblance of continuity was provided by Ayllón's reassuring presence, and Luisa would always remember her old nurse fondly. In a letter she wrote in London two years before her death she fondly recalled what her old nurse used to say. 'Laziness, my child, never got anyone anywhere.'[15]

While waiting for the marquis to return from his tour of duty in Prague and Vienna, Luisa inhabited another renaissance palace, one that was larger than the Descalzas Reales. Dominating the main square of the town of Almazán, the front of the palace abutted the church dedicated to St Michael, and at the back the arches of its long open gallery looked out over a steep drop that fell away to the river Duero. When lessons were over, as she recalled in an unusually lyrical passage from her autobiography, she and her cousin María were free to

go out to the fields and riverbanks along the Duero, which are absolutely delightful, and with such abundant wildlife on the lovely hills that the little birds and deer would come out and cut across us right before our very eyes, and the rabbits would run hither and thither, and the hares jumped out when we least expected it, something which happens all the time there.[16]

About nine months after Luisa had left Madrid, Francisco Hurtado de Mendoza and his wife returned to Spain, probably in October 1576.

Luisa claimed she cried for joy at being with them, but her uncle could stay only a few days before he had to travel on to report to the king, leaving behind his wife, to take charge of the new household. Whether he had any interest in looking in on Luisa's brothers, who were left behind in Madrid, we do not know.

The marquis eventually established an intimate relationship with his 13-year-old niece. So close did they become that, when distinguished visitors came to pay their respects, he would order Luisa to hide behind a curtain until they had gone. Her feelings of closeness can be gauged from something she wrote in the earliest of her letters to survive. In 1598, six years after his death and while she was living as a recluse in Madrid, Luisa announced her intention of giving away all her possessions, including the portrait of her beloved uncle, whom she gladly acknowledged as her intercessor in heaven.[17]

The marquis was attracted by her fearsome intellect. She would listen for hours as he explained the mysteries of the Christian religion, claiming that it was through sitting on his knee as he read devotional material that she acquired her good knowledge of Latin. It was her aunt the marchioness who had started her off, though Luisa loyally claimed she never got much beyond the nominative case before her uncle's return from Madrid. The marchioness also made sure that she could read and write her native tongue to a very high standard, arranging for her to be taught the arithmetical skills required of a great lady who might one day be left in charge of an absent husband's estates. That Luisa received such a good education is not surprising as Spain was in the vanguard of female aristocratic education. In large measure this was down to the strenuous efforts of Luis Vives, a close friend of Erasmus, who earlier in the century had championed women's education and who, in an early instance of headhunting, had been brought over to England by Henry VIII's first wife, Catherine of Aragon, to oversee the education of their daughter, the Princess Mary. Though she is better known to history as 'Bloody Mary', Mary and her half-sister Elizabeth were both outstanding examples of the short-lived fashion of educating girls as much as boys in the classics as well as modern languages.

Considering the easy intimacy which grew up between Luisa and her uncle, it is puzzling that she had not gone to live with his family earlier. Certainly that is what he had hankered after, and several times after his sister's death he had demanded in writing—'hizo mucha fuerza por carta'—that Luisa be handed over to him. She had cried at the thought of being taken away by her uncle, and she remembered Chacón's reply word for word. 'Don't be afraid, my child, no one will take you away from me, because I won't let them.'[18] Did María Chacón know a family secret? Luisa's uncle was obsessed by mortification of the flesh.

2

Blessed Discipline

FROM its earliest days, Christianity despised the human body and the temptations that came with it. This was not merely a rejection of the religion of ancient Greece and Rome, with its voluptuous myths about the hedonistic living of the gods on Olympus and their shady sexual dealings with mortals on earth. The Old Testament story about the Garden of Eden was centred on a denunciation of all that was sensual. Adam had been tempted by Eve to eat the Forbidden Fruit, and it was their expulsion from Paradise which led them to be ashamed of their own bodies. In the Gospels, Christ himself had gone for forty days into the wilderness in order to subject his body to every kind of deprivation and torment, and by the time of the Desert Fathers in the second and third centuries it was taken for granted that the inflicting of pain upon the body was purgative of sin as well as an inducement towards spiritual intimacy with an almighty God. From his monk's cell in the eleventh century, Peter Damian called it the Blessed Discipline.

Golden Age Spain viewed mortification of the flesh as part and parcel of religious life. Not only was it a sign of devotion, it was also considered a method of reaching ever greater holiness. It could range from relatively innocuous practices, such as fasting, to beatings which were intended to draw blood. It goes without saying that these so-called 'religious exercises' must be viewed in the context of an age when acute physical pain was commonplace and could rarely be relieved. It is not hard to imagine mortification as a means of blocking out an uncontrollable pain with an even greater one over which the individual had some element of control. Indeed, there was a degree of 'lifestyle management' involved in suffering and an element of fashion was surely involved. For example, the *disciplina* or whip given Luisa by her uncle when she was barely 14 years old was made from silk and was clearly not intended to inflict much suffering, yet this prompted Luisa to steal a silver clasp from one of her grown-up cousins to ensure the whip would cut into her flesh.

On the surface, Luisa's uncle, Francisco Hurtado de Mendoza, was a conventional Christian. His father had been universally regarded as a saintly man who had turned his back on worldly goods. Don Francisco succeeded his father as fourth count of Monteagudo, being elevated in 1575 to the rank of the first marquis of Almazán by that most pious of monarchs, Philip II. This was a reward for having held the sensitive post of ambassador to the Viennese branch of the Habsburg family for six years—King Philip's sister, María, was married to the Emperor Maximilian—and on the 44-year-old marquis's return home in 1576 he was promptly promoted to the immensely powerful Council of State.[19]

Of average height, possessed of sparkling eyes but extremely pale, the marquis was the epitome of a Spanish gentleman. In a society obsessed socially and legally with purity of the blood, a white skin was taken to suggest that he numbered neither Jews nor Moors among his ancestors, as well as confirming that he had never laboured in the fields.[20] He spoke clearly and without affectation, and Luisa liked to believe he tried hard to reconcile himself with his enemies, though she allowed he had many. She remembered him as very even-tempered but tellingly let slip this was not invariably the case. Luisa can be forgiven for thinking he was 'the most experienced and important minister the king had' but the Venetian ambassador in Madrid knew otherwise.[21] Accepting that he was 'molto gentile e trattabile' ('a real gentleman and approachable'), he reported how the marquis's appointment as viceroy of one of Spain's ancient kingdoms after only two years in Madrid was a sideways move, designed to remove a councillor who had failed to live up to expectations.[22]

While serving as a regular member of the royal council the marquis was obliged to spend most of his time in Madrid. Even when Philip II went to live in the Escorial, the various royal committees carried on meeting in the old royal palace which looked out over the river Manzanares to the park which Luisa's great-grandfather had sold to the Emperor Charles. In her uncle's continued absence, Luisa was left to carry on her relatively carefree life for another two years in Almazán, where her nurse provided a last link to her parents. Ayllón was allowed a great deal of leeway in caring for Luisa. The marchioness did not care for the nurse because she was jealous of her closeness to one of her own daughters, and they kept out of each other's way. This rivalry may be the reason why it was left to Ayllón to teach Luisa the social courtesies expected of someone of her rank. She kept her obsessively clean, not just her clothes but her hands and face as well, and the strictness she had previously demonstrated in the Descalzas Reales now bordered on the fanatical.

Ayllón was fixated about what Luisa might do in bed—or have done to her, perhaps—and she would not allow her to sleep on her left side, fearful that harmful humours might reach the heart. Her concern was not quite as fanciful as it sounds, since early modern medicine was based on the idea that the human body was conditioned by four vapours or liquids that made one predominantly sanguine, choleric, phlegmatic, or melancholic. In fact, it was believed that vapours from the genital area could even reach the head, causing a woman to become hysterical, a term that has its origin in the Greek word for womb. Curiouser was that she made Luisa

fold my arms across my chest in the form of a cross, and she would then pull my nightdress down to my feet and make a crease in it between my knees, and in the summer she would sew up the sheets on both sides, for my health and my modesty.[23]

Long before her uncle's return from Madrid, Luisa experienced 'shame and mortal embarrassment' at catching sight of her naked body.[24] Romantic love was shameful, her nurse drilled into her, and she was ordered not to listen to tales of love. Required to stand up straight, she was forbidden from leaning on anything for support for fear that her nurse would mockingly reprimand her by saying, what more would you do if you were 80 years old? If she did step out of line, 'my arms paid for it'.[25] Luisa's bruises were probably caused by a stick, as Ayllón had given up lashing her once she ceased to be a child. Just as she had done in the royal convent in Madrid, she kept quiet about her nurse's harsh punishments. Her aunt the marchioness was not a woman who approved of beatings.

There was a more considerate side to Ayllón, and, sharing the family's preference for members of the Society of Jesus over the regular parochial clergy, she continued to encourage Luisa to persevere with the newfangled meditative prayer. This way of praying was popularly associated with the founder of the Jesuits, St Ignatius Loyola, and it placed less emphasis on recitation of formal prayers or praying with a rosary; it stressed instead the need to imagine the anguish of Christ and the saints as if one were actually witnessing their torments. One of the singular features of Luisa's temperament was that suffering always gave her a sense of relief. As she contemplated Christ's last hours in Jerusalem her experience was not one of great agitation but of 'great tranquillity, rapture, and deep consideration'. Luisa later became an enthusiastic teacher of this method, passing on her ardour for mental prayer to the marquis's youngest daughter, who was almost exactly the same age as Luisa.

Many years later Cousin María recalled the words Luisa employed to set the mood for a prayer about Christ's time in the Garden of Gethsemane, just before he was to be betrayed by Judas: 'Consider the noises of the night and the great quiet and silence of that place, and Our Lord, amidst so much anguish, praying.'

In September 1577 the two girls took their first communion together in the parish church of San Miguel, which was attached to their house in Almazán. The 11-year-old Luisa's spiritual imagination had become so vivid that she trembled as she climbed the many steps leading up to its high altar, while all the time she and her cousin pondered the eternity of pain and glory, rather as St Teresa of Ávila and her brother, Juan, had done when they were children. In the opening chapter of her autobiography, Teresa related how she and her brother delighted in saying that pain and glory endured evermore, and how they were thrilled by chanting the words, 'for ever, and ever, and ever'. Luisa's recollection was characteristically far more wordy and melodramatic, with her and her cousin saying: 'For more than ten times a thousand years and twenty times a thousand there will be no hope of an end, and even that is nothing, not even many times a million. How frightful!'

This passage has been described as 'probably an echo of Teresa of Ávila's life story'. Tall trees cast long shadows, but the saint's model of female spirituality was not the only one available in the sixteenth century.[26] Born in 1515, Teresa was a professed nun and undoubtedly the greatest monastic reformer of her age. Before her death in 1582 she had founded reformed houses for women (and occasionally for men) which would henceforth be strictly cut off from the outside world. In recognition of the matchless quality of her spiritual writings, she was named in 1970 the first female 'Doctor of the Church' by Pope Paul VI. Her cheerful autobiography was circulating in manuscript from the late 1560s, and some of her printed works found their way into the marquis of Almazán's extensive library; but returning to the similarities between what Luisa and the saint wrote, they may just as well be coincidental as this is precisely the sort of remark that any intelligent child might make.[27] There are also profound differences between the two stories. Teresa was not pining for the eucharist but referring to an infantile wish for spiritual adventure in the Moorish kingdoms of North Africa. As far as we can tell, Luisa's desire for martyrdom in foreign lands would not begin to crystallize until she started coming into daily contact with her uncle.

The marquis became the dominant person in her life sometime after February 1579, when he took up the largely honorific position of viceroy of Navarre, a medieval kingdom that had only lost its independence to Spain sixty years earlier. A rump state lingered on north of the Pyrenees until it was absorbed by France in 1589, and to this day Navarre retains some vestigial constitutional privileges within modern Spain. The new viceroy summoned his entire family to live with him in the angular and fortress-like (and recently gloriously restored) palace in the capital, Pamplona, gathering around him his son and heir, Francisco, his married daughters, Luisa and Isabel, along with Francisca, who became a Carmelite nun. He also sent for his youngest daughter María and Luisa, her playmate.

The move northwards to Pamplona came shortly after Luisa and her faithful nurse parted company. Ayllón's mother had died, and although she needed to claim her inheritance in person, she hesitated, waiting for the right moment to break the news of her impending departure. Luisa found out about her nurse's loss in a letter from her brother, Gutierre. Ayllón offered to stay on but Luisa insisted she had to leave, consoling her with the words that she was not to worry about the pain that would be caused by their being separated only for a while. Ayllón may have returned if only briefly but Luisa recalled that, once she had moved to Navarre, the love she had felt for her nurse was transferred to her uncle. A few years later, in 1580, she promised her old nurse 100 ducats if she were ever to enter a nunnery.[28]

The marquis rapidly looked upon Luisa as his own child. In the will he drew up in Pamplona, four years after becoming viceroy, he recorded how she had treated him with 'much more of a daughter's love than a niece's'.[29] Luisa in turn acknowledged she was his 'hija muy del alma', his soul-daughter.[30] Nevertheless, the ways in which he expressed his concern for her soul are controversial and deeply troubling.

The marquis was a long-standing supporter of the Society of Jesus. On his deathbed, his father had advised him to seek spiritual consolation from the Jesuits and the future marquis went on to become one of 'those most attached to the Company'.[31] The early admirers of the Jesuits' Spanish founder, St Ignatius Loyola, claimed he personally practised a high degree of self-mortification, but according to S. J. Ganss, the modern authority on the detailed rule laid down by Loyola for his followers, 'the manner of living is ordinary. It does not contain any regular penances or austerities which are to be practised through obligation.'[32] Loyola reasoned that assaults on the body would hinder the Jesuits' *raison d'être*. First and foremost they were missionaries, with the task of converting Protestants or bringing pagans to Catholicism; instead of being placed under the authority of local bishops, as most members of other religious orders were, Jesuits were to be ready to go at a moment's notice wherever the Roman pontiff might send them, be it 'among the faithful or the infidels'. This explains why Jesuits were not expected to take charge of a parish as that would tie them down, and it also clarifies a section in Loyola's rules entitled 'The preservation of the body', where he obligated his followers to speak to their superior (or send him a note if he were forgetful) concerning anything which they needed to make the body healthy, be it food, clothes, or accommodation. In other words, Loyola maintained that excessive mortification of the flesh would impair his clergy's physical ability to undertake without delay a papally ordered mission, and though members of the Company were not forbidden from practising mortification of the flesh as their tastes and the dictates of their conscience led them, it played little formal role in the Jesuitical life.

All the more perplexing, then, that such a devoted follower of the Jesuits as Luisa's uncle should have inflicted on her what to us—and possibly even to her—was a shocking degree of physical penance. Once settled in Pamplona, he began to 'exercise' her in an exceptional way which she was the first to admit 'went against my natural condition, I being then only fourteen years of age'.[33] Her uncle selected as her tormentor a female servant whom he could trust not to breathe a word to his wife about the mortifications and whippings that were being unleashed. These secret sessions often took place in a clandestine chapel. The door would be locked and the servant would adopt a severe expression. Luisa would kneel down naked to the waist. She had only a piece of fabric under her chin to cover her breasts, itself an ordeal for someone so ashamed of her body. Then she would be lashed with a whip made from lute strings for as long as her tormentor felt she could bear. This was no mere ritual. Luisa remembered 'the blows as so well dealt that sometimes I could hardly withstand them'.[34]

On other occasions Luisa was subjected to a ritualistic imitation of Christ's scourging by being

tied to a column that was constructed specifically to this end and my feet on the cold ground, and a hemp rope at my throat, with the ends being used to tie my hands and wrists to the column. Sometimes I could tell how many blows of the whip there were because that very person counted them in a way that I could hear. And I recall that sometimes there were one hundred and at times fifty or more, and it seems to me that there were never fewer. And I think they many times exceeded a hundred, but I can't be sure, because my memory of it is hazy. The pain, as I said, was not little, nor the chill that entered my bones on the very cold days of winter, because the ground was very cold.

As if matters could not get worse, the marquis directed a yet more merciless servant to take over the tormenting of his niece. Luisa's recollections are studded with remarks which indicate how Juana tested her religious equanimity to the full. With her 'usual imperiousness', the new woman ordered Luisa in January 1581 or 1582 to go down 'to a lower, very secret, oratory'. She was expecting one of her by now 'ordinary' whippings where she would kneel down to be lashed on the back, though this session proved to be more painful than usual and when it was over she was made to kiss her punisher's feet. Some days later the first servant summoned her for another whipping but on seeing the condition of Luisa's back, she ordered

me to get dressed again because my back was not ready to take any more whippings than those that were already apparent, and she was amazed that Juana ... had gone so far as to mistreat me like that. And when I went to pick up my dress, I caught sight of my shoulders, the part that I could glimpse by turning my head, all black and blue and covered with welts.[35]

One of Juana's specialities was to tread on her victim while she lay on the floor, and in unusually revelatory detail even for Luisa, she recalled how, while she was being verbally abused, Juana would

put one of her feet on my chest, right in the middle. And since she had on a very heavy shoe with a double sole and let herself press too hard, I felt a great pain inside my chest and all around, so great that had she not quickly let up, I thought my health would be seriously damaged.[36]

Her confessor at this time was a Jesuit, and according to what she revealed to Inés de la Asunción, her closest companion before she left for England, the priest had caught an inkling about what was going on in the palace, broaching with Luisa the subject of why she never brought up the subject in confession. 'Sir,' she replied, 'I don't have anything to confess, as I've always thought the ones who put me through such trials are acting in good faith.'[37]

That Luisa was a willing participant in her mortification cannot be denied. During Lent she was whipped on her uncle's orders three times a week, on Tuesdays, Thursdays, and Saturdays, but on the remaining days it was her own decision to flagellate herself, just as it was she who decided to wear a hair shirt for longer than her uncle stipulated. But the fact that Luisa wholeheartedly embraced these practices cannot be allowed to mean that she was capable of making an informed choice. Orphaned for most of her life, she was easily prey to an overwhelming sense of guilt and terrified of committing a mortal sin. A grave transgression, knowingly undertaken, constituted a mortal sin, and it could lead to eternal damnation if not confessed and rectified, and mortification was viewed as a means of spiritual protection. Luisa's terror at the prospect of being sinful so overwhelmed her that she likened it to having a horrible serpent swallow her alive, body and soul. Nor was she helped by her uncle's startling warning. There was not sufficient water in the ocean to cry over a single mortal sin, he told her, just as there was not enough time in a long life to regret it.

Even when he was not at home, her uncle never lost a need to exercise control. If he went away for the day on the king's business, he would lock her up in the darkest parts of the palace, only releasing her on his return. Sometimes he would forget, which caused her aunt to become angry when she discovered what was going on behind her back. On other occasions he simply denied her permission to relieve herself.

An especially chilling event took place in a little village due south of Pamplona, where the marquis's family went to escape the pressures of city life. A place to pray was set up at the end of a very long corridor, and when everyone else had gone to bed, Luisa went there to whip herself in secret. One evening the entire family was walking in the gallery, each going about their own business. Luisa was at the far end, reflecting on her sinful nature, but as she looked out on a tall almond tree she saw an apparition in the form of a white shadow as big or bigger than the tree. Distressed, Luisa anxiously went to kiss her uncle's hand before going to bed. Noticing her agitation, he wanted to know what the matter was before insisting she went back, there and then, to confront what she had seen. She tried to wriggle out of this by pretending it was only her imagination but he seized her by the arm, and despite her protestations he made her return. She again saw the apparition but this time her uncle was with her and he claimed that he saw the same thing. Luisa went to bed, but after a couple of hours or more—perhaps when his wife and the rest of the household were fast asleep—she was woken up on her uncle's orders and sent back to the corridor where she was to whip herself. She knew her flagellation had lasted two hours as she timed it with her fifteen-minute hourglass, but she added that since she had apparently been all alone in the dark corridor it felt as if it had only lasted half an hour, the usual length of time that she whipped herself. In the opinion of the coolheaded Inés, what Luisa endured at her uncle's hands in Pamplona exceeded 'all the limits of reason'.[38]

Was this sexual abuse? It is easy to jump to salacious conclusions about the hidden motives of the marquis by assuming that he derived an illicit pleasure from tormenting his niece. No less reductive would be to avoid this issue by timorously citing all the sixteenth-century spiritual writers who advocated physical punishment as a means of coming closer to God. No amount of historical information will prove what was going through the marquis's mind as he ordered Luisa's beatings, but what we are entitled to consider is whether her treatment was disproportionate according to the accepted standards of the age.

Despite a reputation for religious excess, there was a robust body of common-sense opinion in Golden Age Spain which held that mortification of the flesh could easily get out of hand. The distinguished American Hispanist Elizabeth Rhodes was the first to point out that, in his dictionary of 1611, the great Spanish lexicographer Sebastián Covarrubias propounded the following definition of penance. When it was 'done under the appropriate circumstances, God unites the said penitent's blood with His and gives him courage and merit. But those who whip themselves out of vanity are abominable foolish priests of Baal.'

Similarly there was a feeling that penitential practices were private, or at least should not involve members of the opposite sex. In 1563 concerns were raised in Castile's parliament about friars who entered nunneries 'carrying out for themselves the penances which they give to the nuns'. The deputies in the Castilian Cortes requested that these punishments should be meted out only by the abbess or her female representatives, with no men being present.[39]

The evidence that Luisa's penance was performed for her uncle's secret observance is entirely circumstantial. But why else would Luisa be woken in the middle of the night or very early in the morning, when the rest of the household was asleep, and be whipped or made to walk from room to room 'naked and with a noose around the neck', if the marquis did not intend to listen or watch?[40] Whether he realized that what he was subjecting her to was improper must remain a matter of conjecture, and, as St Augustine said, the mind can always lie to itself. What is clearly heartbreaking is that Luisa appears unwittingly to have revealed in her autobiographical writings a considerable degree of unease about what was done to her.

'Come ye children, hearken unto me: I will teach you the fear of the Lord.' The psalm *Venite filii audite*—from which this quotation is taken—was unsurprisingly favoured by her uncle and he used to chant it to his family and servants.[41] Yet he was never able to inflict his more extreme religious practices on his daughters, who instead preferred to ridicule them, taking courage perhaps from their mother who did not approve of her husband's predilections. Corroboration for Luisa's claims about the family's unease comes from an impeccable source, the reminiscences of the marquis's devoted daughter, Isabel. Shortly after her death a book was published which set her up as model of Christian femininity and in which the author repeated a number of stories that she had told him which suggest that, in the back of her mind, she was less than comfortable with her father's habits. Insisting he was a highly religious individual, his daughter confessed that he whipped himself so much that his back was nearly always covered in welts. Once, when he was ill with fever he had insisted on taking punishment, which forced her mother to explain that, in his condition, what he had in mind 'would not be penance that would appease God but rather would offend him'.[42]

Reading between the lines, it seems that the marquis and his wife were virtually living apart, coming together only for meals. The marchioness, doña María de Cárdenas y Tobar, was in fact one of Luisa's interminable cousins in her own right, and she kept her distance from her husband and also from her children and the other members of the household, preferring to busy herself in distant galleries writing letters and supervising the large viceregal household. Though Luisa lavished praise on her for her charitable visits to the sick, she also found her 'harsh and unyielding'.[43] At dinner she would come out with snide remarks about her niece's excessive devotions until the marquis demanded that they be allowed to eat in peace, and he conceded that much patience was necessary to deal with what Luisa obliquely referred to as her aunt's 'way with words and her temper'.[44] In a telling phrase, Luisa said that in the matter of religiosity the marchioness could not satisfy her husband, and one of the things that seemingly drove them apart was her aunt's disapproval of beatings of any description. She objected to the visible bruising which could be seen after Ayllón's heavy-handed treatment, something which caused Luisa to remark, with her indefatigable cheerfulness, that her aunt had only noticed 'the least of it'.[45]

The tensions within the family shine out in her uncle's firm instruction that Luisa was to keep what was done to her a secret 'and not to say a word to her aunt or her cousins'. Covering up for her uncle meant that to the rest of the family she appeared devious.[46] For instance, she made a point of asking his permission to leave the palace when her aunt indicated she should go to the shade of a nearby grove, but he would usually say no, which puzzled Luisa and annoyed her relatives, because it was invariably the case that a child, especially a female child, should be under the authority of women. Luisa resolved the issue by telling herself that her uncle was a sort of spiritual superior to be obeyed above all others.

The relationship with her uncle has been said to illustrate the 'perfect submission' that is 'the founding principle of modern domestic abuse'. There is much truth in that statement, as it is not hard to discern in Luisa's own recollections—the only direct sources of information we have—not just unease but an undercurrent of resistance on her part. When the marquis probed her innermost feelings by asking her to describe her sufferings, she felt uncomfortable. As she put it, 'my uncle used to say I was at fault in hiding too much my inner feelings, what I did for penance, and my spiritual exercises', and she owned up to revealing the least she could get away with, preferring to keep what she called her 'treasures' to herself.[47]

One place where she did reveal her treasures was in her poetry. She started to write verse only a few years after these incidents began, and her poems are infused with memories of what she had undergone. Modern critical theory treats poetry in starkly analytical terms and from an ideological point of view which is ill at ease with early modern religious zeal, as is clear when Anne J. Cruz writes that, in her poems, Luisa assumes a 'fictive persona', slipping

in and out of character, creating a defence against painful memories that also serves as a linguistic tool with which to convert the past into poetic imagery. She can then project her suffering onto the persona of her poems, transforming her past experiences into spiritual desire.[48]

Put in a different way, one of Luisa's most memorable poems describes what she believed were her inner feelings on the love of God:

> *¡Ay, si entre los lazos fieros*
> *que a mi gloria aprisionaron*
> *por mi libertad, yo viera*
> *enlazar mi cuello y manos!*[49]

> Ah, if only I could see,
> among the savage bonds
> that imprisoned my glory
> for my freedom's sake,
> my neck and hands bound tight!

This short poem ends when Luisa says that it is through religious suffering that she is set free, Christlike, from her sins.

> Oh, how a thousand times happy
> is that life of a thousand bloodstained sacrifices
> and blistering holocausts
> which offers itself to you, my Christ

> Showing through what is possible
> how impossible it is for that deep love,
> in any way or shape
> to be satisfied,
> or your immense love be repaid.

Her poems provide a link between what she went through in Pamplona and her desire to offer up her life for her religion. This is a connection which we will have to probe later, but we must remember that not everyone who is abused as a child develops a desire to become a martyr. Speculation about her uncle's motives and the effects on her development soon becomes otiose, not least because there is only so much reliance we can place on her personal recollections—the only direct source we have—to help us make sense of her teenage years. Victims often defend the indefensible by clinging to the belief that their tormentors have their best interests at heart. This was perhaps the case when, two years after her arrival in England, she tried to persuade one of her priestly superiors that mortification had been the 'seed which landed in my heart, and which was nourished and helped to grow by various extraordinary exercises of tearful mortification'.[50] Of course, the alternative for Luisa in not coming to her uncle's defence would have been to risk shattering *all* her beliefs, familial as well as religious. This leads us into a paradox. If we take it upon ourselves to disregard her own understanding of what was done to her, we would be accusing the marquis of robbing her of a normal childhood yet, in the next breath, we would become ourselves guilty of denying her the freedom to give shape to her life.

In his stimulating survey of early modern martyrs, Brad S. Gregory has suggested that, if the objective is to understand prospective martyrs rather than to judge them, any account that does not listen to what they say 'fails utterly to comprehend them, the character of their actions, and the basis of their lives'. What Luisa suffered was unquestionably bizarre and quite possibly perverse, yet from these cruel experiences she was able to create a sheet-anchor for her life, one where her sense of purpose embraced the fact that her life might be extinguished by enemies of her religion. Luisa had not been rendered irrational or browbeaten by what was done to her. All Christians of the time, whether Catholic or Protestant, agreed that a desire to be a martyr was a principled calling. Along with all fellow believers, she was consciously operating on the assumption that she would be exchanging a temporary life on earth for everlasting life in heaven.[51]

From her tribulations Luisa emerged with her strength of character intact and fully in possession of every social skill necessary to persuade hard-nosed men of the cloth to let her travel to England, where she would achieve things previously unimaginable for a woman. Out of her ordeals she salvaged something which at least *she* thought brought her closer to the divine.

3
Toledo Street

TALL and slender, with pretty eyes that varied in the intensity of their colour from blue to purple, Luisa was growing into a highly desirable young woman. Her eyebrows were well defined and her large forehead had the fetchingly high hairline that was much prized at the time. Her mouth, if on the small side, possessed ample, sensuous, lips. Admittedly she was 'a little eagle-like' in appearance, as her prominent nose was slightly crooked but overall her face was elegantly framed by rich hazelnut-coloured hair that cascaded the length of her body whenever she sat down. The question of a suitable husband for such a prepossessing and well-connected young woman could not be put off for much longer.[52]

To her utter astonishment her uncle favoured her marrying, contradicting her presumption that she was obviously 'mixed up with so much mortification' that no one could take her seriously as a bride.[53] Marriage also ran contrary to her father's wishes in as much that he had decreed in his will that, before she was 12, she should enter a convent to test any vocation. Perhaps the marquis had his own grubby reasons for not wishing to see her disappear for ever into a nunnery. Given her well-developed horror at seeing herself naked, she was barely able to contemplate matrimony herself regardless of whether it might be on the terms of the saints of old, where husband and wife took separate vows of virginity, and lived together as brother and sister in separate rooms.

Along with adolescent insecurities about who was the most attractive, the issue of marriage soured relations between Luisa and her cousins. Later in life, María—her contemporary and with whom she had innocently played along the banks of the river Duero—admitted she was jealous of how pretty Luisa was and how everyone admired her slender figure.[54] Inés de la Asunción told the story that on one occasion her cousins threw a silver candlestick at her, which, if it had hit her on the head, would have killed her.[55]

Luisa's disgust at the thought of matrimonial intimacy provided her cousins with the cruellest of ammunition for their infantile games. They all slept in the same room, and in the summertime Luisa prepared for bed wearing only a simple nightgown which meant that it was hard for her to run out of the room with the necessary degree of modesty if she annoyed her cousins, as often happened if they became bored with playing the clavichord or when her incessant prayers began to grate. To ridicule her, a pretend marriage contract was drawn by her cousins which included 'all those matters of modesty and decency they saw I was particular about'. The terms of the contract hints at a deep resentment towards Luisa's oddly close relationship with their father. It stipulated that for six months of the year Luisa was to remain at her uncle's beck and call, and during the rest of the time, when she was supposed to be with her husband, the married couple would have to keep to separate rooms, 'without any further relations or dealings'. Mostly Luisa bore her cousins' petty torments patiently, but at other times she admitted how more than once she was forced to flee their shared bedroom without a thought for how little she was wearing.[56]

'Coarse, cold and ugly' is how she would have us believe she found all men, expressly including those who were normally taken as being very handsome.[57] Her uncle worked on her by arguing there was a tremendous need for good people like herself to prove that matrimony could exist side by side with a holy life, and when she was 15 or 16 years old, a caballero or knight of the lay religious order of Santiago showed a particular interest in her. Quite probably this was García de Carvajal, a first cousin on her mother's side, who was certainly a suitor for her hand some ten years later. Her position in society gave her a shield. She told her uncle that her admirer was indeed 'reasonably well off', but if she were to travel down that route she would expect a great deal more money than that! Her uncle was forced to agree she could do much better.[58]

Martyrdom rather than marriage was on her mind by the time she was 17 years old at the latest. To die for the faith would give her 'the greatest satisfaction imaginable and huge delight'.[59] Regardless of whether the humiliation suffered at the hands of her uncle meant that the contemplation of her own annihilation alone offered the prospect of a release from suffering, the plain fact is that she was far too young to have much influence over her destiny. She was still living with her relatives, without whose approval she would be unable to decide on her future spiritual life.

Matters came to a head in 1588, when Luisa was 22 years old and around the time King Philip was launching his first armada against England. Her uncle was recalled to Madrid to preside over the Council for the Military Orders and she and the rest of the family moved into his very grand house off Madrid's principal street, the calle mayor, on the main ceremonial route between the royal palace and the puerta del sol, already one of the city's main meeting places. The house had earlier belonged to a nephew of Cardinal Cisneros, the great Church reformer from the time of Ferdinand and Isabella, and it still survives today albeit in much altered form. In Luisa's time, it was a palatial town house with various balconies leading off the principal rooms overlooking the plaza de San Salvador, then the city's 'most important civic space' and now known as the plaza de la villa.[60] Towards the top of the house and along the length of the building ran an external gallery, and above this was a warren of rooms with two small towers at either end.

Madrid had been Philip II's capital for only twenty-five years, and it would not be granted its own bishop till the nineteenth century and so to this day it is not officially accorded the title of city. For the marquis, his return to the 'town and court' of Madrid allowed him to boost his ties with the Society of Jesus. The Company, as it was already known, was trying hard to establish itself at the heart of Spanish society and it would soon be responsible for commissioning some of the finest buildings in an as yet singularly unimpressive capital. In May 1588 the marquis wrote to his daughter Isabel in Pamplona, where she had remained with her husband, Luis Carillo de Toledo, who had been appointed interim viceroy in his father-in-law's place. He related his delight that the Jesuits had brought the consecrated bread and wine to his house and told him he could keep the Holy Sacrament—the very body and blood of Christ—for as long as he wished. He wanted his daughter and her husband to know this 'because he knew they would be pleased to hear of his contentment'.[61]

Despite her uncle's deep religious zeal, Luisa's request that she be allowed to live a solitary life of 'true and perfect poverty' fell on deaf ears.[62] It was one thing for a person of her status to live out a life of poverty within a nunnery. That was institutionally sanctioned by kings, popes, and bishops, and correspondingly offered no threat to public decency. But for a woman to live a life of poverty *in public* was a scandalous rejection of the female need for male protection. When the subject was broached with her uncle, he naturally tried to steer her thoughts towards testing life in a properly constituted nunnery; after all, one of his elder daughters Francisca—the one from whom Luisa had stolen the clasp for her whip—was already taking her vows. But Luisa had decided much earlier on that a cloistered life was not for her, and so, 'since I wasn't going to be a nun', and because she could not wait any longer, 'I separated myself as best I could from any dealings with my uncle and aunt and all my relatives'.[63] Perhaps Luisa turned her back on monasticism because she was too much of an individualist to countenance living in community, and certainly it tests the imagination to see her actually taking orders from another female. In all probability she feared that the dull routine of conventual life would put paid to any opportunity to suffer real pain for Christ.

A compromise was grudgingly reached. In the attic above the upper gallery there was sufficient room for her to live apart. It was only a tentative step towards a life of poverty. She was still reliant on two or three maids—along with a male servant for decency—but at least she was able to stop wearing the elegant clothes associated with her rank, and all this could be done without publicly compromising her uncle's reputation as a provider for his womenfolk. She was already 25 years old when, in the summer of 1591, this new life began to take shape. Preserved among her papers is a carpenter's receipt dated 7 June from Bartolomé Fernández for the sum of 237

reales or a little under £6 in English money of the time, at the going
rate of 40 *reales* to one pound sterling. A derisory sum today, it was the
equivalent of a month's wages for a large working family. Twelve
items appear on the list:

1. framing 2 large portraits and the image of Our Lady
2. 6 images made of pine
3. 3 small images framed in ebony
4. 1 small image of St Francis varnished
5. 2 small images
6. 3 flower containers
7. 1 wooden frame
8. 2 small shutters and a running bench
9. 1 large shutter
10. preparing 1 desk with seat
11. 1 ivory cross
12. 2 lecterns

Inés de la Asunción was one of the three or four servants who were in
attendance on Luisa and her recollection of these new lodgings was that
her mistress 'lived a more pinched life than she was used to before then'
but it was still not sufficient.[64] As is clear from the monies lavished on her
apartment, Luisa found herself enjoying a still far-too-comfortable life.

Luisa's semi-independent existence was interrupted by her uncle's
death, just over a year later in December 1591.[65] In the will he had
drawn up in Pamplona, Luisa was left the ivory cross which very
possibly her carpenter had installed in her lodgings (and which she was
later to bequeath to the Jesuit college she paid for in the Spanish
Netherlands). The death of her beloved uncle revived her determination to live out a self-sufficient life, and her ambition was assisted by
the death of her aunt six months later. In one of her autobiographical
fragments, Luisa accepted that their deaths meant that for the first time
she felt herself 'completely alone and free to seek, without further
hindrance, the disdain and neglect that comes from following Christ
that my soul so greatly desired'.[66]

Luisa was not always entirely straightforward in her descriptions of
how she left the family home. Her aunt was not prepared to see her set

up house alone without a fight, and she tried stopping her 'with all possible force'.[67] It was plain to her that if Luisa lived independently vicious tongues would blame the family (and her late husband) for not providing for her. The marchioness tackled head-on the threat to move out:

Child, you are to do no such thing, and if by any chance you don't wish to obey me, I shall leave this house and take myself into yours. I esteem the wishes of the marquis very much indeed. How much more should you, whom he treated as a daughter.[68]

On one occasion Luisa was so exasperated that she blurted out to Inés that, though she wished her aunt a long life, it was now up to the Good Lord to remove any obstacles she faced.

With the marquis dead, her mother's last surviving brother, the priest Gonzalo Chacón, intervened between aunt and niece to offer a way out. If she would not marry or become a nun, she should come to live with him, but he died shortly after her aunt, which convinced Luisa that it was divinely ordained that she should depend entirely on God and no one else. She still harboured hopes that her brother, Alonso, might aid her financially but 'old rivalries and enmities resurfaced in the hearts' of those around her and she decided not to worry about money and set out to live in solitude, even though it was 'within the limits of the Babylon of Madrid'.[69]

Luisa found her banks of the Euphrates on the far side of the plaza mayor. Though not far in distance from her uncle's house, the calle de Toledo was a world apart from the aristocratic milieu she was leaving behind. This congested street fell steeply away from the old city, lying beyond the extension to the Arab walls undertaken by Christian rulers in the twelfth century. The surrounding area was peppered with brothels and taverns, and rumour had it (and still does) that tunnels led to and from the royal palace to allow members of the royal family to take anonymous delight in the vices on offer. The Society of Jesus had established itself in the street, partly because it was close enough to the court but also because it was on the main road south that led to Spain's ecclesiastical headquarters, Toledo. It was also a cheap area to acquire property.

In 1594 Luisa took over a one-storey hovel from the Jesuits. Its only positive feature was that it was next door to the church of St Peter & Paul, which the Company had occupied for thirty years. The site is now occupied by a far more magnificent church which was completed, some years after Luisa's death, with money left by Philip II's sister, the Empress María; once built, this new church was intended to serve the school that the Jesuits finally set up in 1603 and which would be called the Imperial College in honour of their illustrious benefactress. Luisa's new home was the result of an intervention by her cousin, the new marquis, who asked a Jesuit confessor to find somewhere for her to live, and the house was handed over in return for a promise to pay 1,000 ducats or around £250. According to a receipt dated January 1603, 300 ducats had been paid over, with the remaining 700 still outstanding. Perhaps she was allowed to take over the house on the condition she would pay off the remaining amount when she received the inheritance mentioned in her father's will.[70]

Luisa did not embark on her religious experiment alone. Three or four servants moved with her, among them Inés, who was to remain at her side for the next eleven years. She has left a most vivid account of Luisa's life at that time. The house had no upper rooms and everything was damp. There was nowhere to receive guests. Visitors had to make do with two broken-down seats as Luisa and her companions preferred to sit on the floor or in hammocks. Unlike her well-equipped attic, there was not even a writing desk, although there were three or four pine caskets for her private papers and those belonging to her little community. The mattresses were rudimentary and the pillows stuffed with straw, with horse-blankets being used to keep warm. Eating off metal plates, they survived in the beginning on bread which they had to tear apart with their own hands and on salt which they ground between two stones. The only luxuries were two or three images and some fabrics to adorn their oratory or private chapel. In her wonderfully blunt fashion, Inés said, 'if she had less she'd have had nothing'.[71] Later, during one of Luisa's recurring bouts of sickness, her companions noticed that her mattress had turned mouldy. They took advantage of her semi-delirious state to carry her to an adjacent house which had a room above ground level.[72]

Long hair in women indicated virginity as well as eligibility for marriage, and Luisa's lengthy hazelnut-coloured hair, already turning 'silver at the roots', was unceremoniously chopped off to symbolize the new life on which she was embarking.[73] She had already taken to wearing the small veil that partially covered her face and which would attract notice in England. All in all she affected garb of almost ostentatious poverty, with earth-coloured tunics of rough wool, and brown shoes or black sandals. Since she shied away from anything that was akin to fashion or 'worldly style',[74] the local lads were quick to call her 'the mother of all witches'.[75]

She was trying to recreate life within a convent on a microscopic scale while simultaneously preserving her right to go out into the world. Her companions were told of her hope that their humble home would be 'a strict house', following the same withdrawn life and rule as in the more exacting nunneries.[76] Naturally enough, the rules were to be of her own devising. She insisted on no longer being addressed as mistress because they were all sisters now, and to hammer home the point she nominated a former housekeeper from the Casa Cisneros to act as their superior. Luisa was well aware that this life was not going to be to everyone's taste and promised to help as best she could anyone who wanted to leave. Within a few days two of her companions turned their back on the experiment.

The doleful charade of pretending to be under the authority of another servant grated on Inés, who had been used to a privileged position as Luisa's best friend. Relief fortunately came within a couple of years when the 'superior' left to join an Augustinian house which Philip II had founded in Madrid, where she adopted the ostentatious-sounding name of Ana de la Transfiguración. The passage of time did nothing to diminish Inés's feelings, and she bitterly recalled how the culinary regime was deeply unsatisfying. The memory of being able to count the chickpeas that floated alongside the sardines' heads in the Friday stews provided under Ana's regime was still vivid a generation later. Inés tried complaining to their true leader, but all Luisa would say was that she, too, shed 'tears of hunger'.[77]

Luisa took to their new life with more gusto than her companions if only because, for them, this grim asceticism was not so very different from the years they had spent as domestic servants. She enjoyed her weekly stint at cleaning or cooking, and her washing and cleaning was a marvel to them all, occasionally to Inés's amusement. She had to ask how to boil water, and not knowing that vegetables needed to be chopped up her stews were looked upon as being 'more for devotion than for eating'.[78] There was always an element of wishful thinking on Luisa's part, and in 1598 she admitted that, if truth be told, her three companions, Inés, Isabel de la Cruz, and Isabel's sister María, had to do all the domestic work as she openly admitted 'I'm just no good around the house'.[79] It was an open secret, of course, that Luisa was really in charge. This was implicit in their daily routine. She got up an hour before everyone else at three in the morning to engage in mental prayer until half past six, when she would break her silence by chirpily asking, 'Is there anything I have to do, sisters?'[80] Mass with the Jesuits at the church next door was a daily ritual, with Inés dutifully in attendance. She never dawdled in the church as she had to be back at eleven to join her companions for their meagre midday meal. An hour's recreation passed, with Luisa usually beginning and ending the session with some edifying words.

If anyone said anything out of turn, the punishments were relatively light, at least by comparison with what went on in nunneries. For example, one punishment was to kiss the ground though, if necessary, something could always be put in the mouth to put an end to frivolous talk. After their leisure time, silence was kept till four o'clock when a religious book was read, but Luisa once more took the lead. She read from Scripture, or failing that from less scholastic saints such as St Bernard or St Bonaventure, with St Augustine making an occasional appearance. Inés grumbled that Luisa spoke so quickly that you had no idea 'if she was reading Spanish or Latin'.[81] A discussion might ensue and it goes without saying that Luisa, the most educated of all the companions, dominated conversation. Around six everyone would come together for another hour of silent prayer, and the evening meal might be a snack of eggs or vegetables. The community would reunite once more at nine to examine their consciences or say the rosary and consider what they would pray about the following day. They went to bed at ten.

At first sight, Luisa's community seems little different from the many *beaterios* dotted around Spain. These were tiny communities of *beatas* or women devoted to religion who, like Luisa, did not wish to lose their independence within an already-established order of nuns. The overwhelming majority of Spain's holy women came from privileged families, though few were as rich as the Carvajals or as exalted as the Mendozas.[82] Luisa's community differed in one crucial respect, however. Whereas other holy women in Spain might seek to transcend the social norms of early modern Spanish society, they did not wish to subvert those values. They might lead lives of modesty and without ostentation, but they still affected lives of refined religiosity, being much given to visions and other mystical experiences, all of which were an acceptable if potentially dangerous sign of female religiosity. Divine inspiration came to them not through their intellect, as it did with males, but rather through their senses, wherein lay the danger. Without the safeguards of an academically trained mind, a holy woman who had visions was open to being led astray by the devil's cunning, just as Eve had been tempted in the Garden of Eden.

Luisa never experienced visions of any great significance, or rather they never formed an integral part of her communal life. Her preference was for a more practical existence, where a life led in the world exposed her to the public ridicule and discomfort so necessary to her understanding of religion. She continued visiting the sick which she had done first with her mother and then more systematically with her aunt but now she undertook these visits in a shockingly radical way. No longer did she dole out fruit or sweetmeats to the patients as she had done as a child; instead she made up beds for the needy and diseased or emptied latrines. Worse still for her highly impressionable companions, she brought sick prostitutes back to the house.

That there was a theatrical side to Luisa's actions need not be doubted, yet her work in hospitals and with prostitutes was of real benefit to the individuals concerned, while remaining a drop in the ocean given the poverty that was endemic in early modern society. Literary scholars place the emphasis differently, however, and it has even been suggested that 'Carvajal and her biographers alike emphasise not the actual poor relief such rejection provided *(which in any case was nil)*, rather the social spectacle of public female degradation.'[83]

If Luisa's attempts to help the genuinely needy were nil, it would be hard to explain why Inés reacted so sharply to her companion's more extreme acts of mercy. She objected to the presence of one wretched woman who suffered so badly from the 'French Pox' that it was nauseating to look at her. Her indignation was made worse because many of their neighbours assumed they were prostitutes too!

Her life of poverty contained one element which above all caused her relatives exquisite embarrassment. By trying to earn a living by manual labour, she was snubbing her noble status. In Spain being noble depended on recognition as such by the community. To be viewed as a don was enough to stake a claim to legal privileges. The position in England was different: to be a true noble required the possession of a peerage, even though it brought few legal privileges apart from the right to attend a parliament, whereas in Spain an aristocratic title merely *increased* one's rank within the nobility. The incompatibility of manual labour and noble status had been engrained in the Castilian psyche since at least the early thirteenth century when King Alfonso X's great lawcode, the *Seven Partidas*, ordained that a knight who worked with his hands would forfeit his noble status. Luisa had elected to spin gold, beating the metal into fine strands to be used in dressmaking and the like, and though we might regard this as an art rather than a trade, it still amounted to earning one's keep. As María Nieves Pinillos has pointed out, if it was almost impossible for the greatest painter of the Golden Age, Diego de Velázquez, to be accepted as a member of respectable society and join the Order of Santiago—a quasi-religious fraternity which accepted members of the laity and conferred on them noble status—it is not hard to imagine what it felt like for Luisa's family when she took to pounding with a hammer.[84]

There were other, doubtless equally hurtful, means of rejecting the values that shored up a family's position in the world. She dropped the more aristocratically resonant of her surnames, 'Mendoza', preferring to call herself Luisa de Carvajal and, eventually, simply 'Luisa', just as poor people did when they had no lineage to boast of. Similarly she negotiated her own way around Spanish linguistic snobbery. Put very simply, high-ranking people were addressed as *vuestra merced* (which can very roughly be translated as 'your grace'), whereas *vos* (or 'thee') was set aside for the lower orders. In so far as words can change the world, Luisa verbally challenged the social structure by trying never again to refer to anyone as *vos*. In England it would be another generation or two before the Quakers antagonized their fellow Englishmen and women by addressing everyone as 'thee' and 'thou', without respect for their position in society.[85]

Among the more open-minded of her neighbours Luisa was gaining a reputation for saintliness but most people just found her plain odd. When a bucket was full, Luisa was not content to empty its contents by the side of the house but insisted on pouring it out in the middle of the road where everyone could see her. Sometimes she did not have the strength to carry the bucket so she contrived to put it on her head, precisely as poor people did. Once as she was doing this several grand coaches passed by and she was recognized by a page who started an argument by telling another servant that the strange creature before them was a relative of the family that he served. On one trip to the plaza mayor to buy food at the open-air market, she came across her cousin Francisco, the second marquis of Almazán. Seated on his horse, he pretended not to recognize her while all around him his entourage was tittering at his poor demented relative.

Contrived though these attempts at self-abasement may have been, Luisa found the ignominy intensely gratifying. With her confessor's permission she begged for food when money was particularly scarce at the great door of St Francis's church. Her refined and confident accent alone made her stand out from those who really had no alternative but to beg. She sounded like a 'very sonorous trumpet', prompting a priest on one occasion to take the precaution of being particularly generous with the bread he was doling out.[86] The massive church of San Francisco on the then western outskirts of the city was a bizarre place for Luisa to beg, and if her family heard about her visits it would have been more than usually uncomfortable: her father's grandparents were buried there in a pantheon of their own. Only one relative could bring herself to visit Luisa regularly at this time, and that was her cousin Isabel, the future marchioness de Caracena.

Luisa did have the odd guest. She had acquired a reputation as a wise woman, and for the most part her visitors were women who were supporters of the Jesuits and who, almost by definition, were intrigued by newfangled approaches to a religious life. She claimed to find such visits a bore, restricting them to between four and six o'clock. It was thrilling for these ladies to come to so pitiable a house and they could also rely on Luisa never to stray too far from treating them as their rank deserved, but there were limits. Doña Aldonza de Zúñiga, a daughter of the influential royal councillor, the count of Miranda, remembered how everything in the house was 'poor in the extreme'. Luisa decided she had to buy a white jug and one plate of Talavera pottery for her more distinguished guests to use in turn. This was not good enough for the duchess of Medina de Ríoseco, who arrived one day with her daughters and servants. She insisted on sending for her own porcelain and glassware that was to be kept for her and her daughters' use on subsequent visits. This was too much for Luisa, who promptly sent the glasses away to the hospital of a nunnery and the little jugs to the sacristy, to be used for the wine at mass.[87] Inés maintained that the ladies who visited always took away something that was 'healing, edifying, and useful'.[88] Luisa confidently agreed that they 'were not wasting their time in the least by coming to see me; and because the life I have chosen, as well as the way I dress and the company I keep, just isn't suitable for visits or striding out surrounded by pageboys, messengers and lay folk, I stay at home, hoping to serve these ladies by commending them to Our Lord'.[89]

Spain's royal ladies caught wind of Luisa's experiment. With Inés again taking on the role of chaperone, she was summoned several times to see the young Queen Margaret, and on one memorable occasion she had to flee when the equally young Philip III—he ascended the throne in 1598—came back to the palace unannounced. She was once more the talk of the Descalzas Reales, and its two most distinguished inhabitants, the Empress María and her daughter, the

Infanta Margarita—known in religion as Sister Margarita of the Cross—were intrigued by her radical lifestyle. The empress was not only a supporter of the Jesuits but had known Luisa's uncle when he was ambassador in Vienna. Apparently, Luisa was also summoned to see her childhood friend, the Infanta Isabel Clara Eugenia, but if so it is tempting to conclude their reunion was not a success.[90] When she went to the Netherlands as regent, Isabel never offered the slightest encouragement during the whole of her time in London.

Apart from a doctor, her male visitors were confined to her Jesuit confessor and his companion, and her early biographers liked to claim that the couple of chairs she possessed were expressly intended for members of the Society of Jesus. This is doubtless hagiographical exaggeration, but her Jesuit friends were wise to keep a close eye on their idiosyncratic neighbour. The Company had more than its fair share of enemies. It had not gone unnoticed that the intellectual swagger of the Jesuits made them particularly attractive to bored rich women and there were accusations of manipulation. They could not afford to allow anyone living literally in their shadow to fall under the suspicion of the Inquisition. The Holy Office, as the Inquisition was properly called, was charged with protecting Spain's moral as well as theological purity and high rank offered no protection. A few years before Luisa was born, the highest-ranking clergyman in Spain, Archbishop Carranza of Toledo, had been seized on suspicion of heresy, and more recently the inquisition had made several investigations into as public a figure as Teresa of Ávila.

When the Jesuits of the calle de Toledo called on Luisa, one of their reasons may have been that they were curious to know whether her tiny community might grow into an order that could work in tandem with the Company. With the notable exception of Princess Juana, the Jesuits were exclusively male in recruitment and, unlike most other religious orders, there was no parallel foundation for women, despite their finances being notoriously dependent on the support of wealthy females.[91] The Society of Jesus was still young, and there might yet be good reason to reinterpret their founder's wishes and harness the talents of remarkable women. Luisa was a woman to watch.

4
'Sweet Manacles'

THOUGH she could appear feisty, argumentative, and hopelessly stubborn, it would take several years for the mature Luisa to discover a way forward in her religious life that gave her a degree of satisfaction. Since those around her had so often died, gone away, or abused their position, it was hard to trust other people and she felt more at ease with a series of immature relationships usually resting on her instinctive social pre-eminence, as in the case of her female companions, or on an exaggerated obedience to a male superior, as with her uncle or confessors. The path she followed during her first years of independence was strewn with a remarkable series of vows which manifested a steadily increasing spiritual maturity and a growing sense of purpose. Her promises were intended to reveal the way towards a more contemplative inner life, and they finally pointed in only one direction. By the end of the 1590s she was prepared to take a formal vow in which she offered herself for martyrdom. Though she would never have dreamt that others should die with her, she was prepared to place her life in danger or suffer extreme hardship in order to profess her brand of Christianity.

Her first solemn oath made in 1593 contained, as yet, no hint of martyrdom. Instead she pledged an irrevocable commitment to poverty, thus formalizing vaguer promises made as a girl in Pamplona. To take the oath she had first to seek the advice and permission of her confessor and superior, almost certainly Juan de Sigüenza, the head of the Jesuit college next to where she lived. She made

a firm promise and vow of perpetual poverty before His Divine Majesty, with all my heart, and an entire and true renunciation to Jesus Christ our lord, and to my superior in His name, of the control and ownership of money or any other thing which might be held to be mine, or which must be spent by my decision or to sustain my life, *without any exception whatsoever.*[92]

For an oath claiming to be a definitive repudiation of all worldly goods, it contained a surprisingly long list of exceptions. This reflected both her character and her intellect. She had survived all that her uncle did to her by never wholly surrendering control over her life, as her robust defence against his intrusive questions indicates, and this deeply ingrained streak of independence explains why life in someone else's nunnery held few attractions. She was shrewd enough to foresee that leading a life of apostolic simplicity would still pose practical problems that needed to be thought through, hence her insistence on being paid for any work she did as well as on the right to collect what was owed her. Money was to be available to cover sickness and provide the bedding appropriate to her choice of life, though she conceded that the adornments for the oratory were to be no more ostentatious than gilded tin. Intriguingly, there was to be money for edifying books or to pay for them to be copied by hand.

Why should a female holding no Church-sanctioned position of authority over a convent feel the need to own works of devotion and theology? The answer is that Luisa was arming herself 'to confound heretics and their errors'.[93] Although the chattering classes of Spain were as one in thinking that the Christianity practised in the remoter parts of the peninsula left a lot to be desired, Luisa was slowly setting her sights further afield. Even at this relatively early stage she and her confessors were sounding out whether her calling was for some form of missionary work, not in God-forsaken parts of Spain, but in a foreign country where Catholicism was under attack.

An unavoidable consequence of her increasing dependency on members of the Company was that it became imperative to go in search of her father's money. In fact, the final clause of her vow of poverty dealt with the paternal legacy she had already been pursuing in the courts for at least a year and a half, and, whatever the sum, she readily agreed 'to make it available without delay'. Though the Jesuits of the calle de Toledo were the likely recipients of her generosity,

Luisa still clutched at a degree of autonomy, and she kept hold of the right to determine, 'in accordance with my own devotion, the pious work which seems to me to be to the greatest glory of Our Lord'.[94]

Luisa's obligation was to maximize the money which she could pass to the Church, whereas the Jesuits had a vested interest in ensuring that the very best lawyers were consulted. One of these was Juan Bautista de Aguiriano, a native of Almazán, who was connected with her uncle and with Diego de Laínez, who had succeeded Loyola as the Company's second general. Despite the lawyer's excellent credentials, Luisa's mistrustful nature caused her to doubt his honesty. Probably through sheer exasperation at the slowness of the case, one Monday in 1600 she jotted down a despairing note to herself, lashing out on paper at Aguiriano for coming to her with claims for his own salary all mixed up with the costs of prosecuting her case.[95]

The Jesuit who guided her most in these worldly matters was Father Hernando de Espinosa. His steadfast if not disinterested support during her legal battles was acknowledged by Luisa, and when she moved to Valladolid it was he who arranged for Juan de Ceráin, a busy bureaucrat from Madrid whom he confessed, to explain how the royal courts of justice worked in what had always been Castile's legal capital.[96]

Despite batteries of legal help, it fell to Luisa to make her own representations by personally visiting those officials who were involved in hearing her case. Invariably accompanied by Inés and dressed in their usual rags, they became the butt of jokes for the hangers-on of all the judges she was trying to chivvy. Their ridicule only intensified when they realized she wanted the money to be able to give it all away.[97]

Not quite all the visits resulted in hostility or incredulity. She found a warm and sympathetic welcome when she called upon the count of Miranda, who, as president of the Council of Castile, was responsible for the day-to-day running of the greater part of Spain, including its legal affairs. An old friend of her uncle's, he would come out to greet Luisa literally 'cap in hand', a great honour in a country where noblemen were segregated into those who were granted the right to remain 'covered' in the presence of the king and queen and those who were obliged to take off their hats.[98] Her studied modesty impressed his wife and daughter, notably her refusal to eat with them and only in the servants' hall. The count's daughter, doña Aldonza, saw her father as 'a man so serious and strict who never showed any inclination for holy women or for the devotions that some women go in for, instead he couldn't stand them'.[99] Maybe it was more than Luisa's practical spirit which appealed to the no-nonsense bureaucrat-cum-politician. Did Luisa reveal a hope that one day she might be able to travel to England in order to defy state-sanctioned Protestantism? When Philip II died in 1598, the court of the new king was agonizing over whether to carry on the war with the English Protestants. Miranda was known as a hardliner who wanted no concessions to heretics either in England or the Spanish Netherlands, and although he was more of a talker than a doer he spoke up in favour of taking direct action against the ageing Queen Elizabeth with the intention of imposing a Catholic regime on England.[100]

There was also an amusing side to her lawsuit. At least one former suitor crawled out of the shadows to propose marriage. For all her privations, Luisa had not yet lost the physical attractiveness that had aroused her cousins' jealousy in Pamplona, and as far as Inés was concerned she remained an attractive young woman, though, despite her height, 'the mortification had caused her to stoop a little'.[101] Luisa regularly drew blood by wearing an iron cross on her back, a wooden cross studded with iron spikes on her chest, as well as chains or ropes designed to chafe her arms and throat. She was constantly ill, often with bronchial complaints and sometimes with palpitations of the heart. Her whole body shook from head to foot, and two of her companions would not be enough to hold her down. The count of Miranda's daughter thought 'it seemed a miracle she could keep going'.[102]

Luisa's greatest attraction was not physical. It was the money she would bring a husband. Her first cousin, García de Carvajal, was relatively wealthy but not to the extent that Luisa would be if she married and automatically inherited under her father's will. He was in all probability the suitor she had rejected ten years earlier, but this time her admirer cunningly asked for her hand in marriage through the Society of Jesus, which to all intents and purposes had replaced her uncle as guardian. Inés could not recall which priest it was, Gaspar de

Pedrosa or Juan de Sigüenza, who relayed the offer, which indicates that this took place around 1596, when Pedrosa took over as confessor. The priest passed on the bid 'as a big joke, as it was for her'. It amused her to the point that she would self-mockingly say she had 'been turned into the opprobrium of the world, scurrying about beneath the feet of my family's horses and servants, and still they want to marry me'.[103]

Despite the anxieties engendered by her court case, she continued to look to her confessors for advancement in her spiritual life. In 1595 she reinforced her links to the Society of Jesuits with a vow of obedience where she promised 'to obey, all the days of my life, the mandates and orders' of her superior, regardless of whether the person chosen was technically her superior. This convoluted formula was to get round the fact that Jesuits were not supposed to accept responsibility for others for fear that it would interfere with their primary duty to be ready at a moment's notice to leave on a mission. Though she naturally chose as her superior Esteban de Ojeda, the rector of the next-door Jesuit house, the aristocrat in Luisa still could not bring herself to extinguish her freedom completely. Every Whitsun she would decide who her superior should be for the coming year. If he should die before that date, she would elect another for the interim, and provision was made for what was to be done in his absence. If matters that troubled her conscience could not be resolved by an exchange of letters, she would make up her own mind 'in conformity to what I understand to be to the greatest service and contentment of Our Lord'.[104]

Two or three years later, probably in 1598, Luisa solemnly made her most important vow to date. She promised greater perfection. At first sight, this might seem a standard Christian duty; in fact, when considered in the light of Catholic theology it marked a huge spiritual gamble. She promised 'to do always in all things that which I understand to be most perfect . . . in the manner for me in which this may be possible'.[105] This was not a promise to be made lightly. If it became known that she had failed to live up to her vows, her standing with the Society would be destroyed.

The significance of the vow of perfection depends on a distinction between venial and mortal sins. Put crudely, a venial sin occurs when the transgressor is unaware that a minor fault is being committed, whereas a mortal sin occurs when the sinner is aware that a serious wrong is being perpetrated. Luisa was therefore laying claim to a spiritual insight that allowed her to discern the most perfect path even when it came to the venial sins that most people would be unaware they were committing. As she explained, the urge to take this vow arose out of her prayer life. She had been asking for God's guidance so as 'not to offend you venially in any way whatever, no matter in how slight or inconsequential a way, even at the cost of my life, finding in me much greater satisfaction in not displeasing you than in having life'.[106]

Luisa never regretted making this promise. To a list she later drew up of each of her vows she appended a note in which she claimed to have felt no scruples since promising perfection, 'only great consolation and contentment for having done so, and a desire to carry it through with all my strength'.[107] The much-read spiritual writer Father Luis de la Puente, who frequently heard her confession after she left Madrid, maintained that for him the greatest proof of her sanctity was that she never once asked to be released from such a challenging promise.[108]

This vow highlights just how different in temperament Luisa was from Spain's greatest Golden Age holy woman, Teresa of Ávila. She had taken a similar oath but failed. In his life of 'Mother Teresa' published in Seville in 1590, just eight years after her death, her friend and first biographer Francisco de Ribera said he had never come across an oath of perfection before. More important for us is Teresa's own cheerful admission that she had been quite unable to live up to her promise and that, in the end, she asked to be released from her oath of perfection. Since Teresa's understandable failure in this respect was a published fact, it is unlikely Luisa was deliberately trying to outshine the greatest reformer of the age, and instead it is possible that Luisa's inspiration in seeking perfection was provided by a man, Ignatius Loyola. His writings are not only full of the need to search for the perfect but are replete with practical advice about how to make the right choices, as we shall see when Luisa uses his most famous work, the *Spiritual Exercises*, to determine where her vow of martyrdom should take her.

A year after she had committed herself to greater perfection Luisa was bullied into questioning her commitment to an independent life. In 1596 or thereabouts, in a fleeting moment of intense vulnerability, she agreed that her experimental way of life was too scandalous. What had gone wrong? She later wrote to her cousin Isabel that she had replaced Juan de Sigüenza as her confessor with someone altogether 'more suitable for me', but it is Inés who provides the real explanation for her temporary capitulation. After one prolonged prayer session with Sigüenza, where they had argued for several hours over her future, Luisa finally agreed to enter a strict convent where the ancient austerities were observed. When she tried to get up 'to go and take the habit', she found herself completely unable to move.[109] As far as she was concerned, God had spoken the last word.

Her new confessor was Gaspar de Pedrosa, and he was to be responsible for many of her most dramatic spiritual advances. In an almost flirtatious manner she dubbed him an angel while he responded by cooing that 'she was unique in the world'.[110] In his mid-thirties, Pedrosa was just a few years older than Luisa and considerably more sympathetic to her spiritual hunger than his predecessor. He allowed her to receive holy communion (*comulgar*) on a more frequent basis.

She attended mass every day but could only receive the consecrated bread twice a week.[111] The sacramental wine was not offered to her as it was consistently denied to all members of the laity, male as well as female, being reserved for members of the priesthood. Much hated by Protestants as a practice that set off the clergy from the congregation, the custom of communion in one kind had spread through the Catholic Church from the eleventh century. It was feared that the consecrated wine—by now miraculously transformed into Christ's blood—might be spilt or otherwise dishonoured by clumsy members of the laity. Not offering the chalice undoubtedly saved the Church a lot of money but theologians insisted that God's grace was available in the consecrated bread just as much as it was in the wine. So, when Luisa campaigned to receive communion more than twice a week, it almost certainly never crossed her mind to ask for the cup as well as the host.

The breakthrough towards more frequent communion came within a year of taking on her new spiritual guide. In the run up to Lent Pedrosa agreed she could receive the host three days in a row but in a way which flagged up his priestly authority. Permission would have to be granted afresh on each occasion, something which gives an inkling into how much day-to-day contact she had with her confessors. Satisfied with her humility towards his munificence, Pedrosa then asked the Company to allow her to receive on a daily basis. A rare concession, others who knew her spiritually would have to be rigorously examined before the 'full knowledge and approval' of the provincial head of the Jesuit Order could be sought.[112]

Pedrosa was paving the way for a yet more exceptional privilege. Two months later, the Cardinal-Archduke Albert of Toledo was at his estate at Campillo between Madrid and El Escorial, and on 14 May 1597 he consented to mass being said daily in Luisa's own house whenever she was present. To prevent her home from becoming a public church, the only others entitled to hear mass were her servants and her visitors, and no other sacrament apart from penance was to be administered, which avoided any erosion of the profits that parish churches in her neighbourhood were making from births, marriages, and deaths. What lay behind this concession were Luisa's frequent bouts of ill health which rendered even the journey to the neighbouring church an ordeal. This is clear from the restriction pertaining to Corpus Christi, a feast in celebration of the eucharist which had become a strongly communal occasion where local communities came together in public procession to manifest their solidarity. Luisa was barred from celebrating a private eucharist during these civic festivities, unless, that is, she was 'so ill' that 'she was unable to go out to hear mass outside the house'.[113]

Before the cardinal-archduke's licence could take effect, the oratory in the calle de Toledo needed to be inspected for decency. Unlikely to have been a separate room, her chapel may well have been tucked away in a corner or a passageway with little to see apart from a few images and some ornamental cloth. Ten days later, the Vicar General of Madrid, Dr Domingo de Mendieta, confirmed he had inspected the chapel and found it suitable.

Luisa had been devoted to Christ's miraculous presence at the altar long before her first mass in Almazán. She would always genuflect before the holy sacrament in any church she passed, crossing the road if necessary, and, with her habitual sense of theatre, if she could not get in, she would abase herself at the entrance, splattering herself with mud if necessary. Luisa realized the privilege of daily communion was 'something so good that I couldn't put it into words'. In a struggle to find the right words, she said it could douse a heart that was on fire with a rush of water from the sea or act as a burning flame on a heart that was frozen. She observed how she

felt my troubles lift from my shoulders, fleeing from my heart, which felt its virtue strengthened and less weak regarding faults and ordinary sins. And in a few days it seemed that I had begun to feel what that freedom was like which makes the children of God truly free.[114]

The suspicion is that some of the relief she felt came from the much-needed nutrition in the eucharistic wafer, but, be that as it may, it is not easy to categorize Luisa as a mystic no matter how much inspiration she drew from communion. As plainspeaking Inés said, she was not thought of 'as a woman of revelations but rather of great virtue and insight'.[115]

Her closest companions claimed no more for her than a vague ability to foresee the future, and even then the usually invoked example was an indifferent story involving the stern Ana de la Transfiguración, the fierce servant who acted out the role of the first head of the community in the calle de Toledo. When she asked Luisa if she would ever want to be a nun, she was reprimanded with the allegedly prophetic words—that's your calling not mine![116]

Luisa could count herself lucky not to have a reputation as a seer, because, as the count of Miranda knew well, women who claimed divine revelation were playing with fire. For a female to assert direct contact with God challenged the institutional authority of the male priesthood, with a further danger being that a mystic might be taken up by unscrupulous courtiers to prove that God was on their side in the factional struggles polluting life at court. The greatest peril lay in the fact that the ecclesiastical authorities might allege that these mystical experiences came not from God but the devil. No one was exempt from danger, not even Teresa of Ávila, who had been investigated several times by the Inquisition to see if she had been duped by Satan.

Luisa would have been unusually vulnerable if she ever earned a reputation as a mystic. Her ties to many of the highest-placed families in the realm, combined with her erudition and strong political views, would have made her many enemies, and she might easily have become another Lucrecia de León, a visionary who also lived in Madrid and whose fate was still fresh in the memory. Lucrecia's visions directly criticized Philip II for imperilling Catholicism at home and abroad by alleging he did not care for his kingdom or for his daughter, Luisa's childhood friend, the Infanta Isabel. She was also the Spanish claimant to the English throne, and the king was accused of having failed in his duty as a father because he had not provided her with a husband. (When she did marry it was to none other than the Archduke Albert, who, as archbishop of Toledo when he still held minor orders in the Church, had granted Luisa licence to hear mass at home.) Lucrecia's five-year-long trial by the Inquisition had ended in 1595, and it was probably only because of her relatively low social status that she was let off with the light sentence of being condemned to public humiliation with two years' incarceration in a nunnery.[117]

Unlike Lucrecia's dreams, Luisa's spiritual experiences were kept almost entirely private, and we only know about them because of the reports she faithfully wrote so that her confessors could mount watch on her interior life. They were jotted down on individual sheets of paper which were gathered together in the attempt to canonize her and which have ended up in Madrid's Convent of the Incarnation in Madrid. These experiences centred on intense moments of ecstasy, mercifully devoid of any obvious message for the world at large. Whereas St Teresa's ability to swoon almost at will lent immeasurable weight to her campaign to reform Spanish religious houses along the lines of strict poverty—often in the teeth of literally violent opposition—Luisa's innermost feelings were harmlessly unconnected with any comparable public role.

It goes almost without saying that Luisa's mystical experiences were centred on the sacrament of the altar. Shortly after she commenced daily communion she became convinced that the Person of the Word Made Flesh—that is, Christ—was embossed on her soul, and that this experience 'has always been growing, and never diminishing'.[118] Ever cautious, she stressed time and again that her experiences were strictly personal. In another attempt to describe what she felt, she stressed three times in as many lines that this presence was deep inside her; it was not a general revelation:

I felt for a long time, months even, I don't know, perhaps a year or more, the most delicate and sovereign presence of the Word Incarnate, which, in my intellect, appeared to me that I possessed in the most intimate way imaginable; and this my soul embraced, and tightly became one with Him, causing me a very notable greatness of the heart and much light, love, and esteem for this Sovereign Lord. Each and every time I came to look deep inside me I felt the same, as it was something deeply embedded in my soul.[119]

Sometimes her sense of the presence of God was so acute that she could single out individual days. One such occasion was a Friday, 12 February, which could only have been in 1599. After receiving the consecrated bread, she again saw the Word Incarnate but this time it was enduring the Passion, with the hands pierced by nails and displaying the head-wounds caused by the crown of thorns. She was reading at the time St Augustine's *Meditations*, a work by a medieval writer then errone-ously ascribed to the great African saint Augustine of Hippo. The *Meditations* described the joy of the everlasting life but she found its words dry and uninspiring, and falling back on the power of imaginative prayer which she had first learnt from her nurse, she imagined herself at one with the suffering Christ, wounded by the same thorns and nails. She asked what other heaven or glory could there be but to suffer his torments and humiliation? From her earliest days pain and pleasure had been inseparable, and she did not suffer as she experienced Christ's torments, feeling only a 'gently penetrating and all-consuming love'.[120]

What can be given can also be taken away. Whenever her confes-sors deemed Luisa had been unworthy and of little virtue, they exercised their hold over her by disallowing daily communion.[121] Her companions bore the brunt of her withdrawal symptoms. Once, in Valladolid, Father Antonio de Padilla ordered her not to go to communion for over a fortnight, and when her deprivation became unbearable, Isabel de la Cruz cried out 'for goodness' sake, communicate!' Luisa snapped back, even if all the world and all the saints told her to receive the bread, so long as her confessor thought differently she would not take communion.[122]

Luisa's mystical writings were never longer than a few sheets of paper and were never prepared for a wider audience. This is just as well, as a harsh critic might say that her prose imagery is unremarkable and lacks the simplicity of the great mystics. She equates God's love with a place, a traditional Christian metaphor deriving from the saying in the New Testament that in my Father's house there are many mansions, an idea subsequently taken up by the real Augustine in his *City of God*. By the early sixteenth century it had become a commonplace of Spanish mysticism, most famously in St Teresa's *Interior Castle*.[123] To this image Luisa added a pungent smell of academe when she used the formal language of architecture to describe her reaction to God's mercies. It was, she said, like entering

palaces of divine love, built in conformity with the instructions of God's will, and where, in this position, the deepest and straightest of foundations are put down. Considering the fastness and beauty of this place, I lifted the eyes of my soul and looked around, only to find immense heights and depressions, wide spaces and plains that cannot be comprehended, full of the richest mines of precious stones and the finest gold and the purest silver, which seven times was tested in the crucible of tribulation, and even when it is most accurately assayed it always retains the same value.[124]

We do not know how her spiritual advisers judged her attempts to put down on paper what she was feeling. It is tempting to think of what Luis de la Puente said about the writings of her close friend in Valladolid, Marina de Escobar. A master of mystical writing himself, De la Puente's down-to-earth opinion of Escobar was that 'really her style is wordy and sloppy; she repeats something several times in order to make herself understood, and with too many words'. The same might be said of Luisa.[125]

Her poetry is a different matter. In her prose the essential thing lacking was discipline but this is emphatically not true of her verse.

Metrical necessity focused her thoughts in a way that is absent elsewhere, and if her prose writings were probably written at the behest
of her confessors her poetry was her personal way of expressing what
she felt. Fifty poems survive, and as far as we can tell they were all
written before she left Spain, with one poem being dated as late as
1597.[126] Her verse deserves to be better known and to rank amongst
the most powerful written in the Golden Age. As Seamus Heaney said
of the poems of Sylvia Plath, their only weakness—if this counts as a
weakness—is that their intensely autobiographical nature detracts
from the universality of their appeal.

   The poems reflect the isolation and disapproval she put up with in
the ten years after she had moved out of her uncle's house. Her
family's lack of sympathy caused countless problems and in the early
days she had not found a confessor to her liking, feeling spiritually
alone, especially during those long periods of illness when she could
not get out of bed.

By the end, when the worst was over, I came to feel that my enemies'
strength was weakening, but I was still very ill in bed. Once more I looked
for consolation from the hands of my Lord, whose presence my soul was
waiting for, but this was not granted me. Instead, he hid from me the more I
desired him, and I underwent a harsh and frightening final test.[127]

This was when she wrote one of her most dramatic poems, 'Por un
áspero viaje' (On a harsh journey). It deals with the isolation felt by her
alter ego, a shepherdess called Silva, a thin disguise for her own name,
Luisa. She goes into the mountains in search of the divine. There,
'alone, with love alone, which accompanied you alone', she searches
for her beloved. A most remarkable aspect of the poem is its far-from-
triumphant conclusion, where she will continue waiting for the person in which she 'has placed all her hope'. Luisa later commented that
the conclusion referred to the 'resolution I had taken not to stop until I
had discovered and found' the way forward she was looking for.[128] Its
reiteration of the theme of loneliness was intended to sum up 'in a most
encoded fashion' all that had passed through her soul during the course
of her life. The same mixture of the certainty of divine love, and her
own inability to find it, is found in other of the 'Silva' poems, her

spiritual sonnets, as she called them. Written when she felt 'afflicted by his absence yet burnt by his love', the poem 'Until when, my Lord?' asks how long she must endure her sense of distance from God.

In her poetry more than anywhere else Luisa makes clear that the mortification she was subjected to as a child had transformed itself into a desire to become a martyr. In 'Sweet Manacles, Coveted Noose', she explains how it would be a fortunate fate ('suerte venturosa') to be burnt alive for the faith. If this message were not clear enough, her introduction to this sonnet expressly stated that it dealt with 'a most enflamed love and desires for martyrdom'.[129]

The series of oaths Luisa undertook in the last decade of the sixteenth century culminated in her final and most momentous vow of all. In 1598, when she was 32 years old, she solemnly swore 'to seek out all those opportunities of martyrdom', vowing to 'face all manner of death, torments, and rigours'. It formalized a wish to offer herself up as a missionary, a desire which, incidentally, her companion, Isabel, felt she had expressed obliquely some five years earlier when composing her poem 'Sweet Manacles'.[130] Suffering was the theme of another poem, 'Madre, siendo niña'. Though it begins with a conventional call for a mother to ease a daughter's pain, it also serves as a reminder of the loss of her own mother.

> Mother, when I was little
> Love seized me;
> with chains of gold
> He left me captive.

She goes on to say her wounds were so great that she needed to offer herself up completely, the ultimate sacrifice was, of course, martyrdom.[131]

There is a noteworthy degree of overlap between Luisa's poetry and her other writings. A common stock of words and ideas crops up in her poems and oaths. As we have seen, when she vowed to seek martyrdom, she used the word *venturosa* to describe the occasion when she might be called to surrender her life, choosing the same word when referring to a martyr's death in 'Sweet Manacles'. All that was blocking a chance to test her call to this fortunate sacrifice was that she had yet to collect her father's money.

5

New Ways of Living

I F her interpretation of her father's will stood up in court, Luisa would be a very wealthy woman. Her income would match that of a comfortably-off gentleman in England or Spain. As an aristocrat's wife she would be a catch indeed, and if she chose to give her money away to a religious institution many a royal patron would be hard put to match her largesse. The terms of the will seemed categorical enough. It stipulated that she should receive the capital sum of 12,000 ducats on marriage, and even excluding the interest that piled up as the legal marathon dragged on, this would be worth around £4,000 in sterling in the money of the time. But there was a snag. It never occurred to her father that his daughter might choose to live alone, outside either the bounds of matrimony or the protective walls of a convent. All he said was, if she chose not to marry and become a nun instead, she was to receive only 2,000 ducats, with a modest annual allowance for clothing and medical expenses. Her father's executors took the not unreasonable view that the life she had chosen for herself meant that she had renounced marriage and had chosen in all but name the religious life.

She was adamant her entitlement was to the larger bequest because she had not formally entered a nunnery. The Church's own rules appeared to be on her side. As it was a serious breach of canon law to force anyone to enter a convent against their will she could tell herself that it was equally wrong to designate anyone a nun who did not wish to profess. The distinction between a religious life inside and outside a nunnery was fundamental to her understanding of what she was trying to achieve. Luisa wanted to establish a new type of religious life for those like herself who wished neither to marry *nor* to enter a convent. She was attempting to combine a contemplative life not disimilar to that in a nunnery with the freedom to remain in the outside world, which in her case meant living and moving among the poor, something which the hierarchy of the late sixteenth-century Catholic Church was keen to prevent. As we will see from a set of rules drawn up when she was in London, she was to carve out a way of living as close as possible to that of the Jesuits, who were already free of institutional shackles which might hinder them from going wherever required.

The novelty of project was not lost on her closest companion, Inés, who in her own limited manner perfectly understood why most people reacted so strongly against the community of the calle de Toledo. No matter which way you looked at her 'new way of living', as Inés called their experiment, the ordinary citizens of Madrid could not accept that young women might live independently and without a whiff of sexual impropriety. People of quality, she said, either assumed Luisa was mad or else blamed her family for allowing her to move freely in public. The lower orders were no better, muttering that her behaviour was disgraceful or complaining that her lifestyle was 'something they could not get their heads round'.[132]

By a strange coincidence, one of the people the Jesuits selected to counsel her when she moved to Valladolid knew all about her from when he had been a teenager in Madrid. The calle de Toledo was on Juan de Ceráin's way home. When he heard the chatter about the strange and saintly virgin who chose to live out her life in poverty, he made a point, 'partly out of devotion and partly from juvenile curiosity', of peering through the windows of her house.[133] Catching a glimpse of Luisa became something of a game, though he said he only ever caught sight of her twice, in the street, and to his evident regret, he never saw her face, not even when he spied on her in the Jesuits' church.

Her little community was at odds with the way the contemporary Church was moving, and Ceráin's prurient interest underlines the revolutionary basis of her new life. In the Middle Ages there had been many attempts to find a type of religious life which would allow women to remain active in the community but three years before Luisa was born the Catholic Church had tried to bring a halt to all such experimentation at the Council of Trent.

In 1545, hundreds of senior churchmen from all the countries that accepted the supremacy of Rome answered a summons from Pope Paul III to make their way to the northern Italian town of Trentino. Their task over the next eighteen years would be to revitalize the Catholic Church, in particular to deal with the criticisms of late medieval Catholicism that had led so many of the faithful to follow Martin Luther and other Protestant reformers. Taking their cue from the practical criticisms of the early sixteenth-century writer Erasmus of Rotterdam, Protestant writers went on to question the theological as well as the social utility of monasticism, reserving particular scorn for the financial and sexual irregularities which they claimed were rampant in monasteries and convents. In its twenty-fifth and final session in December 1563, the Council of Trent dealt head-on with these criticisms by decreeing that 'the enclosure of nuns be restored wherever it has been violated and that it be preserved where it has not been violated'. In Spain the ground had already been prepared by Teresa of Ávila. All over the country grilles were installed and walls put up as nuns in houses not-yet-reformed were turned into virtual prisoners (as some of them complained) in their own convents. Two-and-a-half years later, in May 1566, Pope Pius V issued a papal bull which called for all women living in virtually any type of religious community to be strictly cloistered, irrespective of whether or not they were professed nuns.[134]

The practical ability of local ecclesiastical authorities to enforce papal wishes was, of course, patchy, and all the more so in the case of such a well-connected if unconventional individual as Luisa. So much depended financially on the outcome of her lawsuit that no one was going to order Luisa to conform to the principles of the Council of Trent, especially as her claim to the inheritance rested squarely on the assertion that she was *not* professed.

The interminable courtroom wrangles took their toll on her health. The pursuit of material wealth ran counter to the freedom from possessions she hankered after, also getting in the way of seeking the martyrdom she craved; yet, when she wanted 'to break free from those chains, it proved impossible, and I was not allowed to leave everything behind'.[135] Who could have stopped her from walking away from her legal claims?

The only people in a position to give anything remotely like orders to Luisa were her confessors. When Ceráin enquired why she did not give up the case, seeing how much it irritated her and how it conflicted with her life of poverty, her answer was that her confessor 'ordered her to continue'.[136] By the time she arrived in Valladolid, the Company had guided her for thirteen years, that is, ever since the question of her inheritance had come to the fore after she had left the family home and was no longer under her relatives' control. The earliest surviving payment to a lawyer dated back to 15 July 1592, eight months after her uncle's death and about a year after she moved into the upper rooms of his palace. Then the case was still a joint action by Luisa and her eldest brother against the prevarications of her father's executors.

The Jesuits of Madrid were in no position to turn up their noses at the windfall they might receive from the Carvajal inheritance. The munificent benefaction of the Empress María that would build them their great church was still some way off, and their expanding operations in the city were being run on a shoestring. Luisa's money was of strategic importance to them, and it was an open secret that she intended to give away every last penny she inherited. She needed supervising. Her money almost slipped out of their fingers when, in an unguarded moment in 1600, she tried to pass a message to the Archduchess Isabel through her friend at the Flemish court, the indomitable Magdalena de San Jerónimo, offering to travel to Flanders and give her money away by setting up a convent. Replete with references to the sufferings of the Catholic earls of Northumberland and the malevolence of Queen Elizabeth, she hoped her proposal might bring her closer to her ultimate destination, England.[137]

What dampened her spirits most about her lawsuit was that she never really knew how well it was progressing, and she incessantly tried to cheer herself up by pretending that victory lay around the corner. The very first of her surviving letters, from September 1598, contains the message for her cousin Isabel that the case was 'almost over', though she was not fully certain what the decision would be.[138] In the spring of 1600 she heard the rumour that the king's court would sooner or later decamp to Valladolid, and she accepted she would have to follow the court in order to keep up pressure on the judges.[139] By October Luisa had convinced herself that a favourable decision—against which there could be no appeal—was only days away, and she put this down as being largely due to the count of Miranda's vocal support.[140] Her optimism was misplaced and her frustration became palpable, and early the following year she wrote that one of her lawyers was doing her in ('me mata') with messages about a payment allegedly due to a colleague for his legal advice.[141]

Within days of this outburst, an apparently definitive decision was handed down, sometime before the end of January 1601. She complained the judgment had not gone entirely her way yet she still expected to receive the huge sum of over 23,000 ducats, minus various deductions—excessive as she thought, and which finally amounted to some 4,000 ducats—that were deemed to have been spent on her upkeep during the years when she had lived with her uncle.[142]

At the same time as this seemingly final decision was announced, the 23-year-old King Philip III did indeed move his capital to the northern Castilian city of Valladolid. The move out of Madrid was inspired by the young monarch's dependence on the duke of Lerma, another of Luisa's distant relatives. Not only did Valladolid lie close to the duke's own estates, it is highly likely that this, the most pragmatic of Spanish ministers, resented the pious interference that the king's closest female relatives were exercising from their base in Luisa's old home, the Descalzas Reales.[143] Finding somewhere to live in the new capital would be no easy task. She would be competing with literally thousands of bureaucrats, courtiers, and their servants and families who were heading north, and at first she wondered if she could stay with Magdalena de San Jerónimo's sister who lived in the city. Instead two members of the Company came to her assistance.

To her unqualified delight, Luisa found herself being accommodated next to the Colegio de San Albano, usually known as the English College in Valladolid, where on a daily basis she would bump into young men who were steeling themselves to return to their native country and the possibility of dying for their beliefs.

The two Jesuits who found the house were Fathers Jerónimo Acosta and Antonio de Padilla, both closely connected with plans for the reconversion of England although neither was on the books of the College. Acosta had much earlier passed on to Luisa at least one account of martyrdoms in England, and Padilla was one of the favourite teachers of the notoriously hard-to-please English seminarians who were farmed out for teaching across the city. As a pupil of the great philosopher-theologian Francisco Suárez, Padilla was full of new ideas which thrilled his English pupils who had already mounted a boycott against lectures merely repeating what Thomas Aquinas had written 300 years before. It must have been Padilla who informed his sister that Luisa was moving to Valladolid and the countess of Santa Gadea generously offered to take Luisa with her. This was no small benefit, as crossing the mountains which separate Madrid from northern Castile in the middle of winter was not to be undertaken lightly. When she arrived in Valladolid, Luisa stayed for a short while with the countess's mother before she moved into the house next to the English College, sometime before May 1601.[144]

The contrast between the countess of Buendía's mansion and her new home was stark. As Ceráin said, she always chose to live in tiny houses which were 'indecent' for someone of her illustrious rank, which forced him to conclude this was a 'mystical disguise' designed to allow her to conduct a holy life, away from everyone, and especially her family.[145]

Dedicated to England's first Christian martyr, St Alban, the Colegio San Albano occupied the same site as it does today, though then the road that runs past was called the calle real de Burgos, being the highway leading north out of the city towards Burgos. Far enough from the centre of Valladolid for Luisa to boast that she was not really living at court, her new home shared a wall with the English seminarians.[146] Opened by the Jesuits in 1589, the College's principal founder was Robert Persons, who had himself been a missionary in England. Under his leadership and that of Joseph Creswell, the College, along with its counterpart in Seville, served as a training ground for potential missionaries. Luisa's house was probably on the site of what is now the chapel, which replaced an earlier chapel that was pulled down and incorporated into the college cloister. Today's chapel still has its own well, which might partly explain the extreme dampness of where she lived.

Only Inés and Isabel were living with her now, and Ceráin's description of their regime is worth quoting at length, because, despite being an admirer from Madrid days, not even he could disguise his perpetual bafflement at how she lived:

The furnishings in the house and her clothing were intended to keep her hidden away by humiliating her and causing horror in the outside world to make everyone keep away from her, because the single decoration in the house was a rudimentary cross crudely made out of pinewood that hung by itself on the wall. There was an old chair designed to make every visit an experience and two lumps of cork for the women to sit on. I never saw the bed myself, but my wife, who saw right inside, said it was as measly as everything else.[147]

As for her clothes, Luisa followed the fashion she had set in Madrid. By wearing a coarse dark cloth and using a crude rag as a veil, she adopted what was effectively a widow's garb but she also saw herself as spiritually married to Christ. This perplexed Ceráin, as he knew that the Saviour was alive and in glory and therefore could not have a widow, spiritual or otherwise. In a convoluted piece of logic he concluded that she must have thought of herself as dead to the world on the grounds that she was living apart from her husband.

Because he knew the ins and outs of her legal case, it puzzled him that she lived in grinding poverty despite never really needing to want for money. There was more than enough for a compromise with her father's executors and their heirs. This time, the constantly perplexed Ceráin decided she was intending to set an example of how to live according to the lights of the Early Church. Luisa retained fond memories of him, and years after they last met she sent him part of the chest of an English martyr.

Ceráin was on the right track in thinking that the Primitive Church's uncomplicated way of life was a perpetual point of reference for Luisa. In London she pointedly compared the recusants' use of private houses for clandestine religious services with what the earliest

Christians had done when faced with persecution by the Roman emperors. The memory of those martyred in ancient Rome was kept alive by one of the most widely read (and copied) books of medieval and early modern popular piety, the *Golden Legend*, and the cult of the ancient martyrs received a boost in Luisa's lifetime when, in 1584, the Pope decreed that the revised *Roman Martyrology* was to form an indispensable part of the liturgical life of the Catholic Church. Its calculations confidently assigned a saint or martyr for every day of the ensuing four millennia.

Luisa's wish to create a life of pristine simplicity was rudely shattered when, just as the judges were finally making up their minds, her brother Alonso launched a countersuit against her in the summer of 1604. Their last surviving sibling, Juan, a soldier in Italy, had died a few years earlier in 1600, and Alonso was now going back on a promise that he would never take his sister to court.[148] Dealings between the two had, in fact, been sour for some time. He did not take the state of his soul seriously. Their relationship had improved a couple of years before she left for Valladolid when news came through from Jaraicejo of the birth of a daughter, Ana, and his decision to be more earnest in religion.[149] Congratulating him for taking communion and for choosing a holy and experienced confessor, she said he could put in his will that she would look after her niece if this ever became necessary, but she pointedly suggested that the child's financial executor must be someone who could be relied upon to provide accounts whenever asked. The following year she wrote to say how pleased she was to hear that her niece was well, but underlying tensions with her brother were still in evidence; she could not resist using the occasion to justify her own refusal either to marry or to become a nun.[150] Pretending to speak about her niece, she wrote,

although I wish her to lead a holy life, on no account would I try to twist her vocation away from the estate to which Our Lord inclines her, which is the surest way to find salvation, and even those who marry can achieve great perfection if they so wish.

Alonso's legal claim was that the entire sum (after deductions) of just over 19,000 ducats that she was about to receive in fact belonged to the family's *mayorazgo*, the entailment which the crown had allowed his father to set up for the benefit of his eldest son. Alonso's decision is understandable, even if the lateness of his claim must have come like a bolt from the blue. His second child, Francisco, was either already born or on his way, and the future of his growing family was understandably his first concern. It must have riled him that Luisa was intent on giving away her share of the family's fortune to strangers. She initially stood her ground, saying that Melchor de Molina—another highly influential lawyer suggested to her by the Jesuits—was 'defending me bravely against my brother', but after much soul-searching Luisa concluded that she could not let her legal case any longer stand in the way of her calling. Though protesting that her case was watertight, she decided to compromise, being, as she claimed, overly generous. Alonso accepted her offer to hand over 5,000 ducats the moment she received her inheritance.[151] Since it concerned a royal entailment the pact between brother and sister required the king's approval. King Philip III gave his permission on 6 December 1604, only weeks before Luisa set out for England.[152]

6

Generation of Vipers

A glance at an atlas might suggest that the histories of Spain and England had little in common. In fact, dealings between the two countries had been close since the later Middle Ages. What brought them together was a shared hostility towards the French. Spain, or to be more precise Castile, took advantage of friendship with England to counteract the threat from both France and the Crown of Aragon, a medieval federation which included the kingdom of Valencia, the county of Barcelona, as well as Aragon itself. Relations between England and Spain became so intertwined that, in the later fourteenth century, an English army under Edward III's son, John of Gaunt, invaded in order to pursue the claims of his Spanish wife to the throne of Castile. A century later, shortly after the first Tudor had defeated Richard III on Bosworth Field, Ferdinand and Isabella's daughter, Catherine of Aragon, married Henry VII's elder son, Arthur, Prince of Wales, and, after his premature death, she was betrothed to his brother, the future King Henry VIII. When the Emperor Charles V added Spain to an empire that already included the Netherlands as well as much of southern Germany and Austria, the wish for an English counterweight to France was all the greater, with the result that not even Henry's break with Rome could dissolve Anglo-Spanish friendship. When his daughter Mary I restored the papacy she entered into marriage with the emperor's son and heir, Philip. With the accession of her half-sister Elizabeth I, England definitively broke with the papacy and introduced a thoroughly Protestant Church which caused the long-standing ties of friendship to be replaced by almost a half a century of hostility and periods of outright war.

It was against this background of a clash between religions that Spain and England were dragged into a war which neither of their rulers wanted. Even if Queen Elizabeth had wished to, she was in no position to prevent sailors operating out of the West Country and elsewhere from practising their peculiar mix of piracy and trade in the Spanish-dominated Americas. These often devout Protestant mariners had already rejected Rome's spiritual authority, which meant they were never going to tolerate an Iberian monopoly on trade with the New World that hinged on a papal decision to divide up these lands between Portugal and Spain. The English raids in the Caribbean and beyond further jeopardized the already unsteady relations between London and Madrid. In a family as well connected as Luisa's we can take it for granted that she grew up hearing stories about the ungallant and murderous attacks by English corsairs on the Spanish empire. She was 6 years old when a notorious set of skirmishes took place on the Atlantic coast of Panama around the town of Nombre de Dios. On this occasion Francis Drake attacked several nearby settlements, allied with runaway slaves and tried to seize the silver from Peru which was brought overland across the Panamanian isthmus for loading directly onto ships waiting to sail back across the Atlantic. He soon became so notorious that the Spaniards coined their own version of his name, *El Draque*, making play with their word for dragon. By 1578 colonial towns on the Pacific Ocean found themselves vulnerable to English raids.

By the 1580s the two monarchs had been pushed to the edge of open warfare. Elizabeth was being pressed by her privy councillors to send troops to support the Protestant rebels in the Netherlands who were defying King Philip's authority, and it was an open secret that Spain was preparing an armada for the invasion of England. In what must have seemed to Spaniards as something akin to a modern act of terrorism, Drake in 1585 sacked the Galician port of Vigo before crossing the ocean to attack—not for the first time—the city of Cartegena de Indias on the Atlantic coast of today's Colombia. Two years later he raided the shipyards of the Andalusian port of Cádiz, and two years after that he sacked Lisbon, the capital of Philip's newly acquired Portuguese kingdom.

Luisa's inherent curiosity about the wider world is reason enough to assume that from an early age she was alive to the growing antagonism between her country and England. At the root of this hostility was a religious rivalry between an aggressively Protestant England and an implacably Catholic Spain, so it naturally followed that she took a keen interest in what was going on inside Queen Elizabeth's kingdom. The English state persecuted its religious opponents more harshly than many European countries. Under 'Bloody Mary' hundreds of Protestants were burnt at the stake for heresy and many more were driven into exile, and this brutality continued in Elizabeth's reign when scores of priests were executed as traitors. Lay Catholics were not normally executed just for following their religion but they were excluded from public office and subjected to an increasingly severe set of laws designed to harass and bankrupt those who would not worship once or twice a year in the Church of England. If they did shelter priests, then they too could be found guilty of treason. Not even women were exempt. In 1601 the well-to-do Anne Line was executed for abetting a priest, precisely as Luisa was to do in London.[153]

The Society of Jesus quickly assumed a leading position in the English Mission. The return of the first English Jesuits during the summer of 1580 under Edmund Campion's leadership marked the beginning of a particularly aggressive stage in the struggle to reconvert England. The outcome of this first mission was to mark Luisa for life. In the first half of Elizabeth's reign, most of the secular Catholic priests active in England were survivors from Queen Mary's reign or earlier, and on the whole they were prepared to administer the sacraments without calling too much attention to themselves. The arrival in the 1570s of English priests trained on the Continent posed a greater ideological threat to Elizabeth's government, but the real turning point was the coming of the Jesuits, who, as members of a cosmopolitan religious order operating under Rome's direct authority, were hell-bent on reminding English Catholics of their primary allegiance to an international community of believers. Robert Cecil, chief adviser to both Elizabeth and James, appreciated the danger. Secular priests belonging to no specific order offered little threat to the state but Jesuits he regarded as the spawn of serpents, 'that generation of vipers'.[154]

Campion was put to death in London on 1 December 1581 when Luisa was almost 16 and living in the viceregal palace, at the height of her uncle's mortifications. The king of Spain and Queen Elizabeth were still managing to keep diplomatic channels open, and the post of Spain's ambassador was occupied by Bernardino de Mendoza, one of Luisa's more distant relatives. He composed a brief but dignified letter describing Campion's death that poured scorn on the Privy Council's assertions that Campion and the three co-religionists who died with him were killed for the secular crime of plotting to overthrow Elizabeth. According to Bernardino, it was evident when Campion mounted the scaffold that his nails had been pulled out during months of torture. In a masterly understatement he wrote that the death of Campion and his friends needed no miracles to consolidate the faith of England's Catholic community; it was enough that their calm dignity had set an example in imitation of the sufferings of *la primitiva Iglesia*—the Early Church—just as Luisa's friend Ceráin had described her new way of life. In a comment that foreshadows her career in London, Bernardino de Mendoza described how the faithful 'were putting themselves in evident danger' to collect relics of these holy men.[155] A handwritten copy of the short despatch may have reached Pamplona, and thinking about Campion's death helped crystallize Luisa's desire for martyrdom in England. She elected to think of Bernardino's account as an instrument of God.[156]

The next significant stage in her developing thoughts about martyrdom took place after she had moved out of her uncle's palace in Madrid. Living next door to the Jesuits proved to be a constant reminder of the sufferings of the English Catholics, and since she was already receptive to the idea of martyrdom Luisa must have imagined that divine intervention had once more placed her close to people intimately connected with England. Sooner or later she would have learnt she had not been the only person transformed by the first mission. A young member of a landed Norfolk family, Henry Walpole, was so taken by Campion's bravery in his final moments that he lost his faith in Protestantism. He eventually turned up at the English College in Valladolid, which had its own direct connections with the first Jesuit martyr in its main founder, Robert Persons, who had been with Campion in England.

In 1595 the English College celebrated its own first martyr when news came through that none other than Henry Walpole had been put to death in London. Before the year was out, Persons's deputy in Spain, Joseph Creswell—who had also known Campion—had completed an account of Walpole's trial and execution. Creswell wrote this slim volume in Spanish and not Latin in order to maximize its readership at a time when the long-term future of the English seminaries was precarious, and it played strongly on the fact that Walpole had been captured within 'twenty four hours of setting foot in England'. Just what could he have done in that time to threaten the Elizabethan regime, Creswell demanded to know? Perhaps disingenuously, Creswell did not mention the fact that both he and Persons had passed highly disloyal, even treasonous, messages from potentially rebellious English Catholics to Elizabeth's enemies, the king of Spain and the Pope. The effect of this hand-sized book on Luisa was electric. It became her inseparable companion even at night, being stowed under her pillow while she slept.[157]

The power of reading descriptions of the deaths of Campion and his supporters was intensified by the fact that Luisa forged a personal link with both Creswell and Persons. As leading lights at the Colegio San Albano, they were riding back and forth to the Jesuits' headquarters in Madrid. Though she never saw Persons again after he was summoned to Rome in 1597, she often mentioned him in her letters from London, even staying with his sister in the Low Countries before crossing the English Channel. In fact, she actively sought out the company of anyone connected with the English Mission, and if

she knew that any father from the Company or any priest from the English Colleges had arrived, her confessor would bring them along, as he knew she liked this and she spent ages talking about what was happening in England and the terrible persecution which the Catholics suffered . . . and the more cruelties and harassment they told her was like wood for the fire burning in her heart.[158]

We can assume that Henry Walpole was not among the English priests who called on her in the calle de Toledo, if only because, had he befriended her, Luisa would have been completely incapable of not shouting this from the rooftops. Nevertheless, three of his brothers numbered among her closest friends, Richard, Christopher, and Michael. The latter acted as her principal confessor in England and was at her bedside when she died.

The fact that when Luisa left Madrid for Valladolid she once more found herself living next door to people closely connected with the English Mission could only have seemed to be a further providential sign that she should abandon the safety of Catholic Spain. The young priests, her neighbours, were angels, she confided to a friend, and their presence gave her great consolation.[159] Her momentous vow of 1598 had not indicated where she might find martyrdom, only committing her to seek out 'all those opportunities of martyrdom which are not repugnant to God's law', but England was the obvious place.[160]

England was far and away the most persecuting of the larger European states. The Netherlands no longer provided good hunting ground for martyrdom. Despite the war that was being fought against the United Provinces, half the population in the north states remained true to the Old Religion, with a blind eye being turned towards Catholicism so long as it was practised without public scandal. With the Wars of Religion over, France was fast becoming a receding challenge. In 1602 Luisa praised the Discalced Carmelites for their eagerness to travel into a France that had been torn apart by religious wars. Carmelite legend has it that she recommended Mother Ana de Jesús to lead the party of six intrepid nuns, yet by the time they set out in August 1604 the formerly Protestant King Henri IV presided over an essentially Catholic France.[161]

From the point of view of modern psychology, thoughts of a heroic death can be seen as displacing pain and suffering, so reading about the deaths of men like Campion and Walpole may have merely channelled Luisa's childhood experiences in a particular direction. But it is not that she had thoughts of martyrdom that makes her stand out; what is remarkable is the acumen through which she achieved her objectives. Far from being rendered emotionally inadequate, Luisa's upbringing gave her the wit and the strength to vie for twenty years with her spiritual advisers, first for the right to live a life of independent poverty and then to travel to the land that had persecuted Edmund Campion. Luisa was not mad—that is, if we define insanity as an inability to interact with the world around you—since it is undeniable that to achieve her goals she was able to listen, persuade, and, if need be, bide her time. Nor was she cruelly deluded into wanting to force others to suffer with her, being able always to distinguish between what was right for her and the vocation of others.

It is all the more startling that the adult Luisa has been presented as largely powerless, with her thoughts and memories portrayed as the result of gross manipulation on the part of those to whom she looked for spiritual guidance. To prop up this view doubt has been cast on whether Luisa had always felt called to seek martyrdom in England. The distinguished American Hispanist Anne J. Cruz has written:

In her autobiography, Carvajal explains her abandonment of Spain for England...as a long-planned act compelled by her religious zeal. Her letters, however, expressly contradict her autobiographical narrative on this and other points.[162]

Cruz propounds the view that 'her "desires for martyrdom" did not rise up when in her youth' in a number of ways.[163] By suggesting that the Society of Jesus wanted Luisa out of the way the moment she had handed over her inheritance, it is argued that her 'close connection with the Jesuit order has been understandably *downplayed* by her Jesuit biographers',[164] while elsewhere it is claimed that Luisa's twentieth-century Jesuit biographer Camilo Abad had 'obvious reasons' for wanting to suggest that Luisa had made up her mind to leave for England before she handed over her inheritance to the English Mission.[165] It is further stated that Luisa's autobiographical memoirs were drawn up 'while in London', in which case they would postdate her arrival in England and cannot therefore be adduced to provide evidence for her pre-existing desire for an English martyrdom.[166]

The question of when the autobiographical sketches were written can be dealt with relatively quickly. The complicated set of drafts and rough copies which comprise the memoirs are now preserved among the evidence gathered together to support her case for canonization. Since they are undated, any assertion that they were composed in London and during her last years (or indeed at any other time) is as yet unprovable, though it must be conceded that there are indications that they were at the very least revised after her arrival in London. The evidence that they were written up after her arrival in London at Easter 1605 comes in the main from a single memoir that deals with her longing to go to England, a feeling she elsewhere said she had had since she was 17 years old or less. It contains a phrase referring to 'this land', which is taken to indicate that it was written when she had already crossed the Channel. In fact, the passage taken in context reads as follows:

And whenever I thought about England, it seemed to me that, if I were to find myself there, it would be the greatest comfort I could have . . . And I was thinking many times over how to reach *this* land.

The use of one word—this/*esta*—is insufficient to demonstrate that Luisa compiled this memoir after arriving in England, as the actual significance of this word might just as easily be grammatical and refer back to England/Inglaterra. Put simply, the passage may actually mean this land *that I am in now*, but the point is that it could just as easily refer to this land *which I have just mentioned*.[167] More powerful evidence would come from the fact that Luisa refers to her cousins as the marquis and marchioness of Caracena, a title granted in 1606, the year after her arrival in London.[168]

Splitting grammatical hairs will not resolve the problem of dating, and until a full textual analysis is undertaken of her writings, including an assessment of the watermarks of the paper she wrote on, any alternative dating is equally conjectural. It remains conceivable that Luisa began composing her life story in order to justify 'her worthiness to undertake her English mission', which would mean that she started to think about her recollections in Valladolid or while she was whiling away her time in the Low Countries.[169] Since the content of her strictly autobiographical material ends abruptly before she left Spain, one possible explanation for this unexpected interruption is this: if Luisa was composing her *spiritual* memoirs with the intention of satisfying her male superiors, she may have stopped writing up the initial draft of her life story at precisely the moment she was given permission to set out for England.[170]

Fundamentally, when her memoirs were written is a red herring, as, quite frankly, Luisa's intention to seek martyrdom is indisputable from the moment she took her vow in 1598—at admittedly the ripe old age of 32—which was itself the affirmation of sentiments that went back by her own recollection to when she was in her teens. Even then she was conscious of the outlandish nature of her project, being self-aware enough to realize that those around her would think her utterly unhinged if they knew she wanted to live in Elizabeth's England. The most she risked was talking to her cousins in very general terms about the glory of martyrs. Not a word was said to her uncle or confessor, perhaps because she herself 'did not understand what God wanted of me'.[171]

After three or four years of adolescent indecision, Luisa decided to seek the guidance of two of the most famous religious leaders of the day, Fray Luis de Granada and María de la Visitación. Born in late 1504, Luis de Granada had earned a reputation for being one of the finest of all mystical writers, which predictably aroused the interest of the Inquisition. His opinion was that the ignorance of the ordinary people posed a graver threat to religion in Spain than the spread of Lutheran teachings. Luisa could not fail to be attracted by his belief that, whereas the God of the Old Testament demanded his chosen people to be good, the God of the New Testament graced his followers with the strength to achieve whatever he commanded. Luis de Granada was probably already in his eighties when she wrote to him in Lisbon, where he had lived for almost thirty years. He was asked to hand over a letter to his protégée, Sor María, who would then explain Luisa's predicament to him. Sor María was also known as María de Las Llagas (of the Wounds) on account of miraculously bearing the imprint of Christ's wounds on her body, the so-called stigmata, which had appeared for the first time on the body of St Francis of Assisi in the early thirteenth century.

Why did Luisa want to pass on a message through Sor María? We can only conjecture, but perhaps it was easier in the first instance to unburden herself to another woman who also seemed manifestly to suffer for her religion. As Luisa tried to express in her poem 'Sweet Manacles', her own indebtedness to God was so great that she felt compelled to suffer and die for his cause, and it may be she saw in María de las Llagas a kindred spirit. In the message intended for Fray Luis, she cogently explained that England was her ultimate destination because there she would find many opportunities for martyrdom 'or at least to suffer greatly for his holy love'.[172] Fray Luis wrote back saying he had delivered her letter but as yet had not been told the contents.

Sor María never replied, which was perhaps as well. Shortly after, she was denounced as fraudulent and her stigmata revealed as bogus. Far more than even Lucrezia and her dreams, María had become embroiled into the highest matters of state through her opposition to King Philip II's annexation of Portugal after the death of King Sebastian I, the last monarch of the Portuguese royal house of Avis. Sebastian was born in 1554 after the death of his father, the crown prince of Portugal, and his mother was the Infanta Juana who later founded the Descalzas Reales in 1554. The infant king's childhood was tragic as shortly after his birth Juana returned to Spain to take over the regency and at the age of 10 rumour has it that he contracted a sexually transmitted disease from a Jesuit confessor. Brave to the point of recklessness, Sebastian died in 1578, leaving no direct heir, during a madcap military campaign in North Africa. As for María de las Llagas, once she was exposed as a charlatan her reputation was lost for ever but her gullible protector, Fray Luis, finally recovered from the scandal. He continued to ride high in Luisa's esteem, and during her time in Valladolid, she constantly read his guide to Christian doctrine, which she called 'the best book in the world'.[173]

It took years before Luisa summoned up courage to broach the subject of martyrdom directly with her spiritual advisers. One day in her oratory in Madrid, she asked Joseph Creswell about the possibility of going to England but, as he was only too aware of her chronic illnesses, he told her 'that the body was not always able to follow the soul'.[174] Her reaction was that it would be pointless ever raising the subject with him again.

She was not the sort of person to remain idle while others tried to make head or tail out of her wishes. The usual household tasks beckoned, just as they had done since she first lived apart. The duchess of Medina de Ríoseco came across her as she was buying vegetables in Valladolid's main square. Vitoria Colona ordered her coachman to halt while she tried sympathizing with her friend over her impoverished state, only to be told by a smiling Luisa that it was far more pitiable for a duchess to have to condescend to talk to her![175] Despite her protestations of poverty, Luisa jumped at the chance in July 1602 to offer accommodation to five Englishwomen who were passing through the city on their way from St Omer to the English Convent of Syon, founded only a few years before in Lisbon by Philip II. They were a mixed bunch. Rumour was that one of the women had been in Queen Elizabeth's household, and three of them had allegedly not been confirmed, which allowed the papal nuncio to take time out from the royal court to come to the calle de Burgos for their confirmation. The priest accompanying the Englishwomen was invited to stay next door at the college, which presumably provided the extra bedding and other things Luisa would have needed for her guests.

She was enthralled, praising them not only for their religious zeal but also for their English jollity and the friendly way they treated everyone, including Inés and Isabel. They stayed only ten days. This was not nearly long enough to satisfy their hostess, who tried cajoling their priest, Father Cuthbert, to allow them to stay longer on the grounds that one of the group was ill and had already been bled twice. His concern was to return to Flanders as soon as possible but there was still time for them to be summoned, late one evening, to visit Queen Margaret, who used her husband's attendance at a baptism to sneak the visiting foreigners into the palace.[176] Among that group was almost certainly Elizabeth Smith, who eleven years later would write from Lisbon to thank Luisa for her help.

Luisa also acted as a go-between when a rich widow expressed an interest in founding a nunnery for women escaping persecution in England. On the very morning when her five guests set out for Portugal, doña Mariana de Paz Cortés turned up unannounced in a litter, having only just heard about the Englishwomen's arrival. Doña Mariana had inherited two fortunes, one from her husband, a high-placed official in the city, and the other from her parents, who had travelled to the New World to be with their kinsman, Hernán Cortés, the conqueror of Mexico. It was said she was worth 80,000 ducats, and so was four or five times richer than Luisa would ever be. Her grand house in Valladolid was known as Las Aldabas, behind which was the convent of Portaceli that she had recently founded. She was, however, Luisa's social inferior and completely unknown to her.

Later that same evening Luisa got wind of the fact that a certain lady had just written to the English College to say that, if the five women had left because there was nowhere for them to remain, she would be willing to finance their stay. It was not hard to put two and two together and Luisa concluded the letter was from doña Mariana, to whom she straightaway wrote to find out if this meant she was willing to found an English nunnery. There would be no shortage of high-born recruits, Luisa told her. For over a year Luisa tried to broker the setting-up of a Carmelite convent for Englishwomen; in the end Mariana decided to support a more modest Augustinian foundation.

Luisa was in a position to offer herself up as a recruiting sergeant for two reasons. First there were the many English contacts she had cultivated since her days in the calle de Toledo, and an acquaintance, possibly from childhood days in the Descalzas Reales, Magdalena de San Jerónimo, was now spiritual adviser to another old playmate, the Archduchess Isabel, the regent of the Netherlands. A proponent of 'tough love', this Dominican nun was famous for her innovative ideas about women's prisons. When she moved to the Low Countries, Luisa wrote to say 'that living in Flanders with England nearby was more to be envied than avoided'.[177] Just a short distance across the English Channel, on a route made busy by merchants, the Low Countries were invariably the first port of call for English Catholics, and Magdalena was perfectly positioned to help those wanting to start a new life in a Catholic country. Luisa asked her friend to arrange for the archduchess and her husband to intervene with King Philip and

Queen Margaret in the hope that they would lend their support to any new English nunnery in Valladolid, because once there was royal backing no one could stand in its way, not even the municipal authorities, who would be reluctant to see yet more of the city's wealth sink into a house of religion.

She had no hesitation in seeing if her friend could arrange for Margaret Walpole—sister to the martyred Henry Walpole—to be brought over to Flanders. She believed Margaret had some money to pay the dowry that was always required for entry to a nunnery, but if that would not stretch to cover the costs of her journey she promised to reimburse Magdalena as soon as Margaret Walpole arrived in Valladolid, where she could stay with Luisa's little community or travel on to Lisbon.[178] Nor was Margaret the only Englishwoman on Luisa's mind. She wanted to know how others who had fled England were getting on, especially Mary Percy, the daughter of the seventh earl of Northumberland, who was founding a Benedictine nunnery in Brussels.

Despite being drawn ever more tightly into a circle of priests and friends whose lives were dominated by the English Mission, perhaps what more than anything else confirmed her determination to become a missionary was her unbridled devotion to an image of the Virgin Mary which was honoured in the chapel at the English College. *Our Lady of Hope* was a statue of the Mother and Child that had been disfigured by English sailors during an Anglo-Dutch raid on the city of Cádiz in June 1596. Soldiers ostensibly under the control of the earl of Essex and Sir Walter Raleigh mutilated the Virgin's face and arms while the infant Jesus at her knee was cursorily lopped off. The desecrated image came into the possession of Luisa's benefactress, the countess of Santa Gadea, doña Luisa de Padilla, who placed it in her private chapel in Madrid. With prolix civility the members of the English College wrote to the countess in June 1600 to ask that they might be allowed to care for the statue:

what can be more reasonable than that the misdemeanour and barbarous incivility of English heretics towards her sacred image, in view of the world, should be corrected and controlled with no less publicity by the

Catholics of the same nation, and specially by us as we hope it shall be, and that the reverence which we shall do to the blessed virgin in this her image shall exceed all the trespasses and disloyalties which heresy hath been able to invent, and the folly of our countrymen put in execution against her.

Soon to be universally known as the *Vulnerata*, the wounded image arrived at the English College three months later, with the king and queen in attendance and paying their respects. The countess's brother, Antonio de Padilla, preached a sermon of welcome in which he talked of God's 'divine and most provident plot' to preserve true religion in England by means of the seminaries of the English Mission.[179]

The *Vulnerata* transfixed Luisa, who described in loving detail how, 'since it is just a few steps away from home, I present myself before her every day even if I'm very sick'. She brought to 'this sovereign wounded Virgin' her hard-line political views that conflated what was good for Spain with the best interests of the Catholic Church.[180] Increasingly out of line with the policy of peace pursued by the duke of Lerma, to Luisa it was obvious there could be no truck with heretics. All along the Atlantic coast and the Gulf of Biscay the first of hundreds of Catholic families from Ireland were coming ashore in the aftermath of an abortive Spanish landing at Kinsale in County Cork. Just three or four weeks before Luisa left Valladolid over two hundred indigent Irish men and women had to be inveigled into leaving the court and returning to makeshift camps in Galicia.

Living so close to San Albano meant she witnessed young priests setting out for England in the full expectation that, should they be captured, they would most likely suffer the horrifying death of being hung up until they lapsed into semi-consciousness before being cut down only to have their bowels ripped out and other parts of their bodies, including their heads, cut off. Their torsos would be quartered. This was a punishment reserved for those charged with treachery, and it was scarcely imaginable that a foreign-born noblewoman would ever be permitted the luxury, in her eyes, of such a fate, but if Luisa did go to England and assisted Catholic priests she had no reason to expect she would be treated kindly. Wherever she went after Valladolid, there could be no turning back. Once her inheritance was given away, she would have lost the best protection she had against the interminable suggestions that she should vanish into a conventional religious house. If her future really did lie in England, the time had come for decisive action.

7

The She-Apostle

L UISA has a claim to be one of the first, perhaps even the first, female missionary in the history of Christianity. Such a claim depends on how one defines a missionary, of course, and the word is indisputably a term of art. Yet, if we are content to think along the lines of someone who intentionally travelled to distant lands to champion their religion under hostile circumstances, it is a challenge to find an earlier example. We could go back to apostolic times and the sparsely documented life of St Thecla, who is said to have accompanied the Apostle Paul on some of his journeys, perhaps even being a relative, but as this near-legendary saint never left the Roman Empire she did not cross borders, unlike Luisa. The great eighth-century saint, Leoba, along with other nuns from Anglo-Saxon England, went with St Boniface on his missions to eighth-century pagan Germany, where they founded a number of religious houses, but it could be objected that these brave women did not travel alone. They went as part of an institutional group, whereas Luisa struck out on her own.[181] Above all in the eastern churches, St Thecla continues to be revered as an apostle who was equal to men, and so perhaps no more need be said than to register how an English contemporary derided Luisa in comparable terms, dismissing her as 'the Apostlesse, or the shee Apostle of England'.[182]

What matters is that the year 1604 transformed Luisa's life. Within a little over twelve months she had inherited a fortune, only to give it all away to coax her confessors into letting her travel to England. By Easter the following year she had exchanged a damp hovel on the busy road from Valladolid to Burgos for the transitory delights of a grand country house in Middlesex where the music for the Catholic mass was specially composed by England's greatest living musician.

Luisa may have been staunch in her determination to travel to England but the resolve of a single woman was not enough to make the almost impossible happen. The journey became feasible on account of two unrelated events, the first of which being the death of Elizabeth I in March 1603. Before the month was out news had reached the Spanish court that the queen had died a lingering death, and Luisa revelled at the idea that, though she might have reigned in earthly splendour for a few years in this world, her torments in the next would last infinitely longer. Hopes were high that the new king, James Stuart, would be tolerant in religion since he was the son of Mary, Queen of Scots, though Luisa shrewdly surmised that the English would not have taken him as their monarch if they were unconvinced of his Protestantism.[183] As king of Scotland, James had never been at war with Spain and peace feelers were put out at once, with delegations from Spain and Flanders gathering in London in the summer of 1604 for a conference which took place on the site of what is now Somerset House in the Strand. The result was the Treaty of London. It put an end to hostilities but was harshly criticized among Luisa's circle of friends because the king of Spain had brokered no formal concessions on behalf of England's Catholics.

The second factor that made her journey possible was that the count of Miranda had let it be known he would not be satisfied with anything other than a successful outcome to Luisa's lawsuit. In the cautious words of her first biographer, the mission to England suddenly became 'at least worth considering, and not out of the question, as it has appeared until then'. For good measure, he added there was 'morally speaking not a trace of danger'.[184]

Luisa had reached an age when a decision over her future could not be delayed indefinitely. Not long before her thirty-eighth birthday, and exasperated by the failure to set up the English nunnery in Valladolid, she confided to Magdalena de San Jerónimo that the time had come, with or without her inheritance, to seek the martyrdom to which she was irrevocably committed. With England plainly in mind, she announced she was 'resuelta de irme ahí a vivir o morir' ('determined to go there, to live or to die').[185] Magdalena was to burn the letter. The matter was still of the utmost secrecy.

The process of formally seeking permission had begun early in the year. Her confessor's reaction was to advise her to follow Ignatius Loyola's method for resolving important issues. Precisely when this took place is uncertain; all she tells us was that it occurred some six or seven months before the end of her legal case, by which she was almost certainly referring to the judgment handed down in August 1604. One of the Walpole brothers may have been the priest who gave her this advice[186] yet we also happen to know that another of her confessors, the renowned Luis de la Puente, recommended Loyola's *Spiritual Exercises* to one other woman from the city around this time.[187]

The *Exercises* were designed to resolve spiritual dilemmas by providing a step-by-step means of discerning what to do. As an ex-soldier, Loyola's approach was nothing less than methodical. His main preoccupation was that the end should not be confused with the means, and since the examples he chose to give concerned changes of status, such as marrying or becoming a priest, they perfectly matched Luisa's need to make up her mind about martyrdom. In his view, people usually made their decision first, only then deciding to serve God as best they could in the new stage of their life. For Luisa, this meant it would be incumbent to find out what God's purpose was for her, and only then determine whether this end was best achieved by going to England. Given her passion for mental prayer, it is obvious that one of Loyola's methods of discernment would have been particularly pleasing to Luisa. In her mind's eye, she was to think about someone

that I have never seen or known, and in whom I wish to see complete perfection. Now I should consider what I would tell him to do and choose for the greater glory of God our Lord and the greater perfection of his soul. I will act in like manner myself, keeping the rule I have proposed for another.[188]

This passage echoed not just her vow to become a martyr; as Esteban Ojeda from the Jesuits' college in Madrid later conceded, her oath of greater perfection impelled her towards England just as much as her promise of martyrdom.

The opinions of her non-clerical friends needed to be sounded out. Though she may have hoped their support would be a means of increasing pressure on her spiritual advisors, few of her acquaintances were enthusiastic. Somewhat loftily, the duchess of Infantado and the countess de la Puebla wondered if there was not good work still to be done in Spain and her lawyer, Melchor de Molina, tried hard to dissuade her by counting out the dangers.[189]

The one person who gave unstinting support was Valladolid's resident mystic, Marina de Escobar. Twelve years older than Luisa, she was for much of her life confined to bed through ill health, though this did not stop her from holding court in her parents' house where she fed her many visitors on a constant supply of visions. Summing up the two women, Inés concluded that Escobar deserved to be famous for her 'huge abundance of revelations', whereas Luisa's strengths lay in virtue and intelligence. To indicate the intellectual esteem in which she was widely held, Inés recalled that Father Antonio de Padilla decided to put their respective strengths to the test by asking both holy women for their help in interpreting a passage from Scripture but without letting on that he had asked each of them. The result was startling but indecisive, as they apparently both came up with the same answer.[190]

Escobar shared with Luisa a lack of enthusiasm for the cloister, preferring to gather around her a small community in her family home, but the decisions of the Council of Trent caught up with her, and at the end of her long life she was obliged to bow to the mood of the times and set up a fully enclosed nunnery.[191] She, too, was very much a daughter of the Jesuits, and both were under the spell of Valladolid's most charismatic preacher, the gaunt and hooknosed Luis de la Puente, head of another Jesuit college in the city. Far and away the city's most sought-after confessor, he was increasingly preoccupied with protecting himself from the blandishments of the courtiers and suitors flooding into the new capital. His fame pre-dated the transfer of the court to Valladolid, and Luisa had exchanged letters with him before she left Madrid.[192] Regardless of whether or not he was the person who had recommended the *Spiritual Exercises*, when he finally made up his mind to support her he could only bring himself to do so in roundabout fashion. Weighing up his words with care, he said 'that even if did not advise her to undertake the mission nor did he dare stand in her way'.[193]

As long as she adopted a submissive pose, it was perfectly in order for Luisa to initiate debate about her mission but her religious superiors—all men—retained an absolute right of veto.[194] Their power became apparent when she extended an invitation to another of Valladolid's busy circle of holy women, Inés López, also known as Inés de la Encarnación, to travel with her on her great journey. This Inés told de la Puente of Luisa's invitation when they were together one day in his college's chapel, which prompted him point blank to deny his permission.[195] Luisa could not even protect her long-standing companion, Inés de la Asunción, from the dictates of the priesthood. As late as November 1604 she was still included in the plans for the journey, and though Luisa liked to pretend that she had not revealed their final destination it was not hard for Inés to work out their destination.[196] But after hearing the two women's confessions, Luisa's spiritual director, Ludovico Da Ponte, intervened. Da Ponte was not a Jesuit but he obviously shared Ignatius Loyola's views about making important decisions. Thinking about Inés's decade-long devotion to her mistress, he took it upon himself to say that she was following her friend, not God, and before Luisa had left the church she was instructed to leave her companion behind. Luisa unflinchingly said the matter would be attended to at once.[197] To grant permission for a woman to become a missionary was, quite simply, unheard of, and if Da Ponte was not to be seen as encouraging women to usurp the active roles of men (nor gain a reputation for being under Luisa's thumb) he had to make it plain that her journey was exceptional.

In December Luisa started to make the practical arrangements for an imminent departure. Amazingly, she was ill and largely bedridden until the day she left. For much of the time Father Espinosa was with her day and night, and he described her sickness as 'supernatural', and later he assumed it was to prepare her for what lay ahead.[198] In her infrequent moments of lucidity, she had to keep busy. There was a dowry to be arranged to allow Inés to join her cousin, Isabel, in a nunnery in the nearby city of Medina del Campo, where a more recent friend, Mariana de San José, was prioress. She also had to oversee the final arrangements for divesting herself of the money that was coming her way. There was a flood of letters to her brother in Madrid to make sure he would be bought off with the offer of the 5,000 ducats. More delicate was the transfer of her assets to the Company. Technically, she had arrived in Valladolid still under the spiritual authority of Esteban de Ojeda, the rector of the Jesuit college in Madrid; according to the vow of poverty she made in 1593 she was obliged to take his advice. His impression had always been that she would hand over her legacy to the Jesuits of the calle de Toledo.

The bed where Luisa lay chronically ill in the closing weeks of the year was under siege from a brace of contending priests, each clucking away on behalf of the two Jesuit factions vying for her wealth. One was an unnamed confessor from the English Mission at San Albano and the other was Ojeda himself, who just happened to be visiting from Madrid. Ojeda asked her to send the other priest away but, fearing he would overwhelm her with his arguments, she refused, and instead broke the news to him that 'the money she had come into she had left to the Mission'.[199] The fear that she had been disobedient gnawed away at her till the time of her departure, barely a few weeks away. Ojeda was one of the last people she wrote to from Valladolid. She tried to square her conscience by reminding him that the money had, after all, gone to the Society, and she begged him never to drop her from his prayers.[200]

Without a second thought and with her eyes wide open, Luisa had walked straight into the snare set for her by the Jesuits of Valladolid. The fabled Luis de la Puente was not just an alluring confessor but an avid supporter of the English Mission and it is no surprise that he found firm theological reasons for releasing her from obedience to Rector Ojeda. To follow the orders of an absent superior from Madrid he adjudged to be not only difficult but dangerous.[201] He probably had a hand in choosing his young friend, Ludovico Da Ponte, to be her spiritual director, since as an Italian and a Franciscan it would be harder to reproach Da Ponte for having a vested interest in preferring the English Jesuits from Valladolid over the Spanish

Jesuits in Madrid. Now Luisa was free to dispose of her money as the Jesuits of Valladolid wanted, just as she wanted. For all their guile, the men who kept spiritual watch over her life were doing precisely what she wished.

This is not to say that Da Ponte had been anything less than scrupulous in his dealings with Luisa. Ten years her junior, he was, in fact, somewhat in awe of her. Each time they spoke he had come away astounded by her wisdom and good sense. Plumbing the depths of Luisa's labyrinthine psyche was a superhuman task for anyone, let alone for a young man, but he did his best to subject her motives to the most rigorous scrutiny he was capable of. He was clashing swords with a battle-scarred debater who rebuffed his suggestion that leaving for England was too hazardous by declaring that her suffering was already so great that she doubted it 'was possible to feel any more pain in this life'.[202] Inés was right to think that Da Ponte's opinion was crucial since he was 'her confessor and superior combined' but the poor man had been confronted by two almost irreconcilable propositions.[203] She may have convinced him that it was God's will to go to England but what she wanted to do was unprecedented. His verdict was as cautiously phrased as Luis de la Puente's. There had simply been no grounds to stop her.

On 22 December Luisa drew up her will which was dedicated to the Sovereign Virgin Mary. She had framed it with martyrdom in mind and began by specifying where she wanted to be buried.[204] Out of respect more than anything else, she indicated a preference for the main Jesuit house in Valladolid but failing that she could be buried anywhere that belonged to the Company or in any religious house that would bury a poor person. Richard Walpole of the English College was appointed her principal executor, and in the passage handing over control of her fortune to Robert Persons as head of the English Mission in Rome she made mention of her very first vow of poverty in Pamplona, as if fulfilling a destiny mapped out twenty years before. Persons was given carte blanche to set up a novitiate to train English Jesuits in any kingdom or province, in the world, as she rather extravagantly put it. For all that it was worth, the new foundation was to receive her household possessions but, more important, she bequeathed all her religious images and books. In return, she asked that the prospective students pay special devotion to two objects that had belonged to her uncle: the Crucifix with the Living Christ left to her in his will and a piece of the True Cross presented to him by the emperor in Germany and which his son, the second marquis, had passed on to her.

Arrangements still needed to be made for the costs of Inés's admittance to the convent at Medina (or to another house if the rigours of being an *augustina recolecta* proved too much). The lavish sum of up to 1,000 ducats was made available for her nun's dowry, and since it was impossible to forget the problems caused by her father's will, Luisa spelt out that, if Inés did not enter a nunnery, she was to receive 2 *reales* a day for the rest of her life, clear of all charges and without any suggestion that this depended on whether or not she married. Inés received a marble crucifix while Isabel received an image of the Virgin. Luisa had now divested herself of all her worldly goods. As far as we can tell, the only source of revenue remaining to her was a notional right to ask for help from rent for her house in the calle de Toledo, though, as luck would have it, it was rented to a Scotsman who was slow in paying.[205]

Luisa returned to the issue of her inheritance a few days later. In a document dated 7 January 1605, she reiterated that from the slightly over 19,000 ducats which the courts had granted her at the start of August her brother was to receive his 5,000 ducats before anything else could be done. Only when this had taken place were her other debts to be paid, and she attached a memorandum itemizing what she owed. She also repeated her original claim to be handing over to the English Mission the sum of 14,000 *ducados*.

It niggled Luisa that she was able to pass this precise sum to the Mission. She had probably had a rude awakening once the true costs of setting up a religious house were explained to her. In her will, she optimistically hoped that this sum might generate 1,500 or even 2,000 ducats a year, but by the time of the second document she accepted it might only raise an income of 1,000 ducats, presumably at the fairly standard rate of 7 per cent on government bonds or *juros*. Her debts may have crept up on her, as that would explain why she was obliged to ask the countess of Castellar to lend her 2,000 ducats to ensure that the capital sum of 14,000 ducats was reached. The countess charitably agreed to help if she could, and Luisa wisely left the rector of the English College to sort matters out. Estimating the cost of training a Jesuit priest is little more than educated guesswork—especially as it was not yet known in which country Luisa's novitiate would be set up—but if, as seems plausible, the charges might amount to 75 ducats a year, an annual income of 1,000 ducats a year might stretch to the cost of looking after between ten and fifteen novitiate priests.[206] Meanwhile, her lady friends were offering to defray the cost of her journey but she would only accept beasts of burden or, in the case of the count of Miranda's wife, help in obtaining a passport.[207]

Dated 21 January 1605, her last letters from the court were written to the three most important people in her life, Inés, Isabel, and her brother. The contents of these letters were so moving that they were discussed twelve years after her death during the investigation into her possible canonization, but even if she was thinking that her great journey might eventually lead her to the next world, obligations in this world remained. Top of her list of things to do was to repair the damage the court case had done to her relationship with Alonso. She used the occasion of the death of one of her lawyers, Luis Arias, to encourage her brother to muse on the need to prepare for things to come: 'Given the fragility of our natural lives there is nothing to compare with everyone of us having our debts paid up and settled with Our Lord for when we go knocking at His door.'[208]

She knew that her brother, with his growing commitments as a husband and a father, could not feel anything but aggrieved at the thought of all the money that would be passing from the family's hands, and in her will she had begged Alonso to accept that it was not lack of affection that had made her leave everything to the Jesuits. Now she implored him to include her in his prayers. No mention was made of her destination.

A letter now lost was also sent to her cousin Isabel who was then in Galicia where her husband was governor. They did not resume contact until some years after Luisa had settled in London but when they did her cousin admitted she had not understood what Luisa was hinting at when she wrote about going away. Inés had written to say she was pining for her mistress, and Luisa's reply began with a gentle reprimand that quickly turned into a loving account of the minutiae of her preparations, as if these might ease the pain at having been so peremptorily excluded from the journey. She also enclosed a letter for Isabel de la Cruz, congratulating her on having adapted so well to the enclosed life but asking her to help Inés come to terms with separation. In two days' time, she said, she would be gone.[209]

8

The Most Extraordinary Journey

Luisa set out from Valladolid on 27 January 1605 making a pitiful sight as she bobbed up and down on the high plateau that led first to the Basque Country and then onto the pilgrimage route that linked Santiago de Compostela with France. She had never ridden before and her chest was 'utterly broken' with bronchitis.[210] So impatient was she to leave that she elected to brave the depths of a Castilian winter with its icy temperatures and tracks that normally would be treacherous for months on end, letting herself be encouraged by a report that some particularly precarious routes remained open. To keep down costs she dispensed with a coach and took a mule instead, which required two youths from the English College to walk alongside to stop her falling off. A husband and wife who had agreed to take care of her rode alongside, and at least one other man completed the party. He was a priest in disguise.

Michael Walpole is often said to be the clergyman who accompanied her but in all probability he had gone on ahead to the Low Countries, perhaps to prepare the ground for her arrival.[211] John Blakfan is another candidate for her clerical travelling companion but he had reached Paris long before she left Spain.[212] In his history of the English College he tells the garbled story of a priest who had often confessed her and who, by chance, was setting out from Valladolid shortly before she was free to leave. Refusing to delay his journey, Luisa sent on a letter to San Sebastian, begging the cleric to wait for her there. Blakfan was probably writing about himself when he recalled that this priest had vehemently taken issue with her ambition to travel to England, bluntly warning her that it ran contrary to her 'sex but also to her language'.[213] She could not rebut the charge of not knowing English but she hit back, brandishing the names of saints Engratia, Lucy, and Agnes, and all the other divinely inspired women whom God had allowed to suffer for their faith under the pagan emperors.

Michael Walpole was intimately involved in the genesis of Luisa's journey whether or not he travelled with her.[214] Brother to the English College's first martyr, he was to become her spiritual director in London and with him she formed the strongest attachment of her mature life. He was at her side when she died, taking charge of the first steps to have her proclaimed a saint, and, as her first biographer, he skilfully wove her life's story out of the letters she left behind and the recollections of those who knew her. Nevertheless, the explanation Walpole gave of her journey to England is deceptively simplistic. He claimed that she was allowed to undertake her mission in order to provide England with an example of a holy life. She would be able to offer sound advice, demonstrate pious exercises, and console the afflicted.[215] There may be a smidgen of truth in what he had to say, but his justifications were intended to conceal the machinations which lay behind what Mariana de San José called 'the most extraordinary journey ever undertaken by a woman'.[216]

When Luisa left Valladolid no one in their right minds could have imagined that she would survive for eight years in an aggressively Protestant country. Who could have anticipated that she would be able to offer practical help when her body was wracked with illness? She spoke not a single word of the language, and before she left the Low Countries there were murmurings from Jesuits active in England that her presence would endanger what was in effect a priesthood-in-hiding.[217] Lay Catholics proved no more accommodating, with few of London's recusants prepared to put a roof over her head. Was Luisa even expected to survive for long in England?

To get there Luisa needed practical help. De la Puente and Da Ponte were both known for their holiness rather than as men of action, and all they could offer was spiritual support. It was not for them to provide the logistical assistance required to secrete her into England. Only the Society of Jesus, as custodians of the English Mission, could plan her journey, and the unavoidable conclusion is that decisions about Luisa's future were being taken far from the intimacy of the confessional box. The leaders of the English Mission mulled over the advantages and disadvantages of her mission. Though their behind-the-scenes deliberation has left little or no record, without their collusion Luisa's journey is inexplicable.

The three Walpole brothers, Richard, Michael, and Christopher, are likely to have formed, together with Joseph Creswell and Robert Persons, an inner circle among the English Jesuits on the Continent who weighed Luisa's personal wishes against the needs of high politics. Among those members of the Society of Jesus who had been stationed for a long time in England there were beginning to be worrying signs that they, too, were softening their attitude to the Protestant monarchy. Creswell, Persons, and the three brothers, on the other hand, represented the Continental faction which still hankered after no compromise in the war on heresy. For Luisa, it is true that England represented a bizarre form of emancipation, one where the state's persecution might allow her to achieve the active religious life that was normally denied women, yet there was a limit to what even Luisa could achieve on her own. Her emancipation rested on whether her aspirations suited the calculations of the men who dominated high political life.

The Walpoles had more reason than most to understand the dangers of missionary work. The execution of their brother served as a dreadful reminder of how swift the brutality of England's regime could be. The eldest surviving brother, Richard, boasted that it was a privilege that the Almighty had elected 'to make choyce of my owne flesh & bloode' to defend Catholicism.[218] Any operation involving Luisa required careful planning; to do anything less would be reckless and therefore irreligious. For once, being a foreigner and a woman offered advantages, as Luisa would surely be safe from the full rigours of the law even if it was likely she might be roughly handled if discovered. Richard Walpole boasted he was not worthy of following in brother Henry's 'happie stepps' but he nonetheless possessed a reputation for being reckless. Robert Cecil blamed him for a preposterous plot to kill Queen Elizabeth by the novel method of poisoning her riding saddle. Sir Charles Cornwallis, soon after his arrival in Spain in 1605 as James's new ambassador, branded his fellow Norfolk man 'a hot headed fellow' who was 'full of practices' and looked on him as ultimately responsible for Luisa's journey.[219]

In a remarkable letter which has only recently come to light, Michael Walpole turns out to be someone who became spectacularly convinced that the position of Catholics under King James had turned critical. Either at the start of 1604 or more likely a year later, just as Luisa was setting out from Valladolid, he wrote a lengthy and at times rambling letter from Brussels to Father General Acquaviva, the head of the Jesuit Order in Rome. He had lost all patience with King James, who, in financial terms, lapsed into treating Catholics as harshly as they had been under Elizabeth. The only honour the new king deserved came from being the son of Mary, Queen of Scots. What really aroused Michael Walpole's anger was that true Catholics—that is, those who supported the Jesuits—were under attack not just by false brethren but by 'pragmatic' Catholics as well.[220] He had in his sights the internecine conflict raging among his fellow religionists in England, who were bitterly divided between those prepared to work with the new regime and those who, inspired by the Continental Jesuits and their sympathizers, remained gung-ho. Writing in a highly allusive manner, Michael Walpole was in an anguished state as he described the present calamity in England, and it is easy to see how he might have thought that the arrival of a person as uncompromising as Luisa could force ditherers among English Catholics to make up their minds.[221]

As for Creswell, Luisa may have imagined he had been excluded from her decision-making process ever since he had warned her of the weaknesses of her body in Madrid, but this famously cantankerous individual, who was after all the vice-prefect of the Mission, was probably intimately involved in the power-games surrounding her departure. An inveterate meddler in English politics, he had taken charge of the Jesuit mission to England when Persons left for Rome and he remained a devout interventionist before Luisa's departure *and* after. At the end of January 1603, when Elizabeth I was already ill, he wrote to Philip III saying that the 'queen cannot live for long', insisting that Spain must decide whether to intervene to prevent the Scottish succession. Five years after that, he lent his weight to Sir

William Stanley's plans for a joint attack with the Irish leader Hugh O'Neill, the second earl of Tyrone, and other disaffected Catholic noblemen.[222]

Creswell did make crude attempts to adapt to the new circumstances. Not long after Luisa reached England he wrote a conciliatory letter to King James, suggesting he adopt the French example of limited liberty of conscience. With Henri IV's 1598 Edict of Nantes in mind, James was told that this course of action was 'tan moderno' ('really modern'). Whether an invitation to follow French fashion was designed to encourage or infuriate the new king of England is a matter of opinion, and Creswell may not have realized that James looked on Henri with contempt. The French king had brought the generation-long French Wars of Religion to a halt by his conversion from the minority religion, Calvinism, to Catholicism when he allegedly (and notoriously) decided that Paris was well worth a mass. Henri's decision to give up his Protestantism drew from James the caustic remark—in the context of the new fad for wearing disposable linen shirts—that the French king changed his religion as often as some people changed their clothes. Though Creswell wanted a sympathizer at the English court to present his letter when the moment was opportune, he revealed his true feelings when he told the Spanish king that it would not be handed over at all if James maintained his support for the Dutch rebels.[223]

The most distant but no less influential member of the circle was Robert Persons. From his vantage point in Rome, he oversaw a constant stream of information about the political situation in his native country, and it was he who decided that Louvain in the Netherlands was the best place to open a Jesuit house with Luisa's money. Fully realizing there were hotheads among English Catholics who wanted to attack King James, he was nonetheless far from aware that a plan was being hatched to blow up king and parliament, and he instructed Richard Walpole and Creswell to tell Philip III—at the very time that Luisa was crossing the Channel—that 'the crisis has been dampened in such a fashion that they are not expected to move without your majesty's permission and approval'.[224]

Was Luisa's presence in England intended to be part of the process of dampening down this crisis among King James's Catholic subjects?

This is unlikely in the extreme. There is no indication that she had any involvement whatsoever with the many dubious characters—including Guy Fawkes—who visited Creswell in Valladolid or used him to pass messages to the Spanish court. So why was she given high-level support in her wish to travel to England?

Creswell, Persons, and the Walpoles had calculated they had nothing to lose but much to gain from going along with her wishes. It is, of course, highly probable that they clouded their discussion by talking solely in terms of the need to honour an obligation to someone who had given over her entire fortune to the English Mission, never once mentioning the political calculations they each were making; but whatever way they chose to discuss her request, such a hard-nosed group of Church politicians was not blind to the immense benefits her presence in England, and better still her suffering, would bring to the Company.

The Society of Jesus could not fail to reap reward from backing Luisa. For instance, if she were publicly persecuted, the Continental Jesuits would have triumphantly exposed Spain's peace with England as a sham, with James's regal promises that he would turn a blind eye to the practice of Catholicism revealed to the world as worthless. But, if she were allowed to practise her religion freely, then the Society of Jesus would have achieved much more than the king of Spain in opening up England to a form of toleration. To suffer death en route would be sufficient to write a hagiographical account of why she felt impelled to cross the Channel.

The political advantages come into starker relief if we take the plunge and delve further into the murky power-struggle tearing apart the Catholic community in England. The Jesuits, both within and without England, were fighting with the secular or regular clergy to retain control of the Mission. Despite being allowed to travel round and preach, members of the Society of Jesus belonged to a religious order just as monks might belong to the Benedictines or the Carthusians. They also took their orders from Rome, which set the Jesuits apart from the secular Catholic clergy who adhered to no particular order and were instead under episcopal authority (which in the case of England was exercised by an Archpriest). The enduring rivalry between seculars and Jesuits was further embittered when the so-called 'Appellants' among the seculars appealed to the papacy to appoint a bishop in the hope that, unlike an Archpriest, he would have sufficient authority to rein in the Jesuits. Put very crudely, the English secular clergy were more willing than the Jesuits to consider some sort of agreement with Elizabeth and especially with James. Even lay Catholics were drawn into this clerical dispute, with the recusant community being sharply divided between those who were ministered to by the seculars and those who supported the Company. It was against this background that the Walpoles and their friends made the calculation that, if Luisa's presence were to become a cause célèbre, then the spiritual capital flowing the Jesuits' way would bolster their position not just in England but with the king of Spain and the papal court.

Priests had been trying to get into England secretly long before Edmund Campion was killed. Spies and informants in London's pay were posted along the most likely routes, eager to unmask clerics trying to enter the country in disguise. In 1591, one priest took two months to travel from Seville to Amsterdam, and he advised that special attention should be given to the clothes one wore,

which should not seem Spanish, and they could use Irish, Scotch, German, Polish or any other nation's name rather than English because the name attracts the attention of all who hear it. All Englishmen are considered either great heretics or determined Catholics, and both the one and the other of these things have a danger of their own on these roads.

Another priest, Oswald Tesimond, wrote that it had taken him four months to reach London from Valladolid. (Luisa certainly knew of him and quite possibly met him when she arrived in England.) Choosing to sail from Bilbao, he came aboard at the last moment to avoid suspicion, being unable to take food or water with him. The only place left was near the stove where 'the greatest and almost incredible annnoyance was the smoke, so that I could not open my eyes'. Worse was to come. Nine days later the ship reached Calais, where it hit a sandbar while trying to outmanoeuvre Dutch marauders.[225]

Luisa would have heard many stories about the potential dangers lying in store for the strange calvacade setting out from Valladolid, but the members of her party were relatively safe while they remained inside Spain. The first significant town they reached was Burgos, which provided one of the rare occasions when she permitted herself time to visit the innumerable shrines she would pass along the way, and she went to see the image of the Holy Christ, now in the cathedral. The next stop of note was San Sebastian, where they were detained for three days, partly because of heavy rain, but also because she felt too ill to travel, though she summoned up the strength to visit Ignatius Loyola's house.

In San Sebastian she met up with an Englishman, who was presumably the seventh and final member of her party. This initiated the first scare, as she revealed in a letter to Christopher Walpole. What seems to have happened is that the man had with him a boy who had spent time at the English College in Valladolid, and since he was identified by 'the father' who was with her, she was rightly scared he would recognize the priest, as the suspicion was the boy had once been in the pay of the bishop of London. On top of this the town was overrun with Englishmen on their way to Valladolid for the ratification of the Treaty of London.[226]

The scare passed, and wearing the same outlandish clothes she had worn since she left her uncle's house, she crossed over into France and headed first for Bayonne and on to Bordeaux. She was relieved to be well treated, as France was regarded as hostile territory not so much because of diplomatic rivalry with Spain but because the country was only slowly recovering from a thirty-year-long civil war between Protestants and Catholics. The Jesuits had been allowed back in the country only two years before. Along the way some thought that she had come to found a Carmelite nunnery in France, although in the end she faced none of the dangers that had befallen her friend Ana de Jesús and her party of nuns who, just a few months earlier, had been barracked and feared for their lives as they made their way to Paris.[227]

To pay for her journey, Luisa had borrowed 50 *escudos* from her inheritance. Taking into account the premium attached to gold, this amounted to about £18 or £20 in English money of the time, which covered the costs of the whole party.[228] Out of this she paid for different lodgings each night. Without fail, the day began with mass, and to take maximum advantage of the short winter days the group would eat before it was time to set out. Then

we travelled the whole day without getting separated or anyone getting muddled up, being extremely careful to measure both time and distance so to arrive in daylight at the next village so as to choose a good place to stay, and once there I would retire to my room, securing the door with a lock I had brought for that purpose.[229]

In addition to the snow and rain, there was the danger from the broad rivers and estuaries to be found along France's Atlantic coast. Luisa was petrified of water, a fear made worse by being stranded for two hours among the waterways before her frantic gestures brought a passing boat to the rescue.[230]

In Paris she rested for a week in a city which vied with Prague for the title of the most elegant capital in Europe. The medieval cathedral of Notre-Dame was one of the sights she took in, along with the Jesuit headquarters, and she even caught a glimpse of the royal palace of the Louvre, though King Henri was not in residence. Sightseeing apart, most of the time she spent with the Carmelites whom Ana de Jesús had courageously brought from Spain. A feisty companion of St Teresa, Ana had founded many convents in her own right but at 60 years of age she found it hard to pick up French, which Luisa regarded as easy for a Spanish speaker. As one of Ana's companions recalled in her autobiography, 'it is hard work going to live in a strange land and not know the language, especially if you are no longer a girl, since young people learn so quickly'. One of Luisa's blind spots was not to realize how precocious her own intellectual abilities were, and, prig-gishly, she was shocked to discover that all Ana could say after six months was, 'comment allez-vous?'[231]

Leaving Paris behind, Luisa took the indirect route to the Low Countries. She went via Rouen to avoid Brussels, where she thought her party might be more easily recognized but she was also deter-mined to keep out of the way of the archduchess, who most certainly would not have approved of her childhood friend being sent into England at a time when the Treaty of London was not formally ratified.[232] Isabel had been Spain's preferred candidate for the English throne, having inherited her father's watery-thin claims to represent the House of Plantagenet. Creswell had turned the English College into the heart of the campaign for an Isabelline succession, and Luisa had done her bit to nudge Isabel into taking her dynastic claims more seriously by writing to Magdalena de San Jerónimo from Valladolid and saying that 'my neighbours the English' supported her right to the crown.[233] After her marriage to the Archduke Albert and their creation of an artistically brilliant court, the Infanta Isabel was understandably reluctant to press her claim to the notoriously unstable English throne. By 1603 Persons conceded that 'the matter grew at length to be little esteemed',[234] though Luisa—always the cold war warrior—never quite gave up believing that Isabella might one day be England's second Queen Elizabeth.

The Jesuits' plan was for Luisa to be in position in the Netherlands while a final decision was taken about her future. She rashly thought she might help put in order the novitiate that Persons had decided to found in Louvain, but a property had not yet been acquired and it was to be another two years before it opened. Instead she went to the town of St Omer, home to an English seminary and virtually on the coast. For a month she lodged with Robert Person's sister, Ann. She heard mass every day but otherwise led a secluded life, trying to draw the least possible attention to herself in a town which was crawling with English spies. She feared she would have to wait there several months, since 'Father *M[ichael].W[alpole].* was artfully holding me back while he wrote to Rome'.[235]

Walpole's artfulness? She probably meant that he wanted to be confident that all the pieces were safely in place. First of all he needed assurances from Henry Garnet, the head of Jesuits in England, that she would be made welcome by at least a sufficient number of the forty-or-so members of the Society who were operating there. At the same time, he would have to try to establish from Robert Persons that nothing had come to light at the papal court to cause her to postpone or abandon her mission. In fact, he was in Naples at this time, almost certainly because his enemies in the papal curia did not want him in Rome where they had their own reasons for fearing he might incite opposition to King James.[236] But Person's blessing could be taken for granted, and late in March—before word from Persons was received —Henry Garnet ordered a priest to escort Luisa to England.

One tradition is that it was John Blakfan who took her across the Channel, and as a fluent Spanish speaker frequently on the move between England, Spain, the Low Countries, and Rome, he would have been the ideal escort for the final leg of her journey. The argument against his involvement is that around this time he made a formal request to be allowed to return home to England but was turned down by Henry Garnet, who appears to have sent someone specially over from England to fetch her.[237] News finally came through that Luisa was to pack her bags and leave St Omer within a matter of hours. Divine intervention, she claimed, had dissolved the final obstacle in her way,

and hastened my journey. Because meanwhile Father H[enry] G[arnet], realising my implacable resolution . . . sent a very responsible person with four days left in his passport and orders to bring me straight to his house, which was everything that I could wish for.[238]

Using some of the money left over from selling her pack animals in St Omer, Luisa travelled down the river Aa to Calais where she hired a entire ship for her small party.[239] A French boy was on board, and she allowed two poor English lads to hitch a ride, probably to make her party stand out less. For most of Good Friday the ship battled against the winds and it was known that Dutch warships were on patrol. By the evening there was a bright moon and a favourable breeze, and within two-and-a-half hours the ship had reached England.

Luisa disembarked at Dover on the morning of Easter Saturday.[240] A strange incident took place as she was about to wade onshore. Eager to be the first off ship, but with her powerful aversion to water, she looked over the edge to see how to avoid sinking into the sand. Then

a handsome young fellow of 14 or 15 years of age, manifestly pleased about my arrival, stepped right in front of me, just by my right arm, and extending one of his, happily and graciously offered his help. And resting my hand on his arm, I jumped down without any anxiety or difficulty. And when my party reached land, they wanted to know who had helped me out of the boat. Glory be to the majesty of God!

This story about a mysterious stranger is similar to what she said about the coach journey with her uncle to Olite. Did an angelic-looking young man actually help her, or was it an hallucination brought on by the ecstasy of her arrival? There can be no answer to this, but what is important is that Luisa, by her own admission, did not always include this detail when recounting the story of her arrival. She was in England to do a job of work, not to make claims for her own devotional gifts.[241]

Those first blissful moments on English soil were cut short by the behaviour of the customs officials. She had been advised to change her name, and though reluctant to do so, she compromised by drawing upon her first baptismal name and one of her many aristocratic surnames, and it would appear she entered the country as Antonia Enríquez.[242] A greater indignity followed when the officials impounded some of her books and seized the penitential instruments she wore under her clothes, in all probability her whips too. It was a mortification itself, she said, to see them fall into such hands, especially as the officials found it all very amusing![243]

Her embarrassment was short-lived. She quickly found herself in a 'delightful paradise amidst an inhospitable forest of wild beasts'. She was describing a country house which had been rented three years before by Catholic owners and where mass was readily available, which came as a considerable relief because during the two days she spent getting across the Channel she had been unable to hear mass, the only time this had happened since she left Spain. Everything about the house and garden impressed her. The chapel was beautifully provided for and there were relics and pictures of saints on the walls and by the windows. She was delighted by the 'beautifully arranged music for various voices and instruments, and after lunch and dinner there would be deeply spiritual motets to broaden the spirit'.[244]

The likelihood is that she had finally met the chubby and fair-haired Henry Garnet at White Webbs, a large country house inside Enfield Chase, a few miles north of the City of London.[245] His friend of long standing, Ann Vaux, had lived there since 1600 with her elder sister, the widowed Eleanor Brooksby. They had both known Edmund Campion and were friendly with Robert Persons. The great

English polyphonic composer William Byrd regularly produced music for gatherings at White Webbs, and his own house at Stondon Massey was only about 15 miles away to the east. By a remarkable coincidence we know that around the time of Luisa's arrival a musical soirée was held in Henry Garnet's honour, with several gentlemen being present, including 'Mr William Byrd, who played the organs and many other instruments'. Byrd had known Garnet since the Jesuit's return to England in 1586, and Garnet had helped secure for his son, also called William Byrd, a brief stay at the English College.[246] Among Byrd's more popular compositions was a poem about Campion's death which has been ascribed to Luisa's beloved Henry Walpole.[247]

Garnet soon got wind that White Webbs was being watched, and as a precautionary measure he left Luisa in the more-than-capable hands of the Vaux sisters. He took refuge in Erith, on the Thames estuary to the east of London, in a house he had rented through, by chance, the good offices of a Gunpowder Plotter. Though this summer proved to be his last, Garnet continued to move around, finding time to lead a pilgrimage to the shrine at Holywell in north Wales.

For a month and a half Luisa enjoyed the joys of English country life, albeit by her own admission she had fallen so ill that she was confined to bed for a fortnight. But if she was beginning to harbour any doubts about whether Catholics really were being persecuted, she soon had first-hand experience of the uncertain lives they led. When a warning came through that there was a raid coming, she was forced to dress quickly despite being so infirm that she could barely stand up. With Ann and Eleanor Vaux she was driven in a coach at high speed to London, all disguised as poor women. Other members of the household made their escape as best they could, 'some through the fields, others by the river'. Safer lodgings were arranged for the following day, but the saintly Luisa spent her first night in London in a poor man's tavern.[248]

Finding someone who would take her in was not easy. While he was negotiating her arrival in England, Walpole became aware of the reluctance amongst some of Henry Garnet's companions to take charge of a woman who was 'delicate, sick, physically weak, and who did not know the language'.[249] With understandable exaggeration, Luisa claimed that Garnet was the only person who treated her with civility, coming into London when she needed lodgings. Even the charming Walpole had great trouble 'finding me a room in any Catholic's house, even though they were handsomely paid, and what's more they always let me know they were doing this reluctantly and at a cost to themselves'.

She liked to believe that all she was asking for was a quiet corner of someone's house where she could pray and peacefully acquire the language. Instead, throughout her first English summer she was constantly transferred from house to house, though the recusant community was sufficiently well organized for her to receive communion every day. One of the many Catholics she stayed with may have been the young widow Lady Lovell, a relative of the Vaux family who certainly sheltered priests.[250] Luisa was also caught up in at least one more raid. Twenty men and various magistrates searched where she was staying in the expectation of finding a priest. Perhaps mistaking her for a sickly and tight-lipped servant, they assumed she was English born and bred. They pulled off her cap—doubtless to make sure she was not a priest in disguise—but they could not be bothered to search her room. To the immense surprise of her hosts, the intrusion was conducted with an abnormal degree of civility, and when it was all over they said a heartfelt *Te Deum laudamus*.[251] Normally the merest excuse would have been enough to cart a suspicious person off to prison for further investigation, and there is a story that around this time one recusant was arrested just for possessing a copy of Byrd's more obviously Catholic liturgical settings.

The second raid may have taken place around November 1605, as it allegedly occurred in the last private house where she found shelter before the Gunpowder Plot. In the wake of the attack on the king and his family, Ann Vaux was imprisoned or kept under suspicion and a price was put on Henry Garnet's head. Luisa was forced to put aside her ambition to live as an Englishwoman and reluctantly she made her way to the Spanish ambassador's house in the Barbican, where she was forced to seek protection in the shadow of Spain.

9
Treason and Plot

W HEN Luisa landed in England it was illegal to defend the Pope's supremacy or give material support to Catholicism. To say that King James was a heretic or suggest he was a schismatic and outside the true Church could lead to an accusation of treason, with a similar fate awaiting those who imported copies of papal pronouncements, converted anyone to Catholicism, helped the persecuted escape abroad, or gave shelter to a priest who had come over from the Continent. Since anti-Catholic legislation was carefully framed to apply only to those subjects who had been born in England or awarded letters of denizenship granting them a permanent right of abode, an argument could be made that Luisa was not covered by the penal legislation, but the more she became settled in London the harder it would be to argue she was beyond the reach of the law.[252]

James's accession to the throne had led many recusants to hope they would soon be able to practise their religion openly. As a child he had been baptized a Catholic at Stirling Castle, and the wildly optimistic looked upon him as a martyr's son. One of the last surviving members of Mary Tudor's court, Jane Dormer, penned him a letter of encouragement from her home in Spain. Now duchess of Feria, her wish was that God would make him 'as great a saint on earth, as was your blessed mother'. James's unopposed accession raised unattainable hopes, however. He had shown few favours to the Catholic religion in his first kingdom, and it was unrealistic to expect that he would be any different in his next.

On an individual basic, James was personally indulgent towards practitioners of the old religion, seeing them more as gullible or weak-minded than anything else, but he would not stomach anything he considered an affront to his divine office. For him, 'kings are in the word of God itself called Gods', as he told his parliament four days after the Gunpowder Plot was uncovered.[253] His Danish-born wife Queen Anne was allowed to practise a form of Catholicism in the privacy of her own apartments but on the strict understanding that she always appeared at her husband's side when he took Anglican communion during the great ceremonies of state. To a degree James was even-handed, holding the line between the Roman religion and extreme Protestantism. The ultrapapist notion that Rome had a right to depose kings infuriated him no less than the assertion of some Puritans that they could appeal to Scripture to censure and perhaps even remove a monarch with whom they fundamentally disagreed. There were, however, practical as well as political limits to his compassion. Being a stranger in his own kingdom he had to reign with the help of an entrenched Protestant ruling elite. Elizabeth's chief minister Robert Cecil had cleared the way for his peaceful accession to the English throne, and James relied on him not only to govern the country but also to keep him safe from those, both at home and abroad, who questioned his right to be king of England.

Cecil never changed his mind that the Jesuits were exceptional among the Catholic clergy for the danger they posed, and his king had to listen. He badly needed money and no one knew better than Cecil how to manage royal finances. James was the first monarch to be married and have a family since the death in 1547 of Henry VIII, and so, on top of his natural extravagance—which had advantages for a foreign king needing to make friends—he needed to pay not just for the solitary royal household that had existed under Elizabeth but for those of his wife and children as well. He simply could not afford to alienate either his chief minister or a House of Commons from which Catholics had long since been barred, and when his first parliament met just a few months after his accession, all the anti-Catholic legislation passed under Elizabeth was confirmed. Although James claimed he had given orders that the letter of the law was not to be put into practice, his ability to rein in the apparatus of persecution was more limited than he cared to admit, if only because too many people earned a good living from persecuting Catholics. The year before Luisa arrived, fines for non-attendance at church amounted to a little over £1,400, which was a pittance compared with the last year of Elizabeth's reign, when a total of £8,500 had reached the royal coffers. But by 1605 that amount had risen to £2,200 pounds, and what had seemed like a move towards toleration turned out to have been the result of a calculated desire to make a favourable impression on Spain while the peace treaty was finalized.[254]

By the time Luisa disembarked in Dover the king's honeymoon period with his Catholic subjects was firmly over. By the second half of 1605 dissatisfaction was widespread and in October Henry Garnet claimed the persecution was 'more severe than in Bess's time'.[255] Five days before the attempt to blow up king and parliament, the new Spanish ambassador, don Pedro de Zúñiga, reported that many Catholics were leaving for Flanders to avoid the renewed financial exactions, adding that an indignant delegation of over twenty leading members of London's recusant community had converged on the embassy to complain how the previous Spanish envoy, the count of Villamediana, was spreading rumours in the Low Countries which gave the impression that they 'were not persecuted but rather that they were living without being troubled'.[256]

Hotheads within the Catholic community had begun to contemplate killing or removing James only months after his accession. Once it was obvious that the new king was never going to sanction liberty of worship, they dreamt of imposing a Catholic regime by force, with either Luisa's childhood playmate, the Archduchess Isabel, or, more likely, one of his hapless children at its head. Today, they would unhesitatingly be branded terrorists, and Luisa's sponsor, Henry Garnet, was alive to the fact that conspirators were at work. (It was not difficult to read the signs. Ann Vaux's suspicions had been aroused when she noted that Catholic gentlemen seemed to be stabling unusually large numbers of horses!) In May 1605, just a few days after he had sent for Luisa, Garnet had told Persons that he did not dare 'inform myself of their affairs because of the prohibition of Father General for meddling in such affairs'.[257] Garnet asked for and eventually received assurances from Rome that the Pope categorically did not support direct action against James. In the murky world of early modern counter-espionage, where 'the other side' was always guilty, his detractors would later dismiss his endeavours at pacification as a case of too little, too late.

Matters came to a head in June, when the Gunpowder Plotter (and Ann Vaux's cousin) Robert Catesby apparently asked Garnet if it was licit to undertake a good cause that might occasion the death of innocents. The plan to blow up the king and his heir, along with the assembled members of parliament, was already taking shape. Garnet said that at first he thought Catesby was asking about the moral dangers of taking a commission in the king of Spain's army, to which his reply was that it was acceptable, citing the example of a town that is besieged during a just war. According to his own puzzling (and to some self-incriminating) admission, Garnet soon after felt it necessary to warn Catesby against killing those who, as he put it, were indispensable for running the country. Catesby disclosed full details of the plot to another Jesuit, Oswald Tesimond, whose conscience was so troubled that he raised the matter in confession with Garnet towards the end of July. The leader of the English Jesuits therefore possessed a detailed knowledge of the Gunpowder Plot but at the same time he was doubly constrained. As if the secrecy of the confessional were not sufficiently binding, he had expressly agreed to the unambiguous circumstances in which he *could* divulge what he knew: he had Tesimond's permission to report their conversation only if he, Garnet, were accused of taking part in the plot.

Was Luisa welcomed into England by a traitor? Before Garnet's execution in the spring of 1606, she was active in a letter-writing campaign designed to make him a saint on the grounds that he was a blameless victim of Jacobean intolerance. He had protested his innocence on the grounds that he could not impart what had been said in the confessional and that everything humanly possible had been done to dissuade Catesby. The argument against Garnet is that he had revealed earlier plots against the king when they had been sponsored by the Jesuits' rivals, the seculars, and most important of all it was not he but Tesimond who, it could be argued, had heard of the plot under the seal of the confession—*sub sigillo confessionis*. Even in the seventeenth century, there was an energetic debate about the circumstances in which a priest *should* divulge incriminating secrets he had heard in the confessional, and surely Garnet could have found a way to smuggle a message alerting the king's ministers without ever mentioning Tesimond's name? Catesby may have thought that the members of the House of Lords were, by and large, a worthless bunch, famously dismissing them as 'atheists, fools, and cowards', but he was prepared to countenance the killing of an innocent child, as James was expected to open parliament with at least one of his two sons at his side, the 10-year-old Prince Henry.

The most charitable explanation for Garnet's silence is that he was loath to think the worst of a friend as close as Catesby, through whom, only weeks earlier, he had rented the safe-house at Erith where he passed much of the summer of 1605. Perhaps the Jesuits' leader was guilty of no more than foolishness, believing that their friendship was robust enough for his warnings to be heeded. The less charitable explanation is that Garnet was biding his time. He had disassociated the Company from preparations for that attack yet, if the attack were to succeed, there remained a possibility that Catholicism might rise phoenix-like from the ashes of parliament. But does Garnet's sponsorship of Luisa cast any light on what was going through his mind in the summer of 1605?

Whenever she mentioned the failed plot Luisa condemned it roundly, saying it was 'foolish and imprudent, and no way safe for friends or enemies alike', and she expressed her hope that the death of the plotters might atone for their crimes.[258] There is, however, a gap in Luisa's letters from February to December 1605, and we are forced back onto conjecture. The most that can be said is that it stretches credulity to think that Garnet would have invited Luisa to England if he really expected the royal family and members of both houses of parliament to be blown up. Her presence was danger enough to his priests. Why take the further chance that this exotic creature might lead to the unmasking of a Jesuit who could implicate Catesby and Guy Fawkes?

When the Gunpowder Plot was discovered Luisa was staying in the house of an old married Catholic lady. Her hostess she described as very devout but, as always, she criticized the fact that she had to pay for her accommodation with money left over from her journey. Somewhat loftily she dismissed the idea of 'paying guests' as a peculiarly English and execrable custom which she believed demeaned the honour of her hosts, especially as some were by no means poor. But once the Gunpowder Plot had been revealed, not even Spanish silver could find her a place to stay. She underestimated the dangers if she really believed, as she said, that all she wanted was 'a little corner, which I would pay well for, until I learnt the language'. She cited the terse explanation of her English hosts when they defended their decision not to take her in. It was 'because she's Spanish'! In the face of such recalcitrance, Michael Walpole ordered her to seek shelter with Spain's ambassador.[259]

Luisa was put out by his directive. She had not left her uncle's house to become the ward of a diplomat, and she liked to pretend that it was Pedro de Zúñiga who insisted that she move to his residence in the Barbican, something she had resisted until Walpole overruled her.[260] In fact, the ambassador had been trying to trace her since his arrival in the middle of July but the first he knew of her whereabouts came towards the end of November when he received a letter asking whether she might move into a house near the embassy. She did not wish to pose a threat to her English hosts, she explained, adding that she needed the certainty of knowing the sacraments would be available on a regular basis. At a cost of £200 a year, the embassy compound comprised a large house with its appurtenances, including a chapel and a walled garden. It lay just outside the city wall off Aldersgate Street, centring on today's Bridgewater Place.[261] When she turned up, the ambassador took her in there and then, which obliged his confessor gallantly to offer up his room.[262]

Pedro de Zúñiga was almost 45 years old when he was appointed to the London embassy. Though personally a great admirer of Luisa's spiritual odyssey, he struggled to understand why she had any business in England. The diplomat in him categorized her as a potential source of friction between the two governments. He knew how disruptive well-connected females could be, which explains why he tried so hard to persuade Catherine Fitzgerald, the sister of the rebellious Irish earl of Desmond, to abandon her plans to settle in Spain.[263] Through his confessor, Juan de San Augustín, he explained to Luisa the reasons why she should get out of England.

With a forensic intelligence, the confessor tried to grind Luisa down by saying that if she wanted to be a martyr she ought to realize that the English put to death only the king's vassals. The worst she could expect was to be unceremoniously put on a ship across the Channel. If she wanted to lead a life of prayer, Spain would be much more peaceful, and if she really wanted to set an example of a good life, Spain was still the most appropriate place because, in England, she would quickly be noticed and so lack the opportunity of meeting many people. He also invoked his authority as a priest. Did she not realize it would be impossible for her to convert anyone, as it was out of the question for a woman to dispute with heretics?[264]

He had met his match. She told him it was already a martyrdom to see how God was despised and how English Catholics were mistreated. Secure in the knowledge that he had his master's full confidence, the confessor kept up the pressure and more than once she buckled under. Juan de San Augustín cowed her into letting him write to Mariana de San José to say that, if she were willing to leave Spain and go to Flanders to set up a strict Augustinian convent, Luisa would join her. It was almost impossible to find words which would allow a woman to defy a directly expressed order by a man, and all the more so when he was a priest in holy orders, which forced Luisa back on her natural guile. Rather than confront him she subtly manipulated the poor priest into thinking he had won. She had calculated that, since Mariana was still in Medina del Campo, she would not be able to give up her position as prioress at all quickly, and so it was most unlikely that a rapid decision would be forthcoming. Nor was this the only trick she could play. She resorted to the same ruse she had employed in Madrid when her confessor, Juan de Sigüenza, had tried to bundle her into a convent. Instead of confronting the priest, she invoked higher authority. No doubt with all due meekness and humility, she told the ambassador's confessor that she had failed to sustain her decisions whenever she had prayed about the matter.

The first six months spent as Zúñiga's guest were the lowest ebb of her life in England. What was the point of being cooped up in an embassy? In January 1606 she told Mariana of the extent of her confusion, with those around her telling her to go home as soon

LA VENE
RABLE VIR
GEN D'LUI
SA DE CAR
BAJAL Y
MENDOZA

1. Commissioned in the second half of the 17th century, Antonio de Novoa's portrait is to be found in the English College in Valladolid, where Luisa lived at the start of the century.

2. This anonymous portrait is thought by many to be the earliest and most accurate depiction of Luisa, possibly being derived from a depiction made shortly after her death in London.

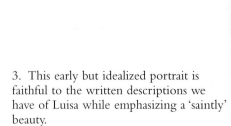

3. This early but idealized portrait is faithful to the written descriptions we have of Luisa while emphasizing a 'saintly' beauty.

4. Luisa´s companion for many years, the down-to-earth Inés de la Asunción later worked closely with Mariana de San José, becoming a notable reformer of several convents.

5. The Gunpowder Plotters were subjected to the public spectacle of being drawn by horses to the place of execution, then hung and quartered. The fire is to burn their entrails.

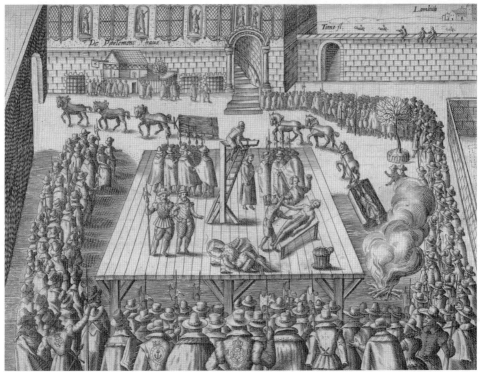

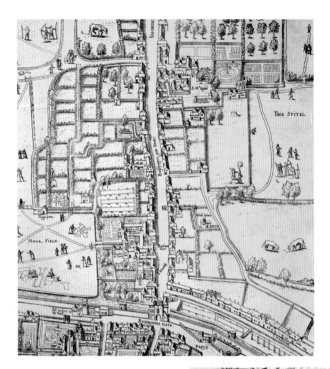

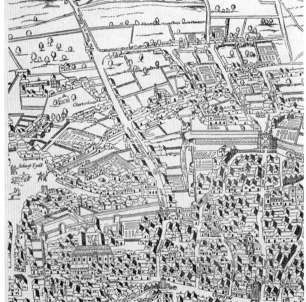

6. This mid-Tudor map brings out the rural nature of Spitalfields. With Bishopsgate Street and country lanes leading to it, Luisa´s house was built just to the north of the pulpit marked with a cross which can be seen next to S[aint] M[ary] Spitel.

7. This part of the Agas Map includes the area beyond the city walls known as the Barbican, where the Spanish Embassy and Luisa's first house in London were to be found. The commercial thoroughfare of Cheapside was the site of Luisa´s first arrest.

8. Luisa was especially devoted to the Vulnerata, an image of the Virgin and Child which was defaced by English Protestant solidiers before being placed in the English College. The damage to the face and arms is evident, and the Christ Child is completely lost

9. Henry Walpole carved his signature into the walls of the Tower of London, and his fate proved to be an inspiration to Luisa.

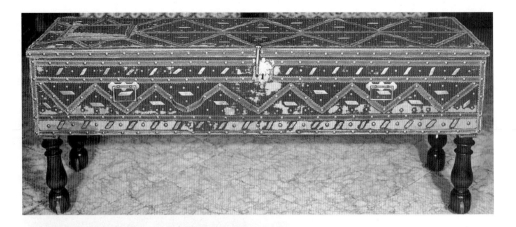

10. Luisa remains unburied and he casket containing her body has been in the reliquary room of the Convent of the Incarnation in Madrid since 1615.

11. St Engracia was one of the Roman female martyrs whose stories were popular in Luisa's day. Despite its harrowing nature, with its similarities to what Luisa endured as a child, The Flagellation of Santa Engracia by the Andalusian painter, Bartolomé Bermejo (*c*.1440–98) originally hung in a Spanish church.

12. Luis de la Puente was a much sought-after spiritual adviser in Valladolid.

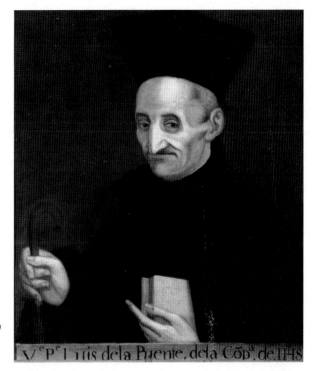

13. The Royal English College was founded by Philip II in 1589 and still occupies its original site in Valladolid.

14. Leader of the English Jesuits, Henry Garnet met Luisa on her arrival in England and was executed the following year for his alleged implication in Gunpowder Plot.

15. With Madrid's royal palace in the background, the two infantas Isabel Clara Eugenia, and Catalina Micaela were Luisa's playmates in the nearby convent of the Descalzas Reales.

16. The Infanta Isabel was ruler of the Spanish Netherlands when Luisa was in England.

17. The Casa de Cisneros, (with Madrid's former town hall to the right) was the marquis of Almazán's townhouse in the ceremonial heart of Philip II´s new capital. Older drawings show an open upper gallery.

18. Born in Guildford, George Abbot (1562–1633) later became archbishop of Canterbury and was known for his virulent anti-catholicism. Luisa described his complexion in highly unflattering terms.

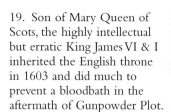

19. Son of Mary Queen of Scots, the highly intellectual but erratic King James VI & I inherited the English throne in 1603 and did much to prevent a bloodbath in the aftermath of Gunpowder Plot.

20. The church Luisa's grandfather built in Jaraicejo.

21. Luisa was baptized in this font in January 1566.

22. This house in Jaraicejo is traditionally said to have been Luisa's parents' home.

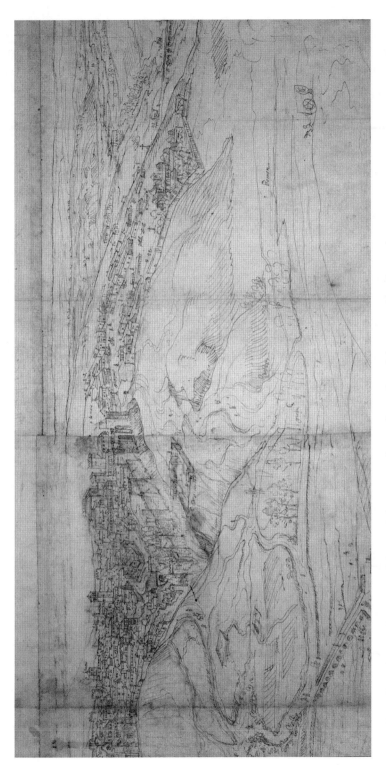

23. The calle Toledo spilt out south beyond the city walls (to the right of the picture) and was the unfashionable area of Madrid

24. Though much altered, the scale of the former royal and viceregal palace in Pamplona is impressive. It is now an archive.

25. The Convent of the Incarnation in Madrid was founded in 1611 by Philip III and Margaret of Austria and still houses an enclosed order of nuns.

26. This bird's-eye view of London is an unromanticized view of the city. London Bridge was the only crossing over the Thames, and Luisa had to walk across it to visit the Clink Prison in Southwark.

27. Luisa´s house in Spitalfields was unusual for being made of brick and the foundations of the little round tower confirmed it as her home.

28. Her 'Oran' is now buried under the modern buildings of Spital Square, London E1

29. The sumptuous reliquary room at the Descalzas Reales, where Luisa lived after the death of her parents, illustrates the value attached to the relics of saints and martyrs.

as spring arrived but how, time and again, she was gripped by an inner feeling that she was meant to stay. Whenever she went to 'His Majesty', her habitual term for God, 'I receive such *super* relief and a great sense of assurance that I have his protection and am fulfilling his holy will.' An indication of how perplexed she was is that, a moment after writing these words, she contradicted herself by saying she did 'not entirely trust' her own emotions, and she felt compelled to continue probing what was expected of her.[265]

Political pressure was being brought to bear from Brussels, and at the start of 1606 she flatly denied the rumour going the rounds in the Low Countries that she intended to convert King James's idiosyncratic consort, Anne of Denmark.[266] In May she complained that Magdalena de San Jerónimo 'has time and again used quite unusual force to get me out of this country'.[267] Even Luis de la Puente, who had been instrumental in allowing her to make her way to England, told her to leave and to accept her return as the martyrdom she was seeking. Slowly Luisa regained some of her old self-assurance, and to the charge that she had received word that the Archduchess Isabel expressly wanted her to leave, Luisa cuttingly remarked that she had never seen the regent's signature on any letters. As for the scurrilous report that she was providing an excuse for England to renege on the Treaty of London, she dismissed that as absurd, but could not resist adding that it would be no bad thing if the peace were broken!

In contrast to the indecision which had marred the first six months in the embassy, her last six months turned out to be the formative period of her time in England. As Zúñiga put it, this was when she started putting down roots. She was stumbling towards discovering a sense of her own worth, and though suffering for the faith remained her ultimate goal, the daily calvary of trying to help London's Catholics made her aware that she could be useful while she was alive.

In the embassy she did her best to follow the life of prayer and good works she had adopted in the calle de Toledo, and the way she dressed continued to set her apart as she chose to clothe herself as an old lady. Polonius-like, she wore a long black garment that went down to the ground and which, being heavily pleated, was similar, she said, to what was worn by members of the Council of State in Spain. The sleeves were tight-fitting, and on top of this she wore an apron that went up to her neck. She wore a simple headdress. It was only when she left the embassy that she allowed herself any adornment, when, for safety's sake, she made a nod in the direction of English fashion by putting an embroidered circlet over her clothes.[268] One of her former companions in Spain heard that she wore shoes when going outside so as not to attract attention.[269] To follow a strict routine, she needed a clock. Not an alarm clock, just one that chimed, she told Magdalena de San Jerónimo, adding that they were difficult to get hold of in England. Her worry was that she did not know whether it was time to get up, or that she might start eating after midnight![270]

Two Catholic Englishwomen were sharing her new way of living. It is not clear whether she brought them with her or whether they joined her at the embassy, though she later remarked that they had nowhere else to live and that many Catholic families had recently been forced to let some of their servants go.[271] They shared the rooms vacated by the ambassador's confessor, which were connected by a private staircase leading directly to the chapel. Isolated from the rest of the embassy, the apartment was next to the orchard, which caused Luisa to think of the Desert Fathers. The rooms were kept locked, even when Luisa was inside, and perhaps she used the bolts she had taken with her on the journey through France. As a lone female, Luisa had to make it abundantly clear that her maidenhood was never to be called into question. Her first companions were a 40-year-old woman and the 20-year-old Ann Garnet, the daughter of one of Henry Garnet's brothers.

According to a letter dated August 1607, Ann had been with Luisa for one year and eight months, which probably meant she had either joined Luisa as a consequence of the Gunpowder Plot, or even as late as January 1606, when her uncle's guilt was first officially proclaimed.[272] According to what John Blakfan said in a letter, admittedly written some years later, Ann had been sent to Luisa by her uncle, and, despite many ups and downs, the two women remained together till the end.[273] She was the sort of girl who was 'prepared to try her hand at anything; she sews well and makes lovely hosts and wax candles, and although this is not so important she knows her way around the kitchen; basically she's good at everything she tries'.

Unlike her uncle, whom even his adversaries regarded as exceptionally gentle, Ann was feisty, being 'a little lion' when it came to religion. The thought occasionally crossed her mind of going to Spain, presumably to profess as a nun, but she would never leave without her mistress.[274] What happened to the older companion is uncertain, as by the summer Luisa was talking about a new girl, also in her twenties, whom she called Marcharo, which may be a corruption of Margery.[275]

Her companions' first duty was to teach Luisa English. Presumably she had made some headway in the private houses she had stayed in, and early in 1606 she gave what seems an objective assessment of how far she had progressed:

And as long as I don't have to tell long stories, I get by quite well in everyday conversation; and though without much in the way of explanation I can talk to them often about Our Lord and make myself understood.[276]

Impatient to learn, Luisa was profoundly aware of the infantilization which takes place when learning a foreign language. Ceasing to be an adult, she found herself 'reduced to the age of the smallest children in everything'. Her lack of fluency prevented her from helping her fellow Catholics as much as she liked, causing her to complain that her good works were as childish as her language, and she compared herself with St Francis Xavier. When faced with a similar situation as part of the Jesuits' mission to Japan, he also fancied that his innocence might be taken as childlike.[277]

What irritated her most was the realization that until she had mastered the language she would not be able to live an independent life outside the embassy, and her frustration spilt over into cruel jibes about her companions as teachers. Accusing them of being difficult and unenthusiastic, Ann and Marcharo were like 'a pair of stone statues', deaf to her need to progress in the language.[278] By the end of 1606 she was seething with resentment at the fact that they were not, in her opinion, devoting enough time to improving her English. Normally not being very talkative was a good thing, she conceded, but this was emphatically not the case when you needed to learn a language.[279] There were few books available to help her. Her irritation continued into the following year, and in April, she griped that they would not spend a whole day giving her lessons. She had to ask questions two or three times, and, in a mechanical voice as if they were just waking up, all they would say was, 'No, it's very good'.[280]

Apart from conversing with those for whom English was their mother tongue, few alternative ways of learning the language presented themselves. Dry but authoritative, the standard reference work was John Minsheu's *A dictionaire in Spanish and English* of 1599, but in the year of her arrival, Lewis Owen, who had not yet achieved notoriety as a Jesuit-hater, brought out a more manageable vocabulary book that included various dialogues. With quite considerable wishful thinking, these dialogues might have been of use to their intended audience, English-speaking merchants trading with Spain and her dependencies, but at least the long alphabetized word-list covered day-to-day vocabulary, which was precisely what Luisa required, and one of its curiosities would have been of no consequence to her as a native speaker of Spanish. Owen placed the indefinite article before English nouns yet omitted the all-important *un* or *una* which indicated the gender of their equivalents in Spanish. His book began with a useful if brief grammatical introduction, and its partial lists of verbs were probably of most use to her.[281]

Luisa had long ceased to write poetry but the images she had employed constantly resurfaced in her letters. She bemoaned the fact that she had escaped from one set of chains when she had put her lawsuit behind her only to find another in the language. Five years on she was still adamant that, though she had learnt to speak English reasonably well, she had done this 'without any teacher at all, as I have never found anyone, in or out of the house, who could be bothered to teach me just for a week'.[282]

Who could have satisfied Luisa as a teacher is frankly unimaginable, but she eventually mastered the language. Her capacity for discussing theology was remarked upon innumerable times, and it was said her English flowed better when she was arguing about religion than in day-to-day talk.[283] Indeed, with her guttural Spanish accent, and her preference for King James over Queen Elizabeth, she was often taken for a Scot.[284]

The dark evenings were probably when she spent her time trying to engage her companions in sober conversation, since during the hours of daylight she would have given priority to writing about the sufferings of the recusants to her influential circle of friends. At last she was beginning to see the good she could do. Her accounts were indisputably biased in their assumption that the Protestant regime had nothing to fear from Catholicism, yet they carried an air of authority because of the exceptional amount of verifiable detail they contained, something all the more remarkable given that she had been in England barely six months before she took advantage of the diplomatic bag to convey her letters safely out of the country.

Her first concern was to provide a running commentary on the fate of her adored Henry Garnet. He was captured at Hindlip Hall in Worcestershire on Monday, 27 January 1606, and taken at once to London. His interrogations began in earnest in the middle of February when he was removed from the relative laxity of the Gatehouse Prison in Westminster to the Tower of London. The trial started on 28 March in the Guildhall, and just over a month later, on 3 May 1606, he was put to death in St Paul's churchyard.

As a female, it was not for Luisa to prepare for publication polished accounts of the suffering of martyrs, since so-called 'true relations' were the preserve of the clergy. At the inquiry into her canonization, it was admitted that in letter-writing she had taken on herself 'the office appropriate to men' but in her defence it was pointed out that this could not be construed as an example of 'disorder or boldness' as she did this with God's help and with the requisite humility.[285] She evaded these unwritten rules by incorporating her detailed knowledge into what was technically private correspondence, although she could not resist the provocation of ending her first surviving letter about Garnet's persecution with the words, 'and here you have it, a true relation'.[286] She spread her version of events to the Low Countries through Magdalena de San Jerónimo, to Spain through her friends at the Spanish court in Valladolid, and, as seems to be the

case, in messages now lost which she sent to Rome. Her letters could
be brief and to the point, as, for example, when she rushed to take
advantage of the departure for Flanders of the marquis of San Germán,
who had been specially sent by the king of Spain to congratulate
James on surviving the Gunpowder Plot. He took with him an
unusually short letter for Magdalena in which Luisa politely wondered if some letters had gone missing since she had not heard from
her recently, adding that if the marquis did not leave quickly they
would hang Garnet 'in his face', as they had only delayed his execution on account of his arrival.[287]

More often her reports were peppered with the providential, even
the miraculous. Though she did this in the matter-of-fact way appropriate for a female correspondent, she was paving the way for others
to turn her simple story into edifying prose. Her report about the
plotter who revealed Garnet's whereabouts was a morality tale in
miniature. She accepted that the sad creature ('el triste') may have
blabbed in a bid to save his own life but she doubted he would be
spared, as another conspirator who had said similar things had already
been put to death. She concluded her tale, naturally enough, by
saying that before he died he had repented of what he had done.[288]

Her stories were imbued with circumstantial evidence of how God
was using the aftermath of the plot to strengthen Catholicism and
confound the Protestants, in much the same way as the Protestants
claimed that the discovery of the conspiracy against King James was
proof of divine favour. The countess of Shrewsbury, as well as ladies
Essex and Clanricarde, had been moved to reassert her Catholicism,
while a noted Puritan had dropped dead in a public house—provi-
dentially named, it seems, the Pope's Head. Another technique she
employed in the service of the growing cult of Henry Garnet was to
meet the Protestant version of events head-on. She told Magdalena
she would feel even more sorry for the way Garnet suffered if the lies
that were being spread about him were true, and she refused to accept
he had revealed the secrets of the confessional, nor that he had begged
to be put to death secretly rather than face the crowd.[289] She also
reported on Ann Vaux's sparkling defence against the accusations that
were put to her. When asked if it was true she and Garnet were lovers,

she replied, if that is all you can say, then obviously you have nothing serious to charge me with. When she was asked whether she had known about the plot, she said, of course—nothing happens in England without the women knowing about it. Another of her alleged remarks was to thank her jailers for their hospitality, as even though she had money of her own, she had been unable to find anyone to take her in, yet they were providing her with free board and lodging![290]

Luisa could not bring herself to witness Garnet's execution, claiming that the journey to St Paul's was too much for her, and she also declined to watch his final procession which set out not far from the embassy. His last words were taken down by a priest who then drew up 'a very true and well organised relation', which she duly passed on to the English College in Valladolid.[291]

The legend of *Garnet's Straw* owes a lot to Luisa, a story which, seven months after his execution, she said was exciting Catholics and Protestants alike. A believer had noticed that a sheaf of straw from the fire where his heart had been burnt was spattered with a drop of his blood. This relic he put away in his trunk, and when he came to look at it again it had transmogrified into a tiny picture of Garnet's face, not only with all its features but with a longish fair beard and the bruise on his forehead from when he had been thrown down from the scaffold.[292]

Given her reluctance to talk about her own mystical experiences, and her preference for the practical, it is not surprising that one can detect a certain uneasiness about this miracle.

At first glance you can't quite make it out, but if you take your time it becomes patently clear, and even more so by candlelight, in my opinion; but you can always see it well enough as if it had been painted by an actual painter, and the eyes are closed, like a little dead figurine.[293]

Ambassador Zúñiga had shown the straw to members of James's Privy Council, including Cecil; the councillors denied it looked like Garnet at all but Luisa said the point was that it looked like him when he was dead. Despite any doubts she may have had, she was effective in promoting Garnet's cult among her circle of friend, with the countess of Miranda's confidante, Leonor de Quirós, being so taken with the story that she asked for a relic or token. She must have been ecstatic when, a year and a half after his death, she received the signet ring which Garnet had sent Luisa just before he was taken prisoner, an opportunity to remind Leonor (and all her friends) that he 'was truly a saint, even when he was alive'.[294] In 1608 Luisa sketched a picture of the straw in the margin of one of her letters in order to correct a false depiction which was circulating which Joseph Creswell had passed on to her. In return, Creswell was promised that Zúñiga would send him one of the two versions which a Protestant painter had made for him, which contradicts later, more elaborate, stories that the image was, by some miracle, impossible to reproduce.[295]

It is to King James's eternal credit that he did not allow the Gunpowder Plot to trigger a massacre of Catholics, as occurred not just in Paris but throughout France after St Bartholomew's Day in 1572. He made it clear to Cecil and his Privy Council that he did not view the actions of Catesby and his treacherous friends as reflecting the sympathies of the Catholic community as a whole. From the very spot where he was supposed to have been blown up only days before, he had the moral courage to say in his speech from the throne that, although their religion had led a few Catholic hotheads to conspire against him, it did not 'follow that all professing that Romish religion were guilty of the same', and he roundly condemned extremism among Catholics and Protestants, singling out the 'cruelty of Puritans'.[296] Sadly, words came easily to James, and the parliament increased the penalties for not attending communion in the state church. Though Luisa characterized the new measures as 'cruel laws', anti-Catholic feeling had calmed down considerably by the end of 1606.[297] She was now convinced that she could live on her own in England.

10

Carrots, Capons, and Plague

L ONDON in 1606 was a warren of buildings constructed mostly
from wooden frames infilled with brick, daub, or plaster, and
which rarely rose above four storeys. In contrast to the more
imposing City of Westminster to the west, only two buildings of note
rose above the trim spires of its medieval churches in what was an
otherwise unexciting skyline. In the heart of the City, and visible
from all sides, was the colossal stump of the Gothic tower of Old
St Paul's—the steeple had burnt down at the start of Queen Elizabeth's
reign—whereas to the east it was possible to glimpse the far smaller but
still intimidating shape of the Tower of London's bleak Norman keep
with its four rounded turrets at each corner, depending on the line of
sight and on how much smoke the city's domestic fires were belching
out on any given day. Hemmed in by its medieval walls, the city
covered little more than one square mile, and its 200,000 inhabitants
were spilling out in all directions. Suburbs of dubious distinction
had long since grown up along the roads leading into the city, such
as around Bishopsgate to the north, or on the far side of the river
in Southwark, which had been famous for its brothels long before
Chaucer's time.

Much new building gave the city the air of a large construction site.
Along the bank of the Thames by the great turn in the river which
marked the genuine, if not the legal, division between London and
Westminster, the great nobles were beginning to put up elegant
palaces reflecting their wealth but also a conviction that England
had become a stable society. King James's chief minister Robert
Cecil was planning the New Exchange near the Strand, one of the
capital's earliest purpose-built shopping centres. Quickly renamed by
a publicity-conscious monarch as Britain's Bourse, the intention was

to promote luxury goods from all over the world. Perhaps the biggest changes to the face of London had taken place south of the river, where Shakespeare and his friends had established their great circular theatres to entertain politically aware audiences with far from uncontroversial theatrical works.

London was unrivalled as the economic and financial centre of the country. With the vertiginous rise in overseas trade, it was more than ever a place where fortunes could be made, because, unlike many other capital cities such as Rome or Madrid, it did not earn an easy living just from the profits of church and pilgrimage, or from servicing a princely court or the courts of justice. The Pool of London was deep enough for the largest ships to drop anchor in the Thames but the economic vigour of Jacobean London contrasts chillingly with the simple truth that it was disfigured by death and disease. The city gobbled up workers from other parts of the country. In fact, London's incidence of mortality was so high that it was unable to sustain its existing level of population without recruiting new inhabitants from the rest of England. The fact that its population was rising rapidly is a reminder of the acute poverty that drove countryfolk to risk all in London, and it was precisely because the city was full of new and often foreign people that Luisa was able to consider living independently. Dozens of nationalities were represented there, and she did not stand out quite as much as would have been the case in less cosmopolitan cities.

Living in the embassy strained relations with Ambassador Zúñiga as soon as it became clear that Luisa would do or say anything not to leave England. Towards the end of her time there, she spoke to him so infrequently that she might as well not be in his house, she said, and she had little more to do with his two priests, Gregorio de Cárdenas and his confessor San Agustín, although she glimpsed them every day at mass. Perhaps they were annoyed at her interference in how the embassy's chapel was run. She made up her mind that the oil in the chapel was too old and she took it upon herself to arrange for a variety of oils to be sent from Flanders.[298] She also insisted that the reserved sacrament—the consecrated bread from mass—was put on permanent display in the chapel.[299]

She had begun to take life in the embassy for granted. Towards the end of her first year there, the ambassadorial secretary, Francisco de Rebolledo Solorzano, was instructed to forbid her from using the diplomatic bag for any letters that were not strictly her own.[300] Whether this order got in the way of her easy relationship with the embassy's main courier, Rivas, is another matter. They normally exchanged incoming and outgoing letters at the midday mass, but, irrespective of his years of experience as a messenger, there could be delays—one packet from Inés took nineteen months to reach its destination—and many letters were simply lost, which meant that important letters were copied and despatched by a variety of routes. On the whole the service was remarkably efficient, and she explained to Inés that, 'once placed in the hands of Father Creswell, they reach Father Baldwin's in Brussels and from his either to mine or don Pedro's'.[301]

By late October 1606 the persecution of Catholics had relented enough for her to think it was time to fend for herself. Living alone would not be easy, and during her stay in the embassy she had been free to come and go more or less as she pleased. On the rare occasions she did go outside she needed chaperoning by her two companions so as to avoid the worst of the anti-Catholic abuse. Her strange garb was enough to indicate that she belonged to some religious movement or order, which by itself was an indication of Catholic leanings.

The Church of England had not yet become a broad church. It was aggressively Calvinist in doctrine with the Elizabeth articles of faith of 1563 proclaiming an unqualified belief in predestination. Though the English Church taught that the doctrine was 'of a sweet, pleasant, and unspeakable comfort' to its believers, it maintained that God had already chosen those who would be saved 'before the foundations of the world were laid', which contrasted starkly with the Catholic view that men could be saved through good works mixed with faith. To be sure, the English Church retained more than a flavour of the old religion, at least in appearance, with its distinctive clothes for the clergy, the office of bishop, and so on, but on the question of contemplative orders there was no compromise. Monks and nuns had been taboo in English Protestantism ever since Henry VIII dissolved the monasteries some seventy years before, and Mary Tudor's earnest attempts to rekindle monasticism did not survive the stutter of her reign. The way she dressed made Luisa stand out in a crowd as someone who observed a very different religion from that of the state church, and if there were any doubts as to her affiliation, the crucifix she sported was plain for all to see. This was a red rag to a bull as many Protestants despised crucifixes for being the graven images proscribed by the Old Testament.[302] At the start of her reign, Queen Elizabeth had kept a crucifix in her chapel but as the clash between England and Spain intensified she reluctantly decided it was prudent to have no truck with a symbol that, for many, harked uncomfortably back to the old religion. Luisa, on the other hand, would be buried with a crucifix.

Shortly before Christmas 1606, a tiny house became available for rent just a few doors down from the embassy. It was so close to where don Pedro lived that she could probably hear the bell being rung for mass in the ambassador's chapel. For a year's rental she paid out 430 *reales*, which left her with nothing for food.[303] As this amounted to roughly £10. 15s. in sterling, it meant she was paying a great deal of money for a modicum of privacy. The house was typical of London, she said, being in a closed-off courtyard which had a gate onto the street. Not only were her immediate neighbours rowdy, they were committed Protestants,

and at times they grind me down with the noise that comes through the wall where I sleep. All you hear is the sound of meat being roasted and others cooking, eating, playing, and drinking. On Fridays it seems to get worse. The wheel of the spit that turns the haunches of a whole cow over the fire reminds me of one that I saw painted in a book about the punishments in hell. As a pious trick, as soon as I hear it, I've got into the habit of praying. But all these irritations, on top of the fact that the house is very narrow and does not have sufficient ventilation for the plague that is raging, I immediately forget as I rush to don Pedro's door where mass and communion is assured.[304]

The plague was a constant worry to her, if only because she secretly feared it might rob her of a martyr's crown. England had more pestilences than Egypt, she once said,[305] and from the relative safety of the embassy she had seen that her new land was indeed the purgatory she had been promised, with the endless bouts of plague 'setting the final seal on it'.[306] It had been a problem for twelve years, she was told, and the doctors had given up trying to do anything, not even bothering to look in on its victims when they were attending other sick people in the house.[307] She was affronted by the attitude of the Puritans as much as by what she saw as the primitive measures taken by the civil administration (the *común gobierno*) to combat its spread.

The Puritans, whom she sensibly defined as 'the most zealous' of the Protestants, insisted there was no purpose in taking precautionary measures as God had decided who would die and who would be saved. For them it was a sign of favour to say that a friend had died 'of the mark of the Lord', wryly adding that they joined in the exodus from London just as much as everyone else whenever the plague turned especially virulent.[308] The city authorities' lack of watchfulness astounded her. In the second-hand clothes' shops the garments of the dead and the living were openly sold all jumbled up, whereas insufficient vigilance was exercised over the supply of food or over houses where plague had broken out. When someone died, everybody went to the funeral together, and only then was the plague house daubed with a red-coloured cross and closed up for a month with its occupants back inside. Those confined were made to pay for their own food, but, as they invariably put an old man or a shady character on duty outside, a piece of bread was all that was needed as a bribe and in effect they were free to go about their business as they pleased. There was no shortage of buyers for the clothes of the deceased or even the bed that they had died in. She had even heard of a case where a cart had taken a corpse out into the countryside only to return piled high with carrots.[309]

Luisa realized that she needed to have a reputable man to act as a chaperone for when she moved, otherwise 'I won't be able to live in a separate house on my own'.[310] Normally she shied away from male company, and what lay behind her decision were practical reasons and not concern for appearances. In the calle de Toledo and next to the English College she had lived in an entirely female household but in

England she and her companions needed a male servant, partly to deflect talk that they were setting up a religious community but also out of concern for their physical safety.

Her friends found her an ideal candidate, a married man who was childless and who, along with his wife, had recently spent some months in prison, losing all his possessions through the application of the penal laws. This old Catholic was a Frenchman, Diego Lemeteliel, who was to remain with her for the rest of her life. There is no indication that his wife joined him, and so he may have been recently widowed. Luisa apparently maintained the fiction of equality among her companions, with one eyewitness remarking she was careful never to give Lemeteliel orders except in the presence of her companions.[311] She now had a virtuous and holy family to support, one in which all its members had suffered for their faith. When she said it would be hard on her poverty she was only half-joking.

House prices in London were astronomical. In April 1607 she reckoned it would cost £100 a year to house, feed, and clothe the four of them, by which she meant herself, her two companions, and Lemeteliel.[312] It cost as much to live in London as in the Spanish court, making the life of the poor very difficult in England. Much of the blame she laid at the door of the mayor and aldermen for not imposing price-controls, standard practice in her home country.[313] The high cost of living was largely responsible for the custom of paying-guests, a habit which she had detested since her arrival, and it never ceased to amaze her that the very rich and the very poor all felt they had to take in lodgers on the grounds that it was 'easier to get by if you share'.[314] This lack of aristocratic liberality—from her Spanish point of view—was also evident in the impoverished way in which even the noblest of houses were run. She granted the fact that the English liked to dress well, but she was surprised that there were only ever two tables—one for the master, his guests and the officers of his household, and the other, *below the salt* as we might say, for the lesser servants—yet they were all fed from the common meal and they drank from the same jug. This struck her as unhygienic but also lacking in a proper sense of hierarchy, which is a reminder that, no matter how much she tried, Luisa never broke free from her upbringing as a great lady. One way to save money was to eat dark bread, which was less expensive since it did not require refined flour, though the staple food comprised large pieces of beef or mutton that might be eked out to last for up to a week.

In her considered opinion, English food was

of poorer quality than in Spain. The food looks good, but has no smell and almost no taste, and is not very nourishing, and you can't keep it, even in winter, for four whole days without it going off. Since they sell things in pieces and not by weight, you are obliged to buy more than you need for a small household. They get round this by roasting things and keeping them as cold meats or by putting them in pastry. Chickens usually cost a shilling to a shilling and a half, but there is nothing to them and, on their own, they are insufficient to the point of being uneatable, as well as being on the small side. This is why they prefer capons, which are like good chickens in Spain, although not really in taste, and these cost half a crown or three shillings, and rarely have I seen them for two shillings.[315]

Her physician Dr Foster, who looked after many in the recusant community in London, agreed. When treating her chronic sicknesses, his orders were, 'Don't eat chickens, which are no good, but the capons instead.'[316] Her way of getting round the extra expense was as practical as it was ingenious. She said eating a quarter of one capon was better than eating three English chickens that tasted of nothing. To use her precise words, she said they tasted like water from Xátiva, a highly irrigated area around Valencia, which must have been her way of saying that English chickens tasted of nothing but Adam's Ale.

Her most persistent image of her new country was that of a dark forest populated with wild beasts. Compared with Spain she thought it unsophisticated and barbaric. Since it had no secure monasteries or as yet no colonies where it could send its criminals, it despatched its delinquents by a different route. Twenty-five or more thieves swung from the gallows every month in London, 'even though some are children of ten or eleven years of age'.[317] Of course, it is common to make invidious comparisons about other countries, and most often these take the form of comments about the food, cleanliness, and the weather. It is intriguing that James's ambassador in Spain was making the same kind of comments as Luisa's about his host country. Whereas she complained there was no difference between winter and summer in England, and that it always seemed to be raining, Sir Charles Cornwallis reported back from Spain he would die if he had to endure another year of so much sun! But what makes Luisa's observations rise above the habitual denigration of the staples of daily living in another country is the precision of her observations. Unafraid of making comparisons with countries with which she ought to have had sympathy, she said that the cost of basic foodstuffs made life difficult for the poor in the Spanish Netherlands just as much as in England. But for all her pretensions to objectivity, she could not for the life of her understand how the English imagined their country was 'paradise on earth'.[318]

How did she manage to pay her way if everything cost so much? When Luisa and her companions moved into the new house, she was down to her last 200 *reales*, or about £5 sterling. She had to ask Magdalena not to buy her the clock that she had asked for, that is, if she had not bought it already.[319] Luisa had learnt to be adept at raising the small amounts of money that she periodically needed to survive. An intended consequence of feeding information back to her friends was to induce them to send her alms in return. She explained to Creswell that the countess of Castellar would let him know all about *Garnet's Straw*, adding that 'if she were to come up with some money over there, it should be sent on with the utmost secrecy'.[320] She promptly received 100 *reales*, and probably a similar amount from the countess of Miranda.[321] Ana María de Vergara in Vitoria offered to send her 500 *reales*, and as word spread back in Spain about her adventure, people began contacting her out of the blue. For example, María Ponce from Valladolid sent her an unsolicited letter and it would be surprising if it, or subsequent letters, did not contain some offer of help. As a settled member of London's Catholic community, Luisa could tap into the various informal means the recusants had set up to help each other, and money could be remitted in a variety of ways. If it could not be passed to the Cornish Jesuit Father William Baldwin in Flanders (where King James's agents were trying to get hold of him for his alleged knowledge of the Gunpowder Plot), it could be sent directly to England, either to another member of the

Company, Richard Blunt or to his father, William Blunt, who belonged to one of England's old gentry families. Money could come via the Fuggers, the German family who dominated Spain's foreign currency dealings, who might even offer some interest on the sum.[322] Occasionally she felt able to decline offers of help, as when the marquis of San Germán visited James after the Gunpowder Plot. As long as Ambassador Zúñiga was providing her and her companions with food, she informed the marquis, she had no need of his help.

Despite their frosty encounters, Ambassador Zúñiga proved to be one of Luisa's greatest advocates. His pride had been wounded by her adamantine refusal to go back to Spain, and although he made it clear that, once she left the embassy, she was to return only to attend mass, he was broadminded enough to accept she was motivated by a higher calling. At some stage he started paying her an allowance of 300 *reales* a month, worth £7. 10s., a generous sum which suggests it was done with royal approval (as Zúñiga himself claimed some twenty years later), but it is unclear whether it was first paid when she left the embassy or later. In April 1607 Luisa praised his liberality and said that she expected him to remain as generous until he ended his tour of duty, which implies payments were being made regularly. At any rate, whatever monies she received had to fund her missionary activities as well as pay for her household, and since her outgoings exceeded her income she led a hand-to-mouth existence.[323]

Ever the entrepreneur, Luisa was constantly looking out for ways to raise money. Her first thoughts were to make perfumed gloves. The ambassador needed a pair, and it would be a way of repaying him for his kindnesses. If Luisa could perfect this art, there was bound to be a ready market, as, in an age where soap was rare and costly, the most common way of dealing with a smell was to cap it with a stronger, sweeter smell. She sent to Brussels for instructions, saying that there must be someone at the archduchess's court who knew how to prepare gloves. She was disappointed with the formula that was sent her, as it was no use, she complained, talking about drying things outdoors, since the sun in England would never be strong enough, and 'especially this year, when it has done nothing but rain'.[324] That was in July. Another idea was to take advantage of the country's renowned sweet tooth by making pastries, and once settled into her new home she wrote to Inés in Medina del Campo for a recipe to make a kind of nutmeg marzipan, saying 'it was what will sell best here'.[325] Why she imagined it was feasible to launch a culinary enterprise is a mystery as she remained a liability in the kitchen. In August she asked Inés to look out for someone who would come to England to buy food or at least cook.[326]

Her most disastrous attempt at moneymaking came when she returned to her old craft of spinning gold thread. Spotting a gap in the market, she saw that this sort of work was not undertaken in England, which led to gold thread being imported at great expense all the way from Italy. Inés was asked to procure her the best scissors she could and to put them along with a spindle in a box for Creswell to forward to London.[327] She was not a natural businesswoman, however, and though a number of people were caught up in the interminable saga of Luisa and her scissors, she was still waiting six years later for a really good pair that would cut gold.[328] In the end, she lost both time and money, as the French constantly undercut the market with false gold.[329] Fortunately there were more important matters to attend to. There were English souls to save.

11

Grand India

CHRISTOPHER Columbus was haunted by the spectre of failure right until his death in 1506 in the landlocked city of Valladolid. His ambition had been to reach the Great Khan in China and the discovery of the Americas came a very poor second. Obstinate to the end, he insisted that what he had come across must be neighbouring islands that lay just to the east of China, which perversely he labelled part of India. Those who sailed with him on his later voyages had no qualms in accepting that they had struck upon a huge landmass—a new continent in fact—as the volume of fresh water projected far out into the Atlantic by the river Orinoco could only have been drawn from a hinterland of almost unimaginable proportions. To justify the violent absorption of so many realms and petty principalities, it was hastily given out by Ferdinand and Isabella's propagandists that the Catholic Monarchy had a God-given duty to Christianize its pagan subjects in the Indies, although not a single priest had sailed on Columbus' first voyage. It became a commonplace to say that anywhere that needed to be evangelized was another Indies, including, for instance, the remoter parts of Spain. For Luisa, England was the 'grand India of the spirit'.[330]

Proof that she was discovering the joys of real missionary work is to be found in the very first letters she sent out from the embassy. By February 1606 visits to Newgate Prison were already an established part of her life as she did her best to console the six or seven Catholics held there on suspicion of being priests. With her face veiled or at least covered by a little mask, and with two companions leading the way, Luisa made what should have been no more than a twenty-minute journey to the jail, which occupied a gatehouse in the city wall, south of the Barbican, yet even this short distance proved almost too much for her frail constitution, at least while the bad weather lasted. New-gate was universally regarded as one of the capital's most insalubrious and fetid jails, but it was not difficult to gain entry. The Catholics were segregated from the common criminals in a part of the prison that had an entrance opening out onto the street, and if you knocked hard enough the jailer would come from his house next door and let you in. On the inside was another knocker to summon him when you were ready to go. He charged sixpence (1 *real*) per prisoner, and you were left to find your own way to where the prisoners were held. On her first visit she spent an hour with the priests and with other Catholics incarcerated alongside them, keeping her little veil on all the time. She tried to avoid speaking English, since at this time she confessed to Magdalena, 'if I knew the language, your grace wouldn't believe the opportunities there are here even for someone as useless as me'.[331]

The following month, in March 1606, Ann Vaux was seized as she knocked on the prison door and was taken away to be questioned about her knowledge of the Gunpowder Plot. This was precisely the type of danger that thrilled Luisa and she was far from being put off, especially as mass was available inside the prison. By and large the inmates were left to their own devices, which meant mass could be celebrated by one of the prisoners if he had already been found out to be a priest.[332]

It seems strange to us that access to the state's adversaries was relatively straightforward but this is a reflection of how early modern society was organized. Prisons were largely privatized—if that is an appropriate term—and the jailer made ends meet by charging admission. King James and his ministers may have been unyielding towards Catholic priests, and Jesuits in particular, but they lacked the means to implement their wishes, which meant that the language of anti-Catholicism outstripped the practice of anti-popery. Important decisions by the government could be spur-of-the-moment responses to circumstances which were usually left to a relatively low-level officer to put into effect. Pursuivants were the officials most feared by the Catholic community, and though some were motivated by an ardent anti-Catholicism, often they were little more than bounty-hunters who went after priests to extort money from the people who were hiding them, or, if that failed, to confiscate their goods. Catholics could never tell when an individual pursuivant might be moved to strike a blow for Protestantism, or when he might be running low on cash.

When Luisa first started going to Newgate the prison regime was relatively relaxed despite the frantic searches underway on account of the conspiracy to kill the king, but by the middle of the following year life at the prison was much harsher. By July 1607 it was housing a number of Catholic women as well as the priests and various laymen, and one day, when they were all gathered in a single large room hearing mass, various pursuivants attempted to force their way in. Four Catholic men held the door and kept them out, but eventually they were overcome and removed to the part of the prison where the common criminals were kept. When Luisa visited them she was so alarmed by the sight of these thieves and murderers that she begged the jailer not to leave her and her companion alone, and when she finally located the friends she had come to see they were in chains.[333]

The clock had turned full circle by the end of the year. In December she visited a newly captured priest who had been thrown into Newgate along with the wretched couple sheltering him. Their furniture was seized, their children put on the street, and their home sealed up, but all three were jolly—and the jailer too. He had not had any priests recently and fee-paying visits had dried up. Luisa turned his necessity into a parable, saying, behold

the greatness of God, who turns the job of this heretic into an effective means of providing relief for many souls. What each one gives him as they enter makes him a goodly year's wage, and it pleases him so much that many should come that he puts no obstacle in their way, something which he arranges as shrewdly as he can; and should he have no priest he gets his friends the magistrates to give him the first one they catch, and every day the padre says mass with usually a hundred or more coming to listen.[334]

The one prison over which the government exercised direct control was the Tower of London, but it was costly and inconvenient to keep a prisoner there, being a royal residence housing a military garrison as well as the royal mint. When important prisoners were removed to the Tower—Ann Vaux for one—Luisa despaired, as 'there was no means of getting in nor having anything to do with it'.[335]

Early on in life Luisa had learnt to ignore whatever she did not like, and a consequence of this was that she convinced herself that she never meddled in politics. When Magdalena de San Jerónimo tried to persuade her to abandon England on the grounds she was jeopardiz-ing Anglo-Spanish relations, she protested, saying she did not 'get involved in temporal matters, as I detest all this war-making and the spilling of blood'. Luisa could be gloriously inconsistent, and before the ink was dry on that passage she let slip that she had no time for lukewarm Catholics who refused to help co-religionists in their hour of need. In her sights was the idea that reasons of state ('razones de Estado') could take precedence over what she called God's glory.[336] This was tantamount to a slur on the efforts by Philip III's chief minister (and her distant relation), the duke of Lerma. Along with the archdukes in Brussels, he was undertaking a series of peace treaties and truces designed to give an exhausted Spain time to lick her wounds and put her military house in order but which to Luisa seemed to be nothing more than a grovelling capitulation to all Protestants, and the hateful Dutch in particular. A by-product of this was that her increasingly resentful letters to Magdalena at the archdukes' court—hitherto her principal correspondent—come to a halt after 1607. Two years later Luisa dismissively told Inés, 'I don't hear a thing about [her], not even if she is alive'.[337]

Luisa was a political animal to her fingertips. If there was any room to dispute this, it vanished when a new statutory oath of loyalty to the crown came into play. After the Gunpowder Plot, the English par-liament had enacted the necessary legislation for a revised pledge to be offered to Catholics and other of the king's subjects. Unlike the Oath of Supremacy, the new Oath of Allegiance made no reference to the monarch's status as supreme governor of the English Church, some-thing intended to appeal to Catholics who could not in conscience swear to a patent affront to the doctrine of papal supremacy; instead, the new oath concentrated on the far less clear-cut question of whether popes could depose secular and especially Protestant princes.

Recusants were invited to swear that they would remain true to King James even if Rome tried to overthrow him.

This undertaking chimed in perfectly with James's image of himself as a monarch who never persecuted people for their religion. He was smugly satisfied that the new oath proved 'I intended no persecution against them for conscience cause, but only desired to be secured of them for civil obedience'.[338] There is genuine debate over what his real intentions were: some believe the oath was a candid attempt to find a way for Catholics to prove they were as loyal as his Protestant subjects; others see it as a 'diabolically effective polemical cocktail', which, by mixing allegiance to the king with the Pope's power to depose princes, was intended to put English Catholics on the spot. What is undeniable is that it split the recusant community into two bitterly opposed camps. It brought to a head the animosity between the Jesuits and the Archpriest George Blackwell who, as head of the secular clergy in England, maintained that Catholics could in conscience take the new oath. Previous spats over promises of loyalty had been largely confined to the clergy, but, regardless of what his intentions had been, the king forced lay Catholics and their priests to stand up and be counted. Intriguingly, the oath provided an opportunity for the French king to stir up trouble among English Catholics by trying to nip in the bud King James's nascent friendship with Spain. By supporting the Archpriest in his endeavours to make the oath the basis for limited public toleration of the Roman religion, Henri IV hoped to weaken the position of the pro-Spanish Jesuit faction in England, and the French ambassador put about rumours that the papal brief against the oath was not the Pope's personal opinion, just that of officials in the Holy Office.

The capture of the long-serving priest John Drury proved a pivotal moment for the new oath. Luisa rushed to visit him in Newgate very soon after he was apprehended on Tuesday, 10 February, in Whitefriars near Fleet Street. A large quantity of Catholic paraphernalia including crosses, pictures, and books, were found in the house of his unfortunate host, John Stansby, who was arrested along with his wife and maid just for harbouring the priest. Another priest, William Davies, was seized at the same time, but of the two, Drury was the more charismatic figure.

He was a keen political operator, fiercely intelligent, and the son of a former sheriff of Buckinghamshire.

He was also a year or so younger than Luisa, had retained his youthful looks, and spoke good Spanish which he had acquired during his time as a leading light in the English College in the years immediately following its foundation. Though he had not stayed on to train as a Jesuit, in court he was nonetheless referred to as a traitor. Why, he asked? Because you are a priest. In that case, he retorted, so was everyone who had ever been a priest in England, including those who were saints. 'My fault is no greater than theirs.'[339] On 19 February he entered a plea of not guilty but the judges had no option but to sentence him to be taken to Tyburn on a hurdle, 'and be there hanged by the neck, and that while still alive he be thrown down, and that his members be cut off, and that his body be divided into four parts, and that his members and quarters be placed where the said lord the King shall be pleased to appoint'.[340]

The question was stark: did James still want to execute priests who were not plotting regicide? Apart from those implicated in the wholly exceptional circumstances of the Gunpowder Plot, Drury would be the first priest to be put to death since England's peace treaty with Catholic Spain. There was beginning to be wild talk that full toleration might be a possibility if only an Anglo-Spanish marriage could be arranged, and James had certainly made a number of fine-sounding attempts to reach out to his Catholic subjects after the attempt to blow him up, even if his officials continued to persecute. In the old queen's time, Drury had made plain he would like to see her rule recognized by Rome and, like many non-Jesuits, he was known to be prepared to swear an oath of fidelity of some sort to his monarch. Even if it was wrong for the clergy to take King James's oath, Drury at least wondered if members of the laity might swear to it—until, that is, he was 'informed by some Catholics' that there was a papal brief to the contrary.[341]

Luisa considered herself to be one of those Catholics. She happened to be with Drury during the evening of 24 February, the day before he was unexpectedly taken away for execution barely a fortnight after his arrest. Though by no means his only visitor, Luisa was convinced she had persuaded him 'as strongly as I could not to let himself be defeated by the audacious arguments they were putting to him just to take the last oath passed by parliament a year ago'.[342] Four years later she was still boasting that the English authorities held her responsible for persuading Drury to stand firm.[343]

She was on dangerous ground. To begin with, she was cutting across Ambassador Zúñiga's behind-the-scenes efforts to save Drury's life through his approaches to the countess of Suffolk, an intimate friend of Robert Cecil. Both in receipt of Spanish pensions, the king's chief minister had blithely promised there would be no further clerical executions. But King James was ever his own master. Zúñiga heard a story that when he was asked by the Chief Justice, Sir John Popham, what to do with the priests in jail, James replied, hang them all. A report sent to Rome claimed that, when James was passing Tyburn on his way to hunt at Newmarket, he went up to the gibbet and sneered, 'all you Jesuits and priests hanged here, pray for me!'[344] The monarch was certainly under pressure from MPs. He had despatched Sir Christopher Piggott, knight of the shire for Buckinghamshire, to the Tower for speaking ill of Scots, while members of parliament were clamouring that it breached their privileges to do so while the Commons was in session. The head of a priest was a dainty dish to serve before a parliament.

As a good Catholic, the French ambassador had no wish to see Drury (or, for that matter, Davies) put to death. He went to James to plead for their lives, but the king was more interested in finding out whether Henri IV had ordered him to intervene. When the Frenchman clumsily replied that he had come out of charity, James was enraged, as he was convinced he numbered among the most charitable of men on God's earth. He became incandescent when the ambassador wondered out loud why he was not more enraged with the Spanish ambassador for having sent cassocks to the priests and for actively encouraging them not to take the king's oath. The Lord Chamberlain was ordered to investigate Zúñiga's interference, which gave don Pedro the opportunity to defend his honour with a bravura performance. He denied sending any vestments, but he added that, had he known they were needed, he would unquestionably have done so. As for the oath there was no need for encouragement because our faith, he declaimed, was encouragement enough.

The finger of blame being pointed at Zúñiga would have been better aimed at Luisa. It was she who had been instrumental in urging Drury to follow the Jesuits' lead in having no truck with the revised oath, and she mentioned in correspondence that a cassock had been smuggled in, as well as a biretta, the square-shaped clerical hat with raised corners. Although the clerical garb may well have been donated by Drury's other visitors, she may have been one of only two Spaniards who could have seen the condemned priest, as Zúñiga and his staff were keeping their distance as they worked quietly to preserve his life. A few weeks later don Pedro reported back to Spain that it was a rogue Spanish barber in the pay of the French ambassador who had been responsible for giving the cassock and the hat to Drury. It is tempting to speculate whether Zúñiga propagated this story in order to play down any part Luisa played in this hiccup in Anglo-Spanish relations, but what is clear is that the ambassador knew that the French would do almost anything to blacken Spain's name, and it must have been a constant concern to him that Luisa—his personal loose cannon—might do something to lend credence to French disinformation.[345]

Between seven and eight in the morning of Thursday, 25 February, a jailer entered Drury's cell and, as gently as he could, he morbidly announced he was the messenger of death.[346] The hurdle was outside ready to draw him to immediate execution. Drury was strapped down feet first while thirty-two condemned criminals were huddled together in a cart, and together they went west—literally that is, to Tyburn, near today's Marble Arch. When his end finally came, Drury was permitted the small mercy of hanging until he was dead before being dismembered. Luisa knew nothing of what was taking place 2 miles away from her home until after the execution rites had been performed but there was one last kindness she could perform. At Drury's request, she took his aged mother under her wing, somehow managing to scrape together a small pension for her to live off.[347] As for William Davies, the Shropshire-born priest tried alongside Drury, his life was spared, probably on account of being almost 70 years of age, and he continued to celebrate masses which Luisa attended. Attracted by his austerity, she pitied him and not just because he had been denied a martyr's crown. It offended her that he was treated 'at every occasion with very little courtesy' just because he was uneducated.[348]

Drury's execution marked the point when Luisa crossed the line and became more than a Catholic oddity in a Protestant city. She had an influential role to play in the vicious dispute between seculars and Jesuits; the new oath had provided her with an opportunity to make waves and this she did with a passion. No longer was she the largely passive embodiment of a lingering Spanish concern for the Catholics of England. By standing by his new oath, James had turned her into an effective agitator in England and a well-informed lobbyist at the princely courts of Europe. In addition to letters to Magdalena in Brussels, she wrote or sent accounts of Drury's defiance to influential people in Valladolid, including her former spiritual director, Ludovico Da Ponte. At last Creswell, Persons, and the Walpoles had their wish. Their gamble in sending her to England was paying off.

Luisa was now self-assured enough to stride into the lion's den. In September 1607 she confronted Archpriest Blackwell, who was being held in honourable captivity in the Clink, the old ecclesiastical prison in Southwark which had once belonged to the bishops of Winchester. It was also the jail furthest from where she lived. The Archpriest's roar was worse than his bite, and in their exchanges he clung to the belief that Catholics could follow his example and take the oath, arguing that the pope's power to excommunicate was only for the purposes of amending a wayward soul, a power which could not seriously be applied to a monarch who was not of his church. His opinions were 'eccentric, wayward, unfounded and pointless', she said, wondering if he had lost his wits. He smiled a lot.[349]

Luisa would not have crossed the Thames just to see an Archpriest she wrote off as unutterably foolish. Given her detestation of water, not to mention her loathing of unnecessary expense, the hiring a wherry from any of the city's three thousand boatmen was out of the question. She would have to brave London Bridge. Though it was nearly four hundred years old, having been completed in 1209, it was the city's sole means of crossing the river by foot until the mid-eighteenth century. Crammed on either side with well over a hundred houses and shops, it was accepted across Christendom as an architectural marvel. It was also narrow, being barely 20 feet wide, which made it an ordeal for Luisa, with her strange clothes, her little mask, and a crucifix audaciously placed around her neck, to fight her way through the crowds and carriages crossing to and from Southwark. What induced her to walk across the bridge and fork left past the bishop of Winchester's palace and his church of St Mary Overie, now Southwark Cathedral, into Clink Street was her self-appointed mission to comfort the elderly Edward Gage of Bentley, the wealthy head of a branch of a notable recusant family, who found himself literally *in Clink* for sheltering a priest from overseas. Unlike many members of his extended family at this time, including his first cousin, Lord Montague, who was the Archpriest's patron, Edward Gage inclined towards the Jesuits' uncompromising arguments against taking the oath of allegiance.[350]

The priest who had taken refuge in Gage's house had done so without the unfortunate owner's prior knowledge. Called Father German, the priest was in all probability a Jesuit who had just arrived from Germany, and he had made straight for where Ann Vaux was living, a couple of miles outside London, possibly near Spitalfields. One morning in July, she became concerned at the number of men she feared were pursuivants who were gathering outside her house, and the priest left for the Gage's new townhouse near the Tower of London, turning up around five o'clock in the afternoon. With all the officials and soldiers going in and out of the Tower, as well as the constant stream of merchants who congregated by the Thames, it was a part of London where it was difficult to pass unnoticed. The Gages had only recently moved into their new home and there had been no opportunity to create priests' hiding-holes or other secret places. German was obliged to sleep in the room of Gage's son, George, and when the pursuivants finally apprehended them they were both asleep in the same bed. Ann Vaux, who had also turned up at the new house, was let off lightly, being released under the terms of her existing bail, but Edward and his son were taken to separate prisons. Mrs Margaret Gage, along with two daughters—one of whom was pregnant—were placed under house-arrest, along with a 6-year-old grandson. Their valuables were gathered together and put in two sealed rooms, with a single constable guarding the house by day and two by night.

The Gages' unmarried daughter had set her heart on becoming a nun in Flanders, and the prospect of being locked up like her father and brother threatened to get in the way of her ambition, as a letter had been discovered suggesting she could lead the pursuivants to where more priests were hiding. Mrs Gage hatched a plan for her escape. Disguising her as a kitchen girl, dirty and in rags, she sent her out with a basket to buy fruit, but instead her daughter crossed London unchaperoned, and headed straight for Luisa's house in the Barbican, where she was immediately taken in. As to the fate of the others, Father German had two lucky escapes from the White Lion prison, also in Southwark. First he avoided the plague from which three of his cellmates were to die, and then one night a young Catholic man who was nonetheless trusted by the jailer helped him break out from what was in fact merely a converted inn. Master George was released by order of the authorities (and is probably the George Gage who went on to take holy orders and to become, some ten years later, King James's semi-official envoy to the Pope) but his father was kept in jail despite his pleas that he had not known he was sheltering a priest. As head of the family, he controlled the family's money, which is what mattered to the pursuivants.[351]

Edward Gage's daughter was welcomed into a tiny religious community. Living with Luisa at this time was the unidentified sister of one Eleanor Dutton as well as the usually dependable Ann Garnet. Strange as it may seem, the three women were already at the hub of what was rapidly becoming an international operation to help place English Catholics in religious houses or with pious families in Spain and the Spanish dominions. Luisa's experience in such matters went back a long way, of course. It will be recalled that while she was still living in Valladolid she had sent word to England that she was prepared to help Margaret Walpole make her way to Lisbon and to the Bridgetine house established there after the death of Mary Tudor; three years later, Margaret Walpole was probably invited to stay with Luisa while final arrangements were made to get her over to Flanders.

To Luisa's irritation, however, she quickly returned to England, claiming her health was not up to the religious life.[352]

Another case of someone who was helped to get out of the country is also unsatisfactory, but for quite different reasons. It concerns a 15-year-old boy called William Richardson whom Luisa befriended while she was living in the embassy. His mother, she said, was a neurotic widow, who, despite opposition from her family, had reverted to Catholicism and who attended mass in the ambassador's chapel. She wanted to place her son in a merchant's household where he could acquire the necessary skills to make a living. If her son stayed in England, that might well mean lodging him with a Protestant family as, generally speaking, wealthy recusants tended to keep a lower profile by becoming craftsmen or professionals, leaving the marketplace to Protestants. William's mother was too timorous to seek out an English Catholic who was prepared to take her son on.

Luisa became interested in William despite no uncertain warnings that it was risky to attempt the conversion of a volatile young man who could easily change his mind and expose her to the authorities. Nevertheless, Luisa quarrelled bitterly with the mother about the future of her soul, and

after some months getting nowhere, I bumped into the youngster on the stairs, and I remonstrated with him for obeying his mother in this matter. Later that day he came to see me at my house, asking me to help him and not to abandon his soul. Even if she threw him out of the house, as she said she would, and even if he had to go begging, he wanted to be reconciled with the Church. I took him to the priests in prison, and they were afraid, as this was undoubtedly a dangerous case. In the end, when he had received enough religious instruction, I had go at them another two or three times, offering to send him to Flanders, which would put him out of danger and where his mother could not get at him. With this promise, they reconciled him and made him a Catholic, and I hope he will remain so for ever.

As for the practical arrangements of getting young William out of the country, the daughter of the venerable English secretary at the embassy, Henry Taylor, offered to escort him to Calais. The next we hear of him is a year later when, in July 1607, Luisa announced that he had finally turned up in the Low Countries. By now she was telling her friends that William was making the journey with his mother's wholehearted approval, adding that he belonged to a family that was related to an Elizabethan martyr. She hoped he would be found a place with a Catholic merchant or else be put to work in a religious house.[353]

Luisa tells William's story as a triumph, with her doggedness over many months finally breaking down a mother's resistance and the circumspection of priests. Another age might read the story differently. She had taken it upon herself to decide where William's spiritual best interests lay and evinced no compunction in applying her force of character and her indubitable intellectual gifts to intimidate a mother she herself described as timid. She had been prepared to contemplate seizing the child without his mother's knowledge. When it came to imposing her will on a child, perhaps Luisa revealed herself on this occasion to be more like her uncle the marquis than we would care to admit.

12

Sovereign Virgin

ITHIN a few years of arriving in London Luisa established a
unique place among the capital's Catholic community.
Her insistence on the presence of the reserved sacrament
and care for details such as the freshness of the holy oil helped make
the chapel in the Barbican the leading place for Roman worship in
London. She had badgered the ambassador into setting up an Easter
Candle, one large enough to burn till Ascension Day, and the Venetian and French embassies were shamed into following suit.[354] At the
inquiry into her possible canonization, members of the embassy staff
agreed she was an inspiration to English Catholics simply by being
present at mass every day.

She even helped out on a practical level, or at least tried to. She had
a hand in making the hosts which were used at the embassy chapel,
which would have been an arduous task indeed as the ambassador
himself calculated that on Holy Thursday in Easter Week of 1607 four
hundred people received communion, and an extra two hundred
turned up on Good Friday, with some arriving in their coaches as
boldly as if it were Spain. But Spain it was not, and the comings and
goings at the embassy were under surveillance from the pursuivants.
Their unwelcomed presence, along with the fact that so many people
were trying to leave all at once, obliged the ambassador to invite some
of the worshippers to leave by the hidden gates in the garden. The
following year, the chapel had become so busy that an additional
chaplain was brought over from Flanders so mass could be said three
times a day, and, although the chapel was extended by knocking
down the wall that divided it from an antechamber, there was still
not always sufficient room for the congregation.[355] The chapel was
enlarged once more at least in Luisa's lifetime.

The London embassy was as difficult a posting as any because 'on it falls in no small measure the honour of Spain and the Holy Catholic Church, the two of which go very much hand in hand'.[356] Her view was shared by the Spanish Council of State, which congratulated don Pedro for keeping his chapel open in 1608 when the other ambassadors had closed theirs because the plague was so virulent.[357] Living so close to the embassy afforded her a degree of protection, and she often expressed her gratitude for being able to live in Spain's long shadow. This protection was far from being total, however, and later that summer she told Ludovico Da Ponte how the capital's Protestants abused her in the street for being a nun. She took steps to protect herself and her companions:

because we dress more modestly than they do, I have to send two of my companions on first to don Pedro's chapel before I set out, so we aren't all seen together, and the remaining one goes with me.

By summer 1608 at least four women had gathered around her to share in a communal life, the most senior being, of course, the increasingly prickly Ann Garnet.[358] Some months before, Luisa had left mass in the embassy flaunting her rosary, which provoked a passing Protestant to snatch it from her hand. Ann stepped in, calling him a bad man and thumping him as hard as she could. Of Joanna Mills all we know is that she was of a contemplative nature and the community became her permanent home.[359] The third companion was Susanna, a strong healthy woman who would willingly lend a hand to anything for the cause despite coming from one of England's nobler families. The most recent arrival was Faith, a little white dove, Luisa called her.

Luisa called her embryonic community the Company of the Sovereign Virgin Mary, Our Lady, drawing up a rule for its members to follow.[360] In fact, it was a treatise on what Inés called the 'new way of living' rather than a traditional monastic rulebook. The first part dealt exclusively with what she termed spiritual instruction, including the need for humility, though it was clear from the outset that Luisa was to be in charge. The opening lines may have greeted her companions with the endearments of equality which were de rigueur in reformed circles but any modesty quickly vanished when she said that divine inspiration would surely make her fit to lead:

Seeing, my dear sisters, that God Our Lord has brought you (so it appears) to my Company, desiring to turn yourselves over completely to Him in the most religious way of life possible for you through His divine help, which I trust will compensate for my faults.

A devotional timetable was laid down that was to be observed 'with the greatest precision and exactitude which your small number and the restrictions of the house permit'. Living this way would be an acceptable offering to God and help to achieve 'the salvation of the souls of your country'. One of her companions remembered she would repeatedly say that they needed to 'be very parfet that ye may appease this great wrath of God with your great virtue and holiness of life'.[361] The Rule's opening section concluded in a way typical of Luisa but shockingly different from anything else written for religious women at this time. It ended with an invocation that 'our path might lead to a violent and fortunate death'!

In the meantime, life had to go on, and she talked more about the need to choose a leader of appropriate age and virtue, which can only have meant herself. In the calle de Toledo it might have been acceptable to allow one of her companions to act out the role of the leader, as in her native Spain her superior rank was indisputable, but in England, where her standing was anomalous and her knowledge of the language imperfect, she could not risk letting others assume a directing role. Interestingly, no mention was made of her own re-election, though in reformed nunneries this was regarded as a necessary innovation which would buttress a female superior's authority against the male clergy.

Since Luisa did not intend her companions to live an enclosed life but go out in the world, it was necessary to talk about dress, and her Rule stipulated that their clothes must be modest so that their enemies could detect no sign of vanity. Luisa went to some pains to explain that the dangers of their way of living had caused her to question whether it was appropriate to take the three traditional vows of obedience, poverty, and chastity. After much deliberation she had decided that it would be wrong to deprive her companions of the spiritual rewards which came from taking such oaths, as she could not imagine how they could conform to a perfect life 'with any less effective bridle than the vow of strict obedience'. Most significant of all, she added a fourth vow, as we shall see later on.

Conversations were to be kept short, but silence was to be preferred wherever possible, which was justified in terms similar to those she had once used to describe her mystical experiences. Her companions were encouraged to listen out for the 'Eternal Word' in all the things divinely made. Manual work was recommended but not just as a means of avoiding the perils of idleness. It had to be undertaken purposefully, as otherwise 'you will do little or nothing for the needs of the house, nor to ease the superior's burden of providing for its upkeep and sustenance'.

The second part of the 'London Rule' dealt with the Distribution of Time. The companions were to rise at the customary hour of five in the morning when it was summer and an hour later in winter, before coming together for an hour of silent prayer. Then parts of the Divine Office were to be recited according to the season, which was to be followed by manual labour, as the superior directed. Two hours after they had woken up, mass was to be said, and Luisa was adamant that any sermon should only take place afterwards. (This is not necessarily wishful-thinking, as there was often a priest living with the community who could provide words of edification.) The sisters were to examine their consciences at 10.45 and then they were free to engage in any religious activity until eleven o'clock when they would have their midday meal. In a further nod in the direction of equality, they were to sit at table in the order in which they entered the room. Following the sixth-century Rule of St Benedict, a religious text was to be read during a meal, which normally would be eaten in silence. Then the timekeeper would turn the hourglass and all would be free to have sixty minutes of recreation and improving conversation, with the rest of the day following the same pattern of silence, interrupted by prayer or work. Dinner was to be served at seven in the summer and an hour later in winter. The day would end with matins at 8.30 in the summer—an hour later in winter—after which they would retire.

Is Luisa's Rule based on the *Constitutions* which St Teresa wrote for her new religious houses? Though 'a marked structural similarity' exists between the two rules, Luisa had many sources of inspiration to draw upon, just as Teresa herself had been open to many influences. What one of Teresa's travelling companions said about her could also be applied to Luisa, with both being like the 'busy bee searching out the best flowers to bring back to her hive'.[362] More specifically, the first half of Luisa's Rule is devoted to spiritual advice, whereas Teresa's Rule is confined to the timetabling of the practical organization of life in an enclosed community, finding no place for the generalized spiritual coaching that Luisa included. That the organization of prayer is similar in both rules is not greatly significant. For instance, their day began at the first hour with *prime* and ended with matins, which had come to be said last thing at night; but the point here is that this structure derives from the Divine Office, or the Liturgy of the Hours, a daily rota of prayers that harks back not just to St Benedict's Rule of the sixth century but ultimately to the Jewish hours of prayer as indicated in the Acts of the Apostles.[363] It is a routine which is common to nearly all Western monastic traditions.

The many coincidences between what Teresa wrote and the 'London Rule' probably owe much to the fact that both women were part of the same general movement for reform which had begun with the Discalced Friars, so beloved by Luisa's mother, and which had been intellectually invigorated by the Jesuits. Luisa also had her own first-hand experiences of reformed practice from the years she spent as a child living alongside the nuns of the Descalzas Reales, and, as we know, she later got to know or corresponded with women who had personally assisted Teresa in founding discalced houses. In fact, it is the *dissimilarities* between the two rules which are more enlightening about what Luisa hoped to achieve.

In the sixth century Benedict had stressed the need for members of religious orders to work. Teresa singled out needlework, whereas Luisa, despite her fascination with threading gold, referred to the value of manual labour in general. Whereas Teresa had said that work was best undertaken in solitude and on no account was there to be a *casa de labor* or communal workroom, this restriction was impractical given the cramped conditions in which Luisa lived, as well as contrary to the spirit of an open community where it might be necessary to perform any number of tasks. True, both Teresa and Luisa agreed that mortification of the flesh should take place on Mondays, Wednesdays, and Fridays outside Lent, but this too harked back to an earlier tradition, being found in the Carmelite constitutions written well before Teresa had felt the need to reform her order. As is to be expected, these had been the very days on which Luisa, as a child, had flagellated herself.[364]

A more detailed inspection of the timetable provides the best clues to Luisa's inspiration. Like Teresa, she emphasized the need for mental prayer to support the spoken prayer of the Office but, unlike Teresa, she spelled out what they were to pray about. From Monday to Thursday they were to spend an hour after getting up contemplating life's end—death, judgement, hell, and glory—and on Fridays and Saturdays they were to think about the death and burial of Christ, and on Sundays the resurrection. Her companions were encouraged to see in their mind's eye Christ in the manger or dead on the cross. Here Luisa was drawing directly upon the practices of the Company that she had first learnt from her nurse, Ayllón, and which had been reinforced while she was living in Valladolid by Luis de la Puente.

What was de la Puente's influence on Luisa? We know that, sometime after 1604, he replied to a professed nun in Valladolid, Ana de Tobar, about the need 'to give oneself over to communing with Our Lord, spending all the time in mental or vocal prayer, in spiritual reading, in examining one's conscience and similar things'. His suggestion was of four hours of mental prayer a day—incidentally an hour more than seems to be the case in Teresa's rule—which were to be split up so that there were, in total, two in the morning and two in the evening. (De la Puente also recommended she acquire one of his own books as suitable spiritual reading.) Though Luisa gave a running timetable for the whole day rather than loosely commenting on the distribution of time, she nonetheless referred to the morning's 'second hour of silence', which indicates that she also expected at least four hours of recollected prayer.[365] There are also precise echoes of de la Puente in the provision of fifteen minutes for the examination of conscience prior to both main meals. We should not think that influence ran only one way. De la Puente told Luisa in the summer of 1608 that she was especially in his thoughts when he recited the morning psalm which she had recommended to him.[366]

The relationship to the male confessor is where Luisa really strikes out on her own. Fundamental to the Teresian reform was to make the enclosed nunnery a place where *female* authority was paramount. Teresa combined what has been called 'a female magisterium with a male apostolate'.[367] That is to say, she tried to make the mother superior as much as a confessor-figure as possible (which was one of the issues that brought her to the attention of the Inquisition). Teresa's *Constitutions* institutionalize the superior's power by stipulating that once a month each nun would privately visit her in order to discuss her spiritual life, but no such procedure was advocated by Luisa. (The closest she came to this was a general requirement for her companions to speak to her in detail about any visions—or 'illusions', as she called them—which they might have in prayer.) A Discalced Carmelite superior was allowed to appoint a general confessor, but— in order to divide and rule the priesthood—Teresa permitted the prioress to bring in extra confessors at will, even at the cost of explicitly acknowledging that this flew in the face of the Council of Trent's decree that additional confessors were to be allowed in on just three occasions in the year. Teresa's bending of the rules enabled a mother superior to undermine the authority of any confessor who crossed her by bringing in a substitute. The 'London Rule' was quite different, reflecting Luisa's strict obedience to her Jesuit confessors and her lack of interest in anything like gender politics. In most un-Teresian terms, her companions were to reveal everything to their confessor in the most straightforward manner possible, obeying him 'not as a man, but as someone whom God has put in His place'.

The inescapable conclusion is that in developing her unique way of living Luisa was influenced more by Ignatius Loyola and the members of the Company of Jesus than by any one else. Unmodish though this may be, Luisa did not look exclusively to females for her role models. The Jesuitical influence is borne out by the title she gave to her community. The Society of the Virgin Mary is a reworking of the

Society of Jesus, and this similarity is even more striking if we look at the Spanish version of the title, where literally she calls it the Company of the Virgin Mary, just as the Jesuits referred to themselves as the Company. But if further proof were necessary we need only look again at the vows to be taken by the companions.

Obedience, poverty, and chastity remain the three Benedictine vows which traditionally define Western monasticism. Monks were under the direct authority of their abbot, not the local bishop, but what made the Jesuits unique and turned them into Rome's 'shock troops' was an additional vow placing them under the direct authority of the Pope. In addition to the three traditional vows, Luisa included what she called

a fourth vow of very special obedience and reverence above and beyond that which is due from all faithful Catholics to His Holiness the Roman Pontiff Paul V and to all his successors canonically elected to the apostolic seat of St Peter.

In other words, Luisa envisaged herself as a female Jesuit. Far from wishing to live in the strict enclosure of a Teresian house, she wanted to follow the Company's example of leading a communal life but actively working in the community for the greater good of the Roman Church. At the centre of Luisa's rebellion against the new orthodoxy of Trent lay her revolutionary insistence that the virtue of religious women did not need to be protected by the bricks and mortar of a convent wall.

The title of the first 'Jesuitess' is sometimes claimed for the Princess Juana, the founder of the Descalzas Reales, but, as we have seen, her membership was strictly honorific. Just as often the title is accorded to Mary Ward, an Englishwoman, but she was twenty years Luisa's junior. Around 1611 she founded what would become the Institute of the Blessed Virgin, first in a house in the Strand, and her community of women would also take Jesuit-like vows to obey the wishes of the papacy. Ward's followers were derided as galloping girls or chattering hussies, and the label of 'Jesuitesses' was meant not as a compliment but to imply an act of perversion. As for Mary herself, in 1606 she undertook Luisa's journey in reverse, travelling from England to

St Omer to join a reformed nunnery, returning three years later to comfort and educate Catholic women. How far Luisa influenced if at all the much younger woman is a matter of conjecture, but we have it on excellent authority that Mary knew Luisa personally and sang her praises. For an unspecified period of time her aunt, she said, had lodged with Luisa. Mary Ward's energy and administrative abilities drew her towards the education of Catholic women, but these two reformers had in common the fact they were both inspired by the Jesuit Order in their efforts to find a more active role for religious women.[368]

When the 'London Rule' was written is not known. There is a reference to a garden where her companions could take exercise, which might suggest it was drawn up after she had moved out from her tenement house in the Barbican, though it could just as easily mean that it was begun while she still had access to the embassy garden. The Society of the Sovereign Virgin was to all intents and purposes in operation by 1609, as the life which Luisa described to her cousin Isabel in Valencia appears to be an ordered one. She hoped that the poor little house she now lived in ('nuestra pobre casita') would be taken by God as a peaceful garden amidst a forest of wild beasts, and she hoped more women would join her, saying, 'It's up to us, through His most holy grace, to spend our time well, and govern ourselves tirelessly in working with our hands, and in the other things which our profession asks of us.'[369]

The 'London Rule' called for mortification of the flesh to play a central role in the lives of the companions. Luisa's close Jesuit friend, John Blakfan, at one stage lived for eighteen months in Luisa's house before he was forced to leave the country. From his Continental exile, he sent the members of the community gifts, including a little rosary for Luisa, adding,

for Mistress Frances I sent yesterday a thick whip which I made myself. Today I'm sending three more, the thickest for Anna, the one with the white thread for Mistress Ann, the one with cords for Joanna, and I will send Helena the first one that I finish.[370]

Blakfan's gifts are significant because they belie the suggestion that Luisa's previous physical penance was a desperate reaction to the suffocating presence of male religious authority, that once she was given the fulfilling role of being a missionary in England she had no need of physical penitence and was subsequently 'able to vent her considerable energies in more positive directions than in flagellating herself'.[371]

It was not only the sound of a cracking whip which disturbed the serenity of the little community, however. In October 1612 Luisa thanked an unnamed clergyman in Valencia for his prayers and she took the opportunity to commend her companions for all the tribulations they had to suffer, calling them 'most virtuous soldier-maidens'.[372] But within two months of writing this she had a near mutiny on her hands.

In December 1612, presumably while her companions were asleep, she wrote a long rambling letter to her confessor which she did not finish until after midnight. She referred to the letter's recipient— Blakfan or more likely Michael Walpole—as well as herself and her companions by a series of ciphers so convoluted that it is a challenge to make sense of her night-time scribblings. Her account seethes with accusations and counter-accusations, so much so her modern Jesuit champion, Camilo Abad, conceded that her 'report says little in favour of Luisa as a teacher or as a superior'.[373] Particularly striking are the criticisms of her long-serving 'companion #1', who, she says, ought more than anyone else to remember the deaths of people near to her. This points to Ann Garnet, who for many years she had praised to the hilt. Now Luisa alleges that from the first day she had been rebellious and ill-tempered, and, whereas she once extolled the fact that she was willing to do whatever was asked of her (even if she was an unenthusiastic teacher of English!), Ann was now accused of doing little more than a few stitches a day and spending too much time in bed. She could not be asked to guard the door because she spent too much time chatting with anyone who would give her the time of day. Perhaps there was a hint of rivalry in Luisa's allegation that Ann's mortification was excessive.

For her part, Ann seems to have raked up old accusations of Luisa's favouritism towards Marcharo, one of the original companions. When Luisa offered to find her somewhere else to live, or find a place for her in a monastery overseas, she accused Luisa of not caring. Perhaps the terrible deaths of Ann's uncle and cousin had finally proven too much for her. This may have been made worse by the physical privations of life in the community and the fact that Luisa had been chronically ill for almost two years before the accusations were launched. Food seems to have caused much resentment. Luisa complained about Ann's slovenliness in the kitchen and how she guzzled sweets and snatched mouthfuls of food in public. She was no kinder about her other companions, with #2 being arrogant and liable to faint at any moment, and as for #3 and #4, it was hard to write anything meaningful about them. At least her fifth and final companion—a youthful 40-something—was of 'much more settled judgement' and had the aptitude and strength of body required to endure a religious life, and guessing from the age, this may have been Joanna Guillen or Mills.

Michael Walpole may have had Ann Garnet in mind when he told the story in Luisa's biography of how he spent two hours trying to help one of the companions deal with her anger. This same companion broke down after Luisa's death, admitting she could not understand how her mistress had been so patient with her for so long. If this was Ann Garnet, the two women were eventually reconciled, as only days after Luisa's death, Blakfan passed on from Brussels to the English College in Rome a meticulous account of what he had learnt about the last weeks of her life. He had no qualms about calling Henry Garnet's niece 'virtuous' nor in recalling a promise he had made to Luisa that, if anything happened to her, he would find places for Ann and her other longest-serving companion in a nunnery on the Continent.[374] Eight years after Luisa's death he told Isabel, her companion from the calle de Toledo, that some of the English companions were still following her example, and prior to the investigation into Luisa's possible canonization she received a letter from a person she called the 'mother' of the companions, one Juanna Guillen. Perhaps her real name was Joanna Mills, as in August 1624 Michael Walpole tried to arrange a pension for her.[375]

Religious communities are notorious for the squabbles that invariably break out in such confined surroundings, and living with Luisa was never easy. The longer she lived in England and the more established she became among the recusant community, the more likely it was that King James's creatures would catch up with her. The threat of prison—or worse—constantly hung over the members of the little community, as they were shortly to discover.

13

Broken English

PRESERVED in London's National Archives is a scrap of paper with just four words scribbled on it, 'Donña Mariana de Caruajal'. This passable rendering of Luisa's name and title was sent back to King James's chief minister, Robert Cecil, by Sir Charles Cornwallis, the first English resident ambassador to Spain after the peace of 1604. Tucked into a letter despatched from Valladolid two months after Luisa had come ashore at Dover, Cecil was informed that 'a lady of this country' was making her way to England to convert Queen Anne. For good measure Cornwallis added that 'she is (they say) very witty & a good speaker'.[376] The ambassador kept up his enquiries, and shortly after he passed on the news that she was being sheltered 'in the houses of some recusants, who could be content she were embarked again for Spain'.[377]

It is a marvel that Luisa was able to live relatively unmolested in London for over three years before being arrested, in July 1608. For at least a year and a half prior to that, ever since she moved out of the embassy, she had been running an incipient religious community which defied the state's religion, had encouraged the king's subjects to embrace Roman Catholicism, even helping some to escape to the Continent. She had also whipped up priestly defiance of the new oath of allegiance which had been specifically authorized by both the king and his parliament.

Why had she been able to elude the authorities for so long? Much was to do with where she lived, since the area around the Spanish embassy in the Barbican lay beyond the city wall and was relatively unfashionable and therefore a less regulated part of the city. Her sex was another reason. Being a woman provided a degree of protection because the men who governed the country were reluctant to concede that a female could harm the interests of the state. Their contempt manifested itself in a number of ways. We have seen how Ann Vaux was arrested after the Gunpowder Plot but eventually released, only to be rearrested again for sheltering a priest from Germany and discharged once more, while the barely culpable male members of the Gage family were kept in prison for the same offence. Another comment from the Cornwallis–Cecil correspondence reveals the general derision. Without a second thought, the ambassador revealed the prejudices of the age when he said something would be as difficult to solve as it would be for 'a parliament of women to agree of a Speaker'![378]

Luisa's Jesuit sponsors on the Continent could be forgiven if it ever crossed their mind why her activities had failed to provoke the English authorities into making an example out of her much earlier on. The idea has been floated that she could 'have got herself killed had she wanted to die' if only her life in England had not become too fulfilling for her to hanker after martyrdom.[379] This may be going too far, since the distinction between constructive suicide and achieving a martyr's crown was well understood: Luisa had little or no right to endanger the women who had chosen to live with her and absolutely none at all to jeopardize the lives of the priests who sought her protection precisely because she was operating a safe-house. All along, it had been improbable that King James would have executed a Spanish aristocrat at a time when he was still fantasizing that his heir might marry a daughter of the Catholic king, yet this does not explain why Luisa was not ordered out of the country at a much earlier date. She goes virtually unnoticed in the voluminous state papers generated under Cecil's ministry, at least until the end of her time in London, but this says less about the government's intentions and more about the ramshackle organization of the early modern state. Luisa was too poor for the pursuivants to make any money out of arresting her; and while Cecil was trying to pretend that Catholicism was never persecuted—only its disloyal practitioners—it made no sense to risk a diplomatic incident on account of someone he took to be as a harmless foreign eccentric and female to boot.

Cecil was wide of the mark to view Luisa as innocuous. From early on in her mission she was involved in illegal book-running. As early as October 1607 Joseph Creswell was asked to send her the four volumes of Juan Basilio's newly edited *Flos Sanctorum*.[380] She referred to it as the 'Lives of the Saints', and the work was intended not for her instruction but for the edification of those she was trying to convert. (Later she asked for the verse version, saying 'it is greatly enjoyed here by the few who can understand the language'.[381]) At the same time she requested a copy of Antonio Nebrija's Spanish–Latin dictionary, and this too was not for her benefit but to help those would-be converts who had more Latin than Spanish. She complained to Creswell of the need for basic devotional books in English, since those who could read Spanish or Latin were usually more theologically advanced. As she bluntly told him, Spanish 'counts for little or absolutely nothing here'.[382] By 1611 she had in her possession 'the book written by the Holy Mother Teresa, in English, very well translated', and her unalloyed praise supports the view that the translator was Michael Walpole, who had been forced temporarily to abandon London for the Low Countries a year earlier.[383]

Creswell was indeed the man to contact. Around the time Luisa arrived in England he had persuaded Philip III to fund a printing press in the Low Countries. In 1616 he asked for the subsidy to be repeated, and eloquently expressed how important books were in sustaining the faith of the English recusants, echoing exactly Luisa's thoughts. She suggested that some books castigating King James and his religious policy ought to be translated into English, 'to encourage and strengthen the Catholics'.[384] In turn, he told King Philip that everyone knew that the devil had spread Protestantism in Germany and England by means of books containing false doctrine, and he went on to say that

experience shows that there is no better way, nor ever has been, of saving the same provinces from total ruin and perdition than continually to plant in them wholesome Catholic books. Some of these are devotional works to maintain the virtue of the well intentioned, while other books reveal the heretics' tricks so as to undeceive those who err and bring them back to the faith. Therefore these books enter where priests cannot enter to offer wise counsel, and by educating and pricking the conscience make others come by themselves to seek out what they need.[385]

Books might take months or years to reach her. For *Flos Sanctorum* to arrive she waited a year and a half, and when it did, at the end of May 1609, six of its twelve parts were missing.[386] One of the problems was having to bribe officials, almost certainly at Dover. When another batch of books arrived shortly afterwards, she explained that 'it didn't come cheap getting them out of customs'.[387] She went out of her way to tell Creswell how grateful she was to Father Silvester from the English College for providing her with books, though it is not clear whether he brought or despatched them. One of the tomes he was responsible for was a gift from 'el contador Saray', none other than Luisa's old admirer from the calle de Toledo and Valladolid, Juan de Ceráin.[388] The main couriers at the embassy, Juan Rivas, his son-in-law Pedro, and Juan Lampe, were all involved in bringing books through customs, and in August 1611 she was still fretting over whether Lampe might be able to bring back copies of *Flos Sanctorum*. She even called for two of the books she had left behind at the convent in Medina del Campo, one about St Francis and the other a manuscript copy of works by St John of the Cross, letting slip that in England there was 'a greater need of such things here than there'.[389]

Her activities were not confined to smuggling devotional books and she inevitably strayed into the political. In 1607 she swiftly passed on to Creswell in Rome a copy of the Archpriest's tract in which he defended his view that it was acceptable for his fellow Catholics to take the new oath of allegiance.[390] She even acquired Protestant books on Creswell's behalf, sending him hot off the presses the new Book of Common Prayer when it was published in 1611. It contained the Church of England's liturgy along with its heavily Calvinistic articles of faith, which would allow him to see for himself 'the most monstrous lies you will have ever heard in your life'.[391] For once, her knowledge of England failed her. She did not realize that it was much the same as the Elizabethan prayer book which Creswell had used before his conversion to Catholicism.

Her interest in the English Prayer Book supports what was said subsequently about her willingness to dispute with people who did not share her beliefs. A chaplain from the embassy went so far as to claim that several Protestants attended her deathbed.[392] Though an earlier chaplain had told her that women were not entitled to dispute doctrine, she clearly relished the opportunity which books provided for polemical debate, and in the Prayer Book she sent Creswell she marked every error by folding down the corner of the offending page. John Calvin's teaching about Christ's descent into hell after the Crucifixion particularly riled her. After pointing out to a learned Protestant the erroneous passages in Calvin's *Institutes*, he obligingly conceded— or so she claimed—that he was saddened that Calvin had written this but he was sure the great reformer would have changed his mind had he still been alive. One wonders if the preacher would have said anything to escape what sounds like a theological rant, and Luisa's reaction was to lament that she did not have Calvin's even more egregious book on St Matthew's Gospel to hand.[393]

The best evidence that she made effective use of her growing array of devotional books is her request for multiple copies. In 1612 she appealed for a dozen copies of the pocket-sized devotional books of John Eck, famous for publicly debating with Martin Luther. Since being caught by the pursuivants with Catholic literature could have serious consequences, it was probably to conceal the smaller books that she urgently requested some dark-leather *faltiqueras*, hidden pockets which Spanish women hung from their belts. As with all missionaries, she was frustrated by the fact her sponsors did not understand the situation on the ground. For instance, she was embarrassed by a well-meant gift from a middle-ranking bureaucrat who came with Pedro de Zúñiga's when he briefly returned to London on a special mission. Juan Pardo de Arenillas presented her with a handful of Cardinal Bellarmine's catechism written in Spanish but, while there was a real hunger for books in Latin or English, Luisa bluntly pointed out that those who read Spanish 'do not need a catechism'.[394] In 1612 she told Mariana de San José that hardly any Englishwomen knew Spanish, but that she was so delighted with the unnamed book Mariana had sent her that she had asked Creswell to put another six into the diplomatic bag, preferably translated into English.[395]

Did Luisa actually convert anyone? Her admirers talked enthusiastically of the countless numbers of people she brought to Catholicism or at least helped to return to a faith they had left behind. Putting her supporters' enthusiasm to one side, we have details about her involvement with a surprisingly varied group of people. As we have seen, she helped 15-year-old William Richardson escape from his Protestant family and start a new life in Flanders. In 1610 she reported on two more people she tried to help, one being the tragic case of a 16-year-old apprentice to a Protestant silversmith who was converted by a young Catholic of Luisa's acquaintance. He asked her to pray for his friend because the silversmith had arranged to hand him back to his puritanical father. The lad was subjected to such harsh beatings, she said, that he died three or four days later. Naturally Luisa envied his martyr's death.[396]

The second case involved Luisa much more directly, causing quite a stir among her friends in Spain who passed on to each other this quaint example of religious repression in England. It concerned an old woman variously described as 80 to 100 years old. Whatever her advanced age was, it made her story particularly appealing to Catholic sensibilities because it linked her to an almost forgotten age, the reign of Queen Mary Tudor, the last time that England had acknowledged the religious supremacy of the Pope. An added thrill was that, since death was not far off, the old woman's immortal soul was saved in the nick of time. As Luisa liked to tell the story, the crone claimed that she had never lost her faith in the Virgin and that, had it not been for fear, she might have taken the veil.

The earliest description of this case comes in a letter written to Inés not long after Luisa had temporarily moved out to Highgate, then a village outside the city, where Pedro de Zúñiga had a country house. In the summer of 1609 the old woman passed by her window several times and, spotting her chance, Luisa shouted to her that 'she was very close to hell if she didn't look sharp'. Some three weeks later, the crone returned demanding to see the *nun*, a term which amused Luisa, who said she did not deserve the name and because it was normally a term of abuse in England. The old woman claimed that twice Christ had told her in a dream that she must return to the Church, and when she replied that she had no means to do so, he told her to go to the Spanish woman who lived next door to don Pedro.

Brought up in the age of the Inquisition, and careful that she should not be regarded as usurping the manly role of priests, Luisa was guarded in her dealings with her guest. Her accounts of the conversion stress that she did not know whether the old woman's revelations were true or false, but she nevertheless resolved to instruct her guest in the faith, and a priest was summoned from London to hear a confession of forty or fifty years—possibly even sixty, Luisa added—and he found it gratifying to have 'brought that soul out of such long sinfulness'.[397] Most days the old woman came to the house, sitting by the fire and praying as best she could, and it did not cost much to feed her. The companions were already planning their return to London, and, rather than leaving the old woman alone amongst the village Protestants, Luisa prayed that she would die before they had to abandon her.

Luisa was also famous for helping convert at least one unnamed Calvinist preacher whom she visited in prison, eventually helping him leave for Flanders and then Spain, where he became a Benedictine. What gives credence to this otherwise thin story is the not entirely flattering circumstantial material provided by Michael Walpole, who asked the preacher how he could have been influenced more by a woman than all the learned men he had spoken to. As her early biographer Muñoz retold the story, he said that 'he had found in her words a force he could not resist, and that he had not felt this fearlessness in what the others had said'.[398]

Much the strongest evidence for Luisa's ability to inspire comes from her carpenter, the Londoner Richard Brough. In his early twenties when he got to know Luisa, he was such a convinced Protestant that he carried around a bible attached to his belt and their meetings would quickly descend into religious arguments, not least because he admitted to feeling a particular venom towards Catholics who tried to convert others. His conversion was a protracted process, and for a time he did not openly declare his Catholicism for fear of losing his livelihood and his family, but after he had witnessed Luisa's death he moved with his wife and children to Valladolid, where he became handyman to the English College.[399] Perhaps Luisa had him in mind when she said how she loved to convert a married man, as it opened up the possibility of converting wives and children too.[400]

A word of caution is essential whenever we talk about her conversions. No matter how many souls she thought she had saved, for most people religious allegiance went hand in hand with the power of either the state or the masters they served. In an age of clientage and obedience, religion was for the vast majority of the population a question of following suit. If the number of people she converted in England was strictly limited, and confined almost entirely to London, perhaps a better claim to success was her part in sustaining the confidence of the capital's exisiting community of recusants, the largest and most influential in the country.

Admittedly Luisa could argue that, as priests could not speak freely in the streets, the duty of converting people fell 'on people of such little importance as me and others like me'.[401] Being a foreigner in a land where her religion was persecuted meant that the normal rules of behaviour could not apply, and whether she was ever self-effacing is debatable, but Luisa was certainly able to stand up for Catholicism on the streets of London with considerable gusto.

Normally she wrote London off as another Babylon but in one of her rare positive remarks about the capital she explained how she was able to converse with more heretics than in a small village. Talk was always about religion, the only topic of conversation she found tolerable.[402] London's principal shopping street was Cheapside, where there were arcaded stalls to keep off the rain and where the shops were fronted by trestle tables which displayed their wares. It was also the site of one of the crosses in London that originally had been put up by Edward I in 1290 to mark the route taken by the funeral cortège of his wife, the Spanish princess Eleanor of Castile. Protestants of the hard-nosed variety reviled it as an outward and superstitious symbol, but for Catholics it was a sign of hope. Whereas Edmond Campion and Henry Garnet could barely manage a nod in its direction on their way to execution at Tyburn, Luisa was able to kneel before it, just as she had done in Spain before a church containing the host.[403] Her genuflexion provoked London's notoriously anti-Catholic apprentice-boys to lean over the shopboards and strike at her with their yardsticks, and for the crowds of shoppers, as one of her companions vividly recalled in a simple unsigned memoir, to cry out, 'a papest a papest hang her hang her'.[404]

A derogatory engraving of the Pope caught Luisa's eye. It was on sale in the Exchange near the Strand, and when she tried to buy it the helpful shopkeeper brought her another, cleaner, copy, which provoked the reaction, 'I wil have this that hangs in the sight of the peepel', at which she folded it several times before tearing it to shreds. On this occasion the onlookers just laughed at her, but a far more serious incident brought about her first arrest and imprisonment, in June 1608. During one of her rare shopping trips to Cheapside, when she was escorted by Lemeteliel and two of her companions, she began talking about her faith. She said she did this all the time but had not appreciated that Cheapside was so vehemently Protestant. She asked a young man who was serving in a shop if he was Catholic. God forbid, he answered, to which she replied that she trusted God would not forbid what was so important for his soul. A crowd gathered, and for the next couple of hours a heated theological discussion took place. She was asked about the mass, about priests, whether the Roman Church was the only true Church, and what were the Pope's powers. Some enjoyed the spectacle but others were angry, and 'so much so that I sensed some danger, at least of being arrested'.[405]

That day in Cheapside was a defining moment of her time in London. For the English government a decision would have to be made whether she should stay or leave, and for Luisa this was a last opportunity to decide whether London would be her home until her death. The argument with the shoppers quickly veered towards politics. Though she claimed she was inspired to speak the best English she had yet spoken, she was taken for a Scot not only on account of her guttural Spanish accent but also for the marked sympathy she showed for King James. An elderly man asked her if the king was not a very wise man to prevent heresy in his kingdom. She recognized this immediately as that malicious question ('la maliciosa pregunta') intentionally designed to lead her into uttering treasonable words. Replying that his religious policy was nothing to do with the king since he had been brought up by Puritans rather than by his saintly Catholic mother, she tried to steer clear of more dangerous ground by adding that he was a more legitimate monarch than Queen Elizabeth, who had been born while Henry VIII was still rightfully married to Catherine of Aragon.

Elizabeth I's posthumous fame had not yet reached the heights that it enjoys today. Many people associated her last years with war, famine, and political uncertainty, and for many she had been wilful in not providing for the succession until it was almost too late. It did not help her reputation that the peacemaking King James was still popular which meant there was no need to use the legend of 'Good Queen Bess' as a stick to beat the House of Stuart. As the direct Tudor line had died out with the old queen, Luisa had reasoned that no one really minded what she said about Elizabeth but the temperature was raised when a voice from the crowd cried out that the Benedictine priest George Garves was a traitor. Sometimes called Jarvis or Gervaise, he had only just been put to death and Ann Garnet, who had every right to be sensitive about the execution of priests, lost her temper. Fearing the most volatile of her companions would say something they might all regret, Luisa turned the question around by asking, why was he hanged? Because he was a Catholic, came the reply, to which she retorted, well don't be surprised if he is called a martyr.

The account written by one of the companions accompanying Luisa that day confirms her mistress's account although it casts a subtly different hue over what happened.[406] Luisa never fully grasped how challenging her new way of living was for the rest of society, and the animus against marriageable females living a communal life was as strong in countries that had abolished nunneries as elsewhere. It is fascinating to see how the mob warned her to go back to where a woman should be, in the home. In rather challenging spelling, it was perhaps Ann or Faith who wrote that the shoppers cried out, 'goe goe you gassop you idel husif haue you nothing to do at home in yor house but that you must stand heere praiting & peruerting the peopol'.

This type of invective is typical of the age, and it was commonplace for women to castigate each other for not being a homemaker. Even the mistress of the shop did not want to believe Luisa could be a woman. She must be a priest in disguise.

After this incident Luisa prudently stayed at home in the Barbican for a week or two. She now had four female companions with her. When she finally ventured out, it was once more in the company of Lemeteliel, Ann Garnet, and now with Faith, who had just joined the companions. Luisa had made more enemies than she realized, and a group of three committed Protestants confronted her on Saturday, 6 June.[407] One of them barred her way, 'fixing me with the eyes of a basilisk', the mythical monster who turned people into stone.[408] She tried to send the newly arrived Faith back to the house with Lemeteliel, but after being dogged for two or three streets the constable and his men arrested her in Lothbury Street, to the north of Cheapside. An ugly crowd gathered and she was taken to the house of the nearest justice of the peace, where two or three men—probably those who had cornered her—swore on the Bible that she had said treasonable words, which 'was to tel them of they popes atorrity'.[409]

Sir Thomas Bennet was the local magistrate, an ageing if prosperous member of the Mercers' Company and a former lord mayor of London. Being the height of summer Sir Thomas was conducting business underneath a canopy in his courtyard, which made Luisa think of Christ before the High Priest Caiphas.[410] She cheerfully accepted that her accusers had given an accurate rendition of what she had said in Cheapside, and when Sir Thomas asked her where she came from, where she was living, and why she had come to England, she leapt at the chance to justify her mission:

I told him my name was Luisa de Carvajal, and that I was Spanish, and I lived close to lord don Pedro, where I went to hear mass, and that I had come to follow the example of the Holy Church's many saints who had freely uprooted themselves out of love for Our Lord from their own countries, their families and friends, to live in foreign lands, poor and unprotected.[411]

What Luisa actually said in her still rough-and-ready English was undoubtedly not as polished as her artfully penned Spanish accounts were, and it is likely that, in her excited state, she was barely intelligible to Sir Thomas. She admitted that he must have found what she said gibberish, and one of her sympathizers glossed the affair by saying she had got into trouble for 'speaking some broken English that was displeasing'.[412] The magistrate's reaction was to laugh at this strange woman with her darned clothes and a piece of torn black taffeta on her head, but there is no denying that Luisa and certainly her three friends were in real danger.

She was principally concerned that Ann and Faith might be manoeuvred into rejecting the oath of allegiance. So, when Sir Thomas wanted to know who had introduced them to her and whether they attended mass she refused to answer. The excited crowd could not be ignored, and the judge went out two or three times to call for calm with one of the companions fearing that if he had not done this they would have broken down the gates. It was not in Sir Thomas's power to release Luisa after an accusation as grave as that of defending papal power, and she had to wait until late into the evening before the crowd had dispersed sufficiently for them to be escorted to the nearest prison, 'and even then some twenty locals followed us'.[413] The three women were led back towards Cheapside and locked up in the Counter, a prison off Poultry Lane. The judge's secretary went with them, and despite having a cousin imprisoned in the Tower for recusancy, it did not stop him from calling Luisa a hypocrite when she tried to hide what she knew about her companions. Even so, he followed Sir Thomas's instructions and ordered the jailer to treat them well. Shakespeare's Falstaff said in *The Merry Wives of Windsor* that the smell emanating from the prison was as 'hateful . . . as the reek of a limekiln'. Luisa and her friends were locked up for the night in a windowless attic without even bread or water, and no light except from the cracks in the tiles. She was ecstatic at being sent to a public prison instead of being confined to house arrest, and though the Counter usually lodged debtors rather than common criminals, her friends played this up as an additional and calculated affront.

Her lifelong fear of having her virtue called into question was evident the following morning when she offered to pay the jailer if he would move her closer to his wife and his female servants. He charged her 40 *reales* or £1 a week for the privilege of being placed in a storeroom next to the kitchen with just one bed for all of them. The jailer's wife and servants treated them kindly every time they came in to fetch something, and their prisoner could not resist trying to talk religion with them. She assumed they were Catholic sympathizers. The women were charged an additional 10 *reales* a day for food, and the Counter had a reputation for providing good food, but only for those who were willing to pay.[414] Luisa was confident that the Lord would provide, which usually meant that don Pedro would foot the bill.

In fact, Zúñiga had no intention of frittering away his influence at James's court on Luisa's behalf. He still maintained she had no business being in the country, and anyway he was several miles away, trying to avoid the plague at his rented house in Highgate. His confessor, Juan de San Augustín, had been left in charge of the embassy and he forbade any of the staff from visiting the women during the first two days of their imprisonment. His writ did not run as far as her other two companions, and Joanna and Susanna gained access to the prison by dressing up as don Pedro's washerwomen. On the Monday a priest smuggled in the consecrated host and heard her confession. This may have been Father Juan, as we know he went to the prison to deliver a message from the ambassador.[415] Luisa must be patient, he said, as his master was not inclined to intervene on her behalf though he was willing to pay her costs. Refusing the offer of a hundred gold coins, she did accept 200 *reales*. Again to avoid a public incident, she was released into the ambassador's custody at ten o'clock on Tuesday evening, and along with her companions she travelled back in a coach provided by some Spanish ladies to the Barbican, where she would spend her last night at her house for some considerable time.

Why was she released so quickly? If Sir Thomas had sent in his report to the bishops, matters would not have been resolved so promptly but he chose to inform Cecil, as the behaviour of strangers was usually a matter for Council. Perhaps it was decided to release Luisa so quickly in an attempt to put flesh on the government's stated policy that it did not persecute Catholics simply for their religion. During her exchange with Sir Thomas, Luisa had touched on this subject when they revisited the question of whether Garves had died a martyr. (When she insisted he had suffered for his religion, Sir Thomas interjected, 'if he did', and these three words in English she incorporated into the account of her arrest she sent Joseph Creswell.[416])

King James had convinced himself that he demanded only civil not religious obedience from his subjects, and at the time of Luisa's arrest privy councillors were considering amendments to the oath of allegiance to make it more palatable to Catholics.[417] Releasing Luisa was a golden opportunity to pretend that no one was persecuted in England for following the Roman religion, but a description of what she looked like was circulated by the bishops for the rest of the year until the whole matter died down.[418]

Luisa preferred to believe that Ireland had come to her rescue. The summer of 1608 was rife with rumours of an uprising and nine months before her arrest the leading Irish nobles, including their once and would-be king Hugh O'Neill, the earl of Tyrone, had fled to the Continent in what became known as 'the Flight of the Earls'.[419] Despite the ambassador's insistence that he was not going to intervene directly on her behalf, there is a report that he was summoned to the Council board, also holding discussions with Francis Cottington, a future ambassador to Spain.[420] At any rate, Zúñiga appears to have given his word that Luisa would cause no further trouble, and the day after her release he ordered her to come to Highgate, where she would be safe from the London mob. A house was prepared for the four companions and Lemeteliel, and though Luisa thought her absence from the capital would be brief, the combination of diplomatic pressure and her own ill health meant that she would not be based in London for another year.

Luisa could not wait to tell her friends in Spain and Flanders all about her arrest. She wrote at least four accounts from Highgate (each dated 28 June, according to the Gregorian calendar, which she always used in England), sending them to her principal correspondents in the expectation that they would also pass on her story. Among the letters which have survived are those for Joseph Creswell, Ludovico Da Ponte, Mariana de San José, as well as to Inés, and we know of several lost letters, including one to the countess of Miranda. Two months later she sent a reply to a now-lost letter from her cousin by marriage, Luis Carillo de Toledo, now marquis of Caracena, in which she enclosed a very full account of her life in England and her recent imprisonment. Married to her cousin Isabel, the count Caracena had left Galicia to become viceroy of Valencia and a marquis. After so many years' silence, he must have been spurred into writing because news of what had happened in Cheapside had reached the shores of the Mediterranean.

The accounts of her imprisonment vary in inconsequential details—crowds get bigger and key events take place later at night—but she consistently described her first arrest as a foretaste of martyrdom. As she put it, she had 'walked between the cross and holy water'.[421] Opening up more to her former spiritual director, Da Ponte, she said how sweet it was to be imprisoned for God but admitted she had been very troubled: 'I wanted to remain, in case sooner or later they would see fit to send me to heaven, yet I wanted to get out, as I feared that they would take me directly from there and throw me out of England.'[422]

She need not have worried. As news spread through the Spanish dominions of her imprisonment in a common jail, a motley collection of people found they had a vested interest in supporting her decision to remain on English soil.

14

Fashionable and Modest

I N the seventeenth century the possession of spiritual capital was no
less valued than amassing gold and silver, with many judging it wiser
to store up riches in heaven rather than lead a damnable life on earth
and risk the eternal flames of hell. The holy was seen as a tangible link
with an all-powerful and interventionist God, and patron saints were
readily called upon to intercede with the Almighty to bless crops,
discover water, find lost objects, make a business prosper, or bring
children to a marriage. Just as eagerly they might be asked to spite
enemies, justify wars, or sanctify a bloody conquest. If they did not
bring sufficient returns, they could be warned to improve their performance or, as actually happened in some Spanish villages, undergo the
indignity of being superseded by more efficacious stock. After her first
arrest Luisa ceased to be one individual fighting for the almost hopeless
cause of Catholicism in England. As a holy woman who had been
persecuted for her faith she was now invested with a series of aspirations,
not all of which she may have liked or even known about.[423]

That is not to suggest that Luisa had ceased being a diplomatic
headache for Ambassador Zúñiga, who was more worried than ever
that her presence might poison Anglo-Spanish relations. In the struggle between his personal and long-standing support for the Jesuits and
his need to represent his king, secular duty won out, and he launched
a torrent of abuse against Luisa's recent misadventures. What would
people think back home or in Flanders once they realized that all she
had been arrested for was bickering with shopkeepers, and, as Muñoz
put it, 'with little authority and fewer results'. Just what was the point,
he demanded to know, of having four maidens dressed up in a habit
that in Spain would be viewed as more fashionable than modest? Just
what *was* she trying to achieve?[424]

Luisa saw no point in challenging him. She knew the embassy was against her staying, as she had found out to her cost when she tried to influence him by suggesting to his confessor how Mariana de San José was one of many distinguished people who supported her wish to stay in England. The priest petulantly denied that Mariana would have said any such thing, and the tittle-tattle that ensued had led to complaints in Spain that Mariana had been interfering in matters that did not concern her. Having failed to learn that lesson, Luisa now tried invoking the name of the entirely venerable Ana de Jesús, though she half-expected him to fire off a letter of complaint to the newly established Carmelite house in Brussels. Zúñiga was a shrewder man than his confessor, however, knowing full well that Luisa would not budge as long as Michael Walpole wanted her to stay. She admitted as much herself, telling Da Ponte that, just as Walpole had finally decided that she should come to England, now it was his advice that kept her in England.[425]

Walpole had been out of London when she was arrested but within days he had eagerly compiled his own version of the arrest for Robert Persons.[426] Walpole related how she had been

in some trouble these days past. I was then out of town, and returned not till the night of her delivery. Some blame her of indiscretion, but as she relateth the matter she could hardly excuse anything she said, and besides spake it with such circumstances and moderation that the hearers took no offence at those words which are most blamed, but only at her being Catholic.

Walpole did not mention the situation in Ireland as a reason for her early release, emphasizing instead that Cecil had taken the opportunity to put Spain's ambassador in his debt by painting what Luisa had said in the darkest possible terms. Walpole generously accepted that Zúñiga really did believe the best way to prevent a further incident was through 'her departure out of this country'.

Walpole's original hopes for Luisa's mission were finally coming to fruition. Her arrest and the latent aggression of ordinary Londoners made it all the more likely that she would be a martyr for the English Jesuits, which is why he asked Persons to comfort and animate her, for so she deserveth, and would be grieved to see her friends forsake her to give content to others by hindering her in her best courses, so long desired, and now at length obtained in great part, and as she hopeth, at length to be accomplished, of these accidents are no bad signs.

There is an outside chance that Persons persuaded Pope Paul V to give her his blessing. The details are hazy but his friend, Bartolomé Pérez de Nueros, who acted as the link between Spain's Jesuits and the hierarchy in Rome, sent some kind of message indicating that the pontiff wanted her to remain. A papal intervention is mentioned in Walpole's life seemingly in connection with the events of 1608, though Luisa herself only referred to support from 'persons of the highest importance' in Italy.[427]

At any rate, Walpole had successfully launched a letter-writing campaign designed to promote Luisa's cause. Luis de la Puente would have heard the news of her arrest from Creswell, and it caused him to alter his opinion about whether she should stay in England, but only slightly. Two years earlier he was telling Luisa the time had come to leave but a month after her arrest he conceded that 'prison is the precursor of martyrdom', even though he left open the possibility that the Almighty might still prefer her to go.[428] Creswell wrote to Juan de Ribera, the 75-year-old archbishop and patriarch of Valencia, who replied saying that previously he had been in favour of her withdrawal from England because her cousins, the viceroy of Valencia and his wife, had shown him a letter from Zúñiga explaining that she was in mortal danger yet powerless to achieve anything substantial in the face of English pigheadedness. Now that he had read Creswell's letter, the patriarch had changed his mind, being adamant she should not leave. Referring to her as Luisa de Mendoza, he wondered if she had heard his name mentioned by his old friend, her uncle, even claiming that he pictured himself being one of her chaplains.[429]

The early modern belief in the power of prayer as a force in temporal politics cannot be underestimated. Just as Luisa maintained that the arrival of Mother Ana and six Carmelites would do more to uphold Spanish sovereignty in the Low Countries than a small army of seasoned troops, the patriarch wanted to enlist Luisa and her prayers.[430] She had become a foot soldier in a controversial campaign he was fighting at the Spanish court. By associating himself with Luisa's sufferings in England, Ribera wanted to draw political strength for his ultra-conservative views at the royal court, now back in Madrid. At stake was whether the duke of Lerma's policy of peace with England and a ceasefire with the Dutch was the best way for Spain to rebuild her strength, or whether it was a dangerous trap which could only assist Protestant rearmament. At the start of 1608 Ribera had dared write a long letter to Philip III saying that his long-standing fears that the peace with England was offensive to God had been proven right because of news filtering through that 'the perse-cution of Catholics was never so bloody in that kingdom, even in Queen Elizabeth's time, as it had been since your majesty made peace' with King James.[431] For Ribera as for others, direct contact with Luisa was a way of bolstering his opposition to Lerma.

She had been preparing for her role as a seer for some time. Though she liked to tell herself she never meddled in politics and had an abhorrence of warfare, her intelligence and upbringing in her uncle's household left her with an acute interest in affairs of state. She consistently articulated what would currently be termed a 'neo-conser-vative' approach to Spain's political problems. After the *Invincible Armada* and other attempts by Philip II to coerce Elizabeth's England into submission, a less belligerent approach to international politics had slowly gained ground. The Spanish Netherlands had been granted an excep-tional degree of autonomy in an effort to spike the Dutch rebels' cause. Even the expeditionary force dispatched to Kinsale in 1602 can be seen as a muddled attempt to move away from plans for an outright invasion of England in the hope that by putting pressure on Ireland Queen Elizabeth could be steered towards a general peace with Spain.

Luisa counted amongst those Spaniards who clung to the older view that not an inch should be conceded. In 1600—in only her second letter to survive—she warned against the peace-feelers under-way between agents of the ageing Elizabeth and the young Philip III. Railing against any concessions to 'that monster of a woman' and her vixen-like ability to deceive, she tried passing on this warning to the Archduchess Isabel via Magdalena de San Jerónimo. Intriguingly, at some early stage in its life, someone inscribed on the back of the letter that it was very much worth reading.[432]

The archduchess featured prominently in Luisa's vision for a post-Reformation England. To most people it was apparent by 1606 that the Archduchess Isabel was unlikely ever to be queen of England but Luisa was overcome with joy when that summer she spied her picture in one of London's shops.[433] A few weeks earlier, she had heard a rumour that Isabel Clara Eugenia was pregnant, and she prayed for a daughter who could be married to her first cousin, the 1-year-old heir to the Spanish throne, effectively reuniting the Low Countries with Spain. Though this would stymie the French marriage that was already mooted for the prince, it would have the advantage, she explained, of ensuring that Spain regained absolute control of the southern Netherlands as a shield against France and to safeguard the Atlantic.[434]

The debate over the future direction of Spanish foreign policy came to a head shortly before Luisa's first imprisonment. The question was whether to enter into a truce with the Dutch Protestants. Six weeks earlier, she sent Creswell a well-crafted letter which was to all intents and purposes a political agenda for the Jesuits.[435] Firmness about the oath of allegiance in England went hand in hand with firmness towards the Protestants in Europe, and so that he was in no doubt about what was at stake she tied her appeal for toughness to a description of the sufferings of the priest whose name she had defended in Cheapside, George Garves.

Luisa described in great detail how he had resisted James's oath, even after being thrown into 'limbo', the deepest and darkest part of Newgate, where he survived on a diet of bread and apples. Her argument was helped by the fact that Garves was not a member of the Company but a priest in the Benedictine Order, whose members did not invariably side with the Jesuits. She recounted his final moments with stomach-churning precision, including his cries in English—'Let me alone'—when the executioner cut open his chest. To play up how he was now a saint (who presumably should not be angered) she told the story of an English lady of quality who had visited her the day after the execution and was inspired to utter King David's warnings from the Book of Samuel about the murder of priests who had been anointed with holy oil. Luisa associated Garves's instant cult with her political vision, using this letter to make clear her utter opposition to a truce with the rebels. Using every ounce of her political savvy, she tried to appear reasonable, wishing the negotiations in Flanders well but immediately qualified this by adding 'through peace or war'. Realizing it would be more effective—and safer—for a women to put the most controversial statements into the mouths of others, she went as far as to say that the English were accusing Philip III of being by nature a coward who would give in to anything the Dutch demanded. She expressed support for an all-out war against the Protestants, but quickly added she had heard this was what the young king of Spain was now proposing to the Pope.

The best indication that this was Luisa at her most artful is that she managed to incorporate a word of praise for the prominent recusant Viscount Montague, ranking him, if only in passing, amongst the more steadfast Catholics. It was as if she wanted to hint that English Catholics were all united and waiting only for Spain to act. Lord Montague was in fact a mouthpiece for the English secular priests and no friend to the Jesuits, favouring the appointment of a bishop in England who would be powerful enough to restrain them, as he was convinced they bore some responsibility for the Gunpowder Plot. Luisa's support for Montague was short-lived and before the year was out she was back on the offensive. She had heard that he had sent his two daughters, Mary and Katherine, to Brussels to *cluck*—as she put it—for an English bishop and for the various English nuns there to be subjected to the authority of the friars. She added disdainfully that she did not know if his daughters would try to blacken the Jesuits' name 'as if they [the Jesuits] were to blame or were the reason why all this isn't happening'.[436]

In Luisa's mind as much as in Archbishop Ribera's, Spanish firmness against non-Catholics abroad needed to be counterbalanced by equal determination on the home front. They both actively supported the expulsion of hundreds of thousands of Moriscos. Descendants of the medieval Muslim conquerors of Spain in the eighth century, the Moriscos' removal had first been aired in Philip II's reign after an unsuccessful revolt in the Alpujarra mountains of southern

Spain. Her uncle the marquis had agitated for this brutal measure, but in the last resort King Philip was too Christian a monarch to expel subjects who had been baptized into the Church. His preferred solution was barely less inhuman, however, and rebels from the south were forced to relocate to northern Castile, far away from the Mediterranean coast, where it was feared the Ottoman navy might appear on the horizon to liberate them. In 1608 the question of expulsion was constantly debated in the royal council, and when early the following year the duke of Lerma authorized a twelve years' truce with the Calvinist rebels in Holland it was felt necessary to reaffirm Spain's Catholicism by a blatant act of ethnic-cleansing. Somewhere in the region of a third of a million Moriscos were callously expelled from the land where they and their ancestors had lived for close to a thousand years. All had been baptized and countless thousands were active in their local churches.

The Moriscos were specially numerous in the kingdom of Valencia, where they were also economically important owing to their mastery of the techniques of irrigation. Since 1606 the viceroy had been Luis Carrillo de Toledo, a militant Catholic who was married to Luisa's Almazán cousin, Isabel, with whom he had fourteen children. He was sent to the Mediterranean after having been governor of Galicia on Spain's northern Atlantic tip, where he had been in charge of receiving perhaps the ten to fifteen thousand Irish refugees who were fleeing the English and Scottish plantation of their country. Caracena favoured an aggressive foreign policy, and his heroes were evident from the pictures which hung in his gallery, which included portraits of Elizabeth I's great opponent in Ireland during the 1590s, the earl of Tyrone, as well as of Luisa herself.[437] If in Galicia Caracena was a liability on account of his attachment to the Irish cause, in Valencia, with its settled Morisco community of not-far-off a hundred thousand souls, he was the ideal man to force through the expulsions, though had matters been left to him he would have allowed several hundred Moriscos at least to remain behind in order to teach the Old Christians how to produce sugar, rice, olives, and that most precious of commodities, silk.[438]

It was also a time of immense political strain for Caracena, which made Luisa's prayers and intercessions more than usually valuable. In turn she was more than willing to play the part of a *saint-in-waiting*, and in her reply from Highgate to his now lost letter she painted herself in charismatic colours. She sent him one of the fullest descriptions of her journey from Valladolid and her first months in England, to which she added a brief description of the latest martyrdoms. She concluded by telling him that he could not believe what English Catholics were suffering.[439]

Now that she was back in contact with her Caracena cousins, she took the plunge and resumed contact with her brother, though judging by the first surviving letter of their correspondence the wounds caused by their squabble over the inheritance had not yet healed over.[440] It turned out that neither her brother nor her cousin Isabel had grasped why she had left Spain in the first place. As the marquesa put it, it was when she learnt what Luisa was up to in London that she began to understand what she had been hinting at in the 'farewell letter of yours saying you were going on a long journey'.[441] From 1608 onwards Luisa never again lost contact with her brother or the viceroy and his wife. In fact she continuously chivvied the viceroy about the need to press on with expelling the Moriscos, promising him three years later that God would recompense him with something more than human pay.[442] Eventually she would send her cousins human remains from the English persecution to serve as objects of veneration to help sanctify their campaigns against the defenceless Moriscos.

Cousin Isabel in Valencia needed little encouragement in the attack on the Moriscos, however. She described it to Luisa as something 'very great, and to the glory of God and the king for starting it and finishing it'.[443] She unstintingly praised her husband's involvement despite his having been obliged to deprive lords of their vassals, yet she occasionally had sleepless nights thinking about what was being done in God's name to the children. In a particularly horrifying report, the vicereine told of how she had snatched a child from its mother's breast—on the orders of her confessor—after the unfortunate woman tried to take her child away with her. Disagreements had broken out even among the religious hardliners in Valencia. Her husband's relationship with Patriarch Ribera broke down when he refused to use his powers to allow even the most devout Christians among the Moriscos to stay behind. Once a fervent believer that their offspring could be assimilated into the wider Christian community, Ribera was now equally fervent in his desire for total expulsion, and he cast a greedy eye over two colleges for young Morisco men and women founded by the Emperor Charles V. Whereas Ribera wanted their endowments to pass to his pet project, a college for Valencia's Old Christians where he was to be buried, Isabel's husband fought to keep the two schools open on the grounds that their pupils were on the way to becoming good Christians. The vicereine confessed to her cousin in London that she was worried about the consequences if any of the ex-pupils strayed and fell into the clutches of the Inquisition.

Luisa was now someone to be cultivated not just by the religious women of Spain but by the country's most senior politicians. Potentially far more significant than the inauguration of her correspondence with the Viceroy of Valencia was that another cousin-by-marriage, don Rodrigo Calderón, wanted spiritually to invest in her. In 1621 Calderón, the count of La Oliva and marquis of Siete Iglesias, would be executed on trumped-up charges of having tried to poison Philip III's wife, Queen Margaret, over a decade earlier. (One of the accusations was that he had employed Luisa's somewhat feeble brother as an assassin!) Put to death in the plaza mayor in Madrid, it was said that Calderón died better than he lived. He had long been the object of great envy. In 1605 an English traveller noted that he was one of 'the men that prevayle most with the duke of Lerma', adding snobbishly that he was 'a yong man of small desert or worth'.[444] Of Spanish-Dutch lineage, Rodrigo Calderón came into the world of court politics as a page in Lerma's household and was quickly married to one of Luisa's fabulously rich cousins on her father's side, doña Inés de Vargas. The duke's right-hand man, Calderón controlled access to the royal favourite and was rightly feared as a bad enemy to have. Hungry to acquire land and property, he earned a reputation for greed and his suave, assured manner alienated the old aristocracy, with

Queen Margaret heartily detesting him. Calderón's position at court was constantly in danger and late in 1607 he came within a whisker of falling from grace for having taken bribes far in excess of what was considered tolerable. Shortly after this he became Luisa's most intense correspondent during her remaining years.

Cousin Rodrigo had occasionally sent greetings and gifts to Luisa through their mutual friend, Joseph Creswell, and early in 1608 he intimated he wanted her to arrange for England's Catholics to re-member him in their prayers.[445] At the time of her arrest she had told Creswell that she would not trouble so important a person as Cal-derón with a letter, making the rather lame excuse that she had promised not to seek the consolation of friends. This reticence van-ished, however, as she became conscious of her spiritual importance and after her arrest she had the confidence to write to more men.[446]

She penned her first letter to Calderón in July 1609, towards the end of her semi-retirement in Highgate. Prompted perhaps by an-other donation, Luisa was instinctively cautious about approaching one of the most potent figures at court. Short (by Luisa's standards) and largely formulaic, her note reminded him of the great good he could do in the world if only he bore in mind the need to protect his immortal soul.[447]

The example of Rodrigo Calderón is still used in Spain as a warning of how power corrupts but his first letter to London throws new light on this enigmatic figure.[448] In an almost childlike manner he thanked Luisa in his and his wife's name for remembering them, asking her never to stop writing as life at court was the ideal place to lose sight of what was spiritually important. He wanted Luisa's prayers so that 'Our Lord will take us away from this Babylon and lead us to a peaceful life at home, because, although one can do the odd good thing here, there is great danger and the chance to fall into a thousand traps'.[449]

Luisa may not have realized how controversial a figure Calderón was, perhaps not knowing that his conduct had merited an investiga-tion by her long-standing supporter, the count of Miranda. Whether Cousin Rodrigo had deemed it politically astute to associate himself with someone whom Miranda regarded as a living saint, or whether his brush with one of the court's 'thousand traps' made him look to his spiritual future is a question that perhaps Calderón could not answer with certainty.

He became her principal conduit for expressing her increasingly bold and, needless to say, irredeemably conservative, political views. In 1611 King James started to think seriously about marrying off his two elder children, Henry, Prince of Wales, and his only daughter, Elizabeth Grace, as Luisa referred to her. At first Luisa told Calderón guardedly that she would say only 'una palabra' ('one word') about James's persecution of Catholics.[450] The maltreatment was worse than ever, and she feigned surprise that James was trying hard to reach agreements with Catholic princes. A year later she was bolder. There was talk that the widowed King Philip might marry James's daughter. The rumour must be false, she told Calderón, but for good measure she made sure to brand the princess a seasoned Protestant. She was at quite exceptional pains to make sure he realized that the idea of marrying Elizabeth to a relatively minor Habsburg prince was also unacceptable. Talks were already underway about marriage to a prince of Savoy and that idea she dismissed as a 'bad seed' which God should not allow to be planted in anyone's head.[451]

Luisa's renewed importance as spiritual capital is most evident from the amazing revelation that Rodrigo Calderón considered coming to London to meet her. That this was even conceivable was made possible by his having been banished from the court in 1612, but to save face, Lerma arranged for his friend to be given the task of informing the Archduchess Isabel of her brother's decision to ally with France. A double wedding was in the offing. To use their papal titles, the Catholic King of Spain would marry his eldest daughter to Louis XIII, while his son, the future Philip IV, would take the Most Christian King's sister as his wife.

The new British ambassador in Spain, John Digby, the future earl of Bristol, picked up a rumour that Calderón intended visiting London. Since he was still on speaking terms with his close friend, Joseph Creswell, the envoy asked straight out if it was true, only to be told that indeed 'he would see london, to visite Doña luisa de Caruajal'. In the margin, Digby unflatteringly described her as 'the old Spanish Lady that hath had greate parte of her mayntenance' from Calderón.[452]

Did the two ever meet? During the attempts to canonize Luisa, Alonso de Velasco, the son of the ambassador who replaced Zúñiga, casually mentioned that Calderón privately visited London in 1612, and he could have hidden behind the comings and goings involved in Pedro de Zúñiga's brief return to England cover for a flying visit.[453] (Zúñiga had the unappetizing task of informing King James that both the king of Spain's eldest children were marrying into the French royal family, which left only a younger daughter as a possible bride for the Prince of Wales.) Luisa offered to go to the south coast to meet Calderón.[454] The ambassador's son would only have been 16 or so when he would have made any visit, and his testimony cannot be relied on, though it is puzzling that his statement, copied out more than once, was never corrected. Neither Walpole nor Muñoz make any reference to a meeting, but given the depths to which Calderón's reputation later sank there was good reason not to play up Luisa's links with a disgraced courtier. Although the fourteen letters she wrote that year to Calderón do not indicate that he crossed the Straits of Dover, it is imaginable that they decided that the quasi-confessional meeting should never be mentioned. Though it seems unlikely they ever came face to face, this does not alter the fact that Calderón desperately hoped Luisa would enter his private nunnery.

In July 1612 Luisa lamented that they had not yet been able to meet as a preliminary remark before she addressed the delicate subject of the 'offer of your own convent'. As part of his plans to establish himself in Valladolid when it was the new capital, Calderón had bought a grand house in the centre of the city from Mariana Cortés, the rich widow who had led Luisa a merry dance when she seemed willing to endow an English nunnery in the city. With his purchase he acquired the rights to the adjoining convent of Portaceli which Mariana had founded a few years before. (Luisa had once visited the convent with Inés and the nuns had made a favourable impression on her. To this day it remains an enclosed order in the very heart of Valladolid, on what is now one of its busiest commercial streets.) Luisa let 'Cousin Rodrigo' down as gently as she could, telling him she had no plans to leave England but leaving open the possibility that, if the Lord decided she should go, 'it would be a notable consolation and pleasure to go to Portaceli and serve the nuns there, with tremendous goodwill and zeal as if it were the gravest and most holy house in the world'.[455] His interest in Luisa continued after her death when he was prepared to fight with the king of Spain for possession of her body.

If Calderón had succeeded in wresting control of her earthly remains, one thing seems certain: he would have moved heaven and earth to have her swiftly recognized as a saint. To demonstrate that he now had his own celestial protectress, he would have encouraged anyone who knew her, or knew of her, to come forward with stories of miracles she had performed, and perhaps he would have gone as far as to make enquiries among England's Catholics for tales of her many conversions in London or examples of her divinely inspired wisdom. We should be in no doubt that he would have fostered a local cult around her mortal remains, enjoining the great ladies of Valladolid, or the officers of the city's many courts of justice as well as the incessant visitors to the English College, to visit the magnificent tomb he would surely have built for her at his convent of Portaceli. As we shall see, Luisa was to be deprived of a permanent resting place where the faithful could gather round and swap stories of her heavenly intercessions, which is ironic. No one knew better than Luisa the transcendental importance of bodily relics for promoting a counter-reformation vision of the world.

15

Pears and *The Last Supper*

A thousand people gathered in the height of summer 1608 to witness the execution of a 33-year-old priest who chose to die rather than take the oath of allegiance. Three hundred of the spectators were wealthy enough to make the journey to Tyburn on horseback—if the figures can be trusted—with Robert Cecil's elder brother, Lord Exeter, being among those present. Only an exceptional person could attract such crowds. The young man about to be put to death was Thomas Garnet, nephew of Henry Garnet and cousin to Luisa's longest-serving companion. His blanket refusal to take King James's oath resulted in his being put to death within a matter of weeks of being captured, prompting Michael Walpole to remark that 'this blessed martyr's death seemeth to have silenced the parliament oath, as his good uncle's did the gunpowder treason'.[456] After only eighteen months of existence, the college Luisa had paid for in Louvain had offered up its first martyr.

She wrote to Thomas in the Gatehouse just a few days before his execution. In her spiritually macabre way, she told him she was jealous of his impending good fortune. Though she knew him well, describing him as her 'friend and master', there was a degree of frustration as she contemplated his fate.[457] She had been released from the Counter after her arrest in Cheapside not long before, and to appease Ambassador Zúñiga she agreed neither to visit Garnet in prison nor attend his execution, 'which otherwise', said Walpole, 'she would have presumed'. She later obtained from the executioner a piece of the shirt that the young man had worn to his death, and the following year she distributed pieces of the holy relic to friends in Spain.

The journey to visit Thomas in his last days would not have been an easy one, as Luisa was living next door to a country retreat Zúñiga was renting in the village of Highgate, some 6 miles north of the City of London. We know almost nothing about her house there, although we could infer that it was at least two storeys high, since the old woman from the village that she so proudly converted had been invited 'up' to see her.[458] She kept on her old house in the Barbican as she certainly intended to return within a matter of weeks or at the very least at the end of the summer, which marked the beginning of the political and commercial year. Instead the plague and her own ill health forced her to make Highgate her principal base for almost a year. Between November 1608 and the following March no letters have survived.

Luisa tried returning to her London base around the middle of 1609 but she was forced to retreat to Highgate for the rest of the year. She was suffering from heart palpitations and for a fortnight during the summer she was unable to put pen to paper. A doctor was called to administer a bloodletting, itself an indication of how ill she was since she would allow only this as a last resort. London's doctors charged extortionate fees, and she thought they were on the whole uncaring. A visit cost about 12 or 14 *reales*, that is about 6 or 7 shillings, and a really deep bloodletting cost about 10 *reales*, though less invasive ones could be had for 4 or 6 *reales*.[459] Nevertheless she was content with one Dr Foster, who treated her over several years and whose medical advice she often repeated to friends.

It was at Highgate that she met a gifted Flemish painter who was working for don Pedro in a little house he had in the orchard. He spoke good Spanish as he had been brought up by Philip II's court painter, Alonso Sánchez Coello. He was accompanied by his young son and a servant, and although she conceded the artist was 'upright and modest' there was no avoiding the fact he was a hardened Protestant whose faith she was quite incapable of shaking.[460] Mariana de San José had asked for a portrait of Luisa, but it is unlikely she allowed her picture to be painted, saying 'the idea seems totally pointless', although the case of Henry Garnet and his Straw should have taught her the value of a true likeness. A later Spanish ambassador stated that no portrait of Luisa was made while she was alive. But what was this unidentified painter working on for the ambassador in the summer of 1609?

One of the great mysteries of early modern Anglo-Spanish painting is the provenance of the two paintings of the Somerset House Conference of 1604. Almost identical in quality, they depict English commissioners seated at the negotiating table with a joint Spanish-Flemish delegation. These two pictures were once thought to be by Pantoja de la Cruz, but the style of both are now regarded as more likely to be that of an artist from the Low Countries. There is even mystery about whether the paintings were produced for a Spanish or an English audience. Though the Spaniards are seated in the place of honour and the English are depicted as suing for peace, the eye is nonetheless drawn towards Cecil as the commanding figure in the bottom right-hand corner. Is it possible that Luisa was chatting away about matters of the faith while her unidentified artist-friend was working on a magnificent memorial to the Anglo-Spanish peace? It would make sense from Zúñiga's point of view. He had left his wife behind in Spain when he came to England in 1605, and her death provided a tragic excuse for him to beg to be allowed to return home. Now 48, this was his last opportunity to break into the inner circle of the king's most trusted counsellors. To commission a pair of magnificent paintings in honour of the Peace of London would be a sure means of currying favour with the duke of Lerma's 'peace party' and their policy of Pax Hispania.

This is, of course, speculation, but it is underpinned by a subtle change in Zúñiga's attitude towards Luisa at this time. He knew Rodrigo Calderón still had friends in high places, and it made sense for Zúñiga to consolidate links with Lerma's close political ally in order to ensure his own smooth return to Spanish political life, and he even used Luisa to pass messages suggesting it was time for Calderón to return to Spain and brave the court.[461] The ambassador came to see her very early one morning in June 1609 to say he hoped to be shot of England within a fortnight. As he would be giving up his house in Highgate, he urged her to move back to London but only to Spital-fields, beyond the city walls, where she was less likely to be harassed.[462]

A year was to elapse before Zúñiga was finally able to leave London, but as soon as Luisa heard of María Coloma's death she started meddling in the process of choosing a successor. A 'prudent

God-fearing man of sound judgement' was needed, one who would stoutly defend the interests of Catholicism but at the same time be generous towards the heretical English and treat them honourably. He must be able to keep the members of his household under control so as not to offend their hosts, and above all he must not be obdurate 'when it comes to taking advice'.[463] She meant advice that came from her. Her arrest had made her think more than ever that she was an indispensable expert on Anglo-Spanish relations.

The new ambassador presented his credentials to King James in May 1610, and he spent the next three years proving correct the initial view that 'by his countenance he gave no great impression to the court of his sufficiency'.[464] The embassy in London had been effectively downgraded with the appointment of don Alonso de Velasco, lord and later count of Revilla. Out of the four names put forward to the Council of State, it was felt that Velasco had the advantage over Luis de Padilla, another, far richer, middle-ranking bureaucrat, as Velasco had been a junior member of the peace delegation of 1604 and it was assumed he was acquainted with English ministers.[465] Luisa was at first hopeful but within a month of his arrival a problem arose concerning temporary accommodation which poisoned their relationship.

Before he departed, Zúñiga found Luisa another place to live in the Barbican. She had probably outgrown the house with the rowdy and carnivorous neighbours as, at any one time, she might have half a dozen companions or guests living with her. Her new home was more secure than ever, being 'right next to the ambassador's house, and I have a key to the door which leads from our backyard into his courtyard'.[466] Still unbelievably cramped, it was 'almost uninhabitable, falling apart, and full of holes', which was eating into the money Zúñiga handed over on his departure, and the problem of noise persisted.[467] All through the night till almost dawn vile-smelling refuse carts trundled past on the way to the new dumping grounds north of the city walls.[468] Shortly after the new ambassador's arrival she had eulogized him as 'a perfect gentleman and honest too', who had instructed her to ask for whatever she needed and offering to help out with the loan of a room in the embassy.[469] A month later she

denounced him, saying that she and her friends had use of the room
for just four days before he had asked for it back, an affront to Luisa's
dignity which sparked a campaign designed to ruin Velasco's reputation. His sense of charity, professionalism, and his health were all
ingeniously lampooned. When he sent her the occasional dish from
his table, she complained it saved her no money as she had no idea it
was coming. He lacked his predecessor's 'perspicacity, shrewdness,
courage and wit' in dealing with the Privy Council. Soon after
arriving he fell ill and thought he was going to die, but he had failed
to include in his household a priest who was licensed to hear confession. He asked Luisa to call for the Benedictine priest John Roberts,
who spoke Spanish, but Luisa said she did not know where he was but
she offered to find him another Spanish-speaking priest, though in the
end he recovered sufficiently to postpone his confession. No wonder
she asked Creswell to burn this indiscrete letter.[470]

Her sense of isolation was intense. Quite apart from the clean air of
Highgate, she was missing two of her closest supporters. Michael
Walpole had been arrested six months earlier—quite possibly while
he was her lodger—and the departing ambassador, for all his faults,
had at least respected her vocation enough to have been financially
generous. Walpole was supposed to have been included among the
half-dozen priests Zúñiga was allowed to take with him when he left
England but in the end, despite all his efforts, Cecil would only agree
to deliver Walpole separately to Calais so as not to antagonize the
House of Commons, which was in session at Westminster. Luisa
was feeling put out because of a rumour among some Catholics—
almost certainly opponents of the Jesuits—that she had not been
arrested for defending her religion but rather for speaking ill of
Queen Elizabeth; she lamented the fact that her co-religionists
would not give her 'a single drop of support or help'.[471]

It was emphatically not a good time to be a supporter of the
Company. Henri IV of France had been assassinated in May 1610,
just as Velasco was entering England, and the murderer was a Catholic
fanatic whom King James was convinced had been led on by the
Jesuits. He reacted by renewing pressure on the entire recusant
community, ordering that the Oath of Allegiance be administered

to all Catholics, including for the first time peers of the realm, causing a Jesuit to quip that 'scarce a beggar hath escaped it'.[472]

Luisa's state of mind was not helped by the fact that her finances were in a parlous state. Zúñiga's money had been swallowed up by repairs to the new house, which threw her back on her old fantasy of threading gold. Acting out of 'my absolute need', she asked Creswell to cover the costs out of whatever alms her lady friends in Valladolid would give her.[473] To make her plight worse, the plague was at its height and her health had completely broken down. From the summer of 1610 she was ill for well over a year, seeing the doctor three times in September. Her weak heart was at the root of the problem, causing her to break out in fevers, and apart from chicken soup the best remedy was to swallow bezoar stones. Formed in the stomachs of animals, they offered protection against all sorts of infections and poisons, and although they were available in England she bombarded her friends for stones from Spain.[474]

Ill health did not stand in the way of Luisa's sense of purpose being almost miraculously replenished before the year was out. King James ordered a new wave of persecution which moved her mission in a wholly novel direction. Skilful at detecting the weaknesses of others, George Abbot was bishop of London for only a few months before the French king's murder made it possible for him to play on James's deep-seated fears of assassination. With the ever-loyal earls of North-ampton and Suffolk in mind, he maliciously enquired why so many privy councillors avoided taking communion in the Anglican Church.[475] Overruling Cecil, he demanded a resumption of priestly executions, successfully demanding that the oath of allegiance be applied to female recusants.

Among those priests caught in the net were John Roberts, a Benedictine, and a secular priest called Thomas Somers. Both were well known. Under the name of Wilson the former had preached to the Spanish embassy's English-speaking staff and was nicknamed the 'parish priest of London', and he was praised for his willingness to comfort those dying of the plague.[476] Roberts was also the Spanish-speaking monk Ambassador Velasco asked for by name, and despite having left the English College in Valladolid under a cloud to join the Benedictines he admired the Jesuits for their uncompromising stance towards the oath. It was a sign of the renewed intensity of the persecution that Roberts was killed. He had returned to England in 1603, but despite several arrests he had always been released, made his escape, or gone abroad.

Clad in the vestments for Advent Sunday, Roberts was captured after celebrating mass on 2 December 1610 and eight days later was put to death. Despite her chronic ill health, Luisa went to see him in Newgate, and this may have proven particularly gratifying since he had briefly been imprisoned with Thomas Garnet, whom she had been warned off visiting. Egged on by Luisa in his opposition to the oath, he declined a chance to make his escape for fear of showing a lack of solidarity with the other Catholics who were about to appear in court.[477] Abbot was one of his judges, and word quickly spread how during a fiery exchange Abbot referred to him as the 'insolent Roberts'.[478] Luisa was at his side when it was time to make the journey back to court to hear sentence pronounced, and being unwell, he was shaking so much he could hardly button up his clothes. Look how much I am trembling, he said, and she made him laugh by telling the story of the Gran Capitán. Gonzalo Fernández de Córdoba was one of Spain's greatest generals in Italy, but when he shook putting on his armour he boasted that his 'flesh was frightened of his heart'.[479] After the two priests' inevitable condemnation, Luisa recorded how 'I prostrated myself before their lucky feet and kissed them, telling them how I was brimming with jealousy for their happy fate'.[480] She also sent him pear tartlets.

Like a scene from a Hollywood movie, one of the most graphic occasions in Luisa's life took place on the evening of Sunday, 9 December 1610. It was the night before a double martydom, and Newgate's jailer, Stephen Houghton, was paid a large sum of money for her and two companions to reach the tower where the condemned men were waiting. John Roberts came out to greet her, fearful she might slip on the stairs. All in all, twenty or more imprisoned Catholics were assembled there along with their visitors who had come for a farewell meeting with the two priests and together they sat down for a final meal. On this occasion Luisa agreed to sit at the head of the table, flanked by the two martyrs, something she had refused 'until that last supper'.[481] Worried in case he appeared too cheerful, Roberts asked whether he should go into a corner and pray, only to be firmly told there could be no better example than for him to be seen 'with such great desire and determination to die for Christ'.[482] He apologized for the circumstances in which he had left the English College, saying he wanted to write to the General of his order requesting that Benedictines and Jesuits should call a halt to their bickering and co-operate, presumably over the question of the oath. She did not know if he managed to write that letter before the night was over but he did hand over a vellum parchment containing an image of a crucified Christ to serve as a peace offering for Joseph Creswell.[483] Luisa's new-found sense of purpose derived from what she was able to do for the two martyrs after they were dead.

After the double execution, the heads of Roberts and Somers were taken for display on London Bridge but their bodies were buried at Tyburn with eight common criminals on either side. Catholic sympathizers rescued the quartered remains of the two priests and temporarily hid them. Priests usually turned up to Luisa's house after darkness had fallen, as did William Scott, another Benedictine, when he came to ask if she would take charge of the bodies. Born in Chigwell, he bore in religion the more exotic name of Mauro de Sahagún after having been converted by John Roberts himself. The carriage Luisa arranged to pick up the bodies was intercepted by men of the night guard but they had the fright of their lives when John Robert's leg dropped out and they ran off into the darkness. One of the guards who was apparently taking instruction as a Catholic let them pass, but the monk's leg ended up on London Bridge. Half of Somers's chest was also lost.[484]

Luisa rejoiced at having the relics with her in the Barbican. Since they were martyrs, she was convinced the two men were not languishing in purgatory but had gone directly to heaven, where they could intervene on behalf of the faithful. As she told the marquess of Caracena,

I considered myself fortunate to have these guests, and to be able to serve them in such great need, being unable to find a nook or cranny that was halfway safe to put them in. In order to prepare them, one arm with half a chest and its back was placed on the floor, and the other with the other half. It was an extraordinary sight and a cause for much prayer to see these so frail weapons that had fought without frailty but with conviction. They flew up to heaven, where they increased the number of intercessors, making my house happy with such rich remains[485]

She was entering unchartered waters. If King James's spies ever found out she was involved in the glorification of those whom the state had killed, she could not expect to be treated as leniently as before. Even some of her clerical friends thought that she had finally overstepped the limit. Angry at their timidity, she said, in an odd phrase for a would-be martyr, that not even for ten extra lives would she have refused to receive the saints. Luisa was entirely conventional in believing that the sufferings of martyrs should be exploited for the sake of the Roman religion, and it was surely deliberate that she followed her description of the body parts on her floor by heaping praise on Caracena for his attack on the Moriscos.

Sadly accepting that the relics were not hers, belonging instead to William Scott and the Benedictines, Luisa's immediate task was to preserve the remains by washing and dressing them.[486] The relics were still with her in April 1611, when she asked to be allowed to keep bits of her honoured guests. She sent Creswell a relic of John Roberts which she unceremoniously described as 'a lump of his holy flesh'.[487] A few months later she asked for a relic taken from Roberts's chest to be passed on to her old friend, Ceráin and his wife, but a more formal approach was required towards those of higher status. Not only did their relics have to be properly encased but the process of desiccation had to be complete, and Rodrigo Calderón was told in February the following year that his relics were not quite ready, and four months after that he was still waiting, because they were not yet 'fully dry and without moisture'.[488]

The political role of relics within international Catholicism is clear from a remark Zúñiga made during his brief return visit in the middle of 1612. He dropped a hint that the duke of Lerma would appreciate a relic. Luisa had already been thinking about contacting the duke and a couple of months later she asked Calderón to pass on directly to the royal favourite one of her audacious statements on Spain's foreign policy. She had got wind of a plan to marry the king of Spain's second son, don Carlos, to a French princess, with the Spanish Netherlands as a dowry. To surrender the Low Countries would create an unstable situation that would leave the way open for Protestantism to spread in Flanders and undermine its position as the shield protecting Spain. She wanted the king's children to be given armies, no matter what the cost, so they could carve out Christian kingdoms 'among those barbarous nations of Moors and Turks, so close to Spain's dominions'.[489]

There is no evidence that her message was ever passed on, and obviously her shrill interventions never caused the duke to budge from his policies of peace. In fact, her highly conservative views on Spanish foreign policy may have had the opposite effect from what she intended. By being connected to such a conservative thinker as Luisa, Lerma and his supporters paradoxically may have found it easier to pursue their agenda; direct contact with her would allow them to pull the rug out from under the feet of the archbishop of Valencia and his friends if they ever tried to support their ideas by boasting of a unique connection with Luisa. In other words, by cultivating friendship with Luisa, Lerma and his allies were subtly defending their version of the Pax Hispanica. It would be all the harder for anyone to say that the duke was pursuing a godless policy when he was associated with someone who knew at first hand just how much Catholics were suffering in Protestant lands.

One area where she did have direct political influence was in ruining Alonso de Velasco's career, which had the additional effect of making any marriage alliance between England and Spain an even remoter possibility. She was unhappy that he had not been able to save John Roberts, who had been reprieved before, and Velasco was quickly forced into making his excuses to Madrid. He had not made any public appeal for Roberts's life, because he had judged it unlikely that James would kill a priest so precipitously when he was talking up the possibility of a marriage between his daughter and a Catholic prince from Savoy. He went on to say that, after the executions had been carried out, Cecil had apologized, saying it had proved impossible to save him while a parliament was sitting.[490] Velasco was too inexperienced to know this excuse had been used before. Two other priests, Napper and Cadwallader, were executed outside of London at the same time as Roberts and Somers. The ineffectual ambassador secured a pardon for Napper on the Monday, only to discover he had been executed the previous Friday.[491]

Luisa had less and less to do with him, and it made no difference to find out his wife had a distant connection with the Mendoza family.[492] Though don Alonso sent her food, they only saw each other in chapel. She could see him seated in his gallery while she remained below, with the English. In a particularly biting remark, she told Zúñiga how keen she was to help him 'with what I have seen and been through, or now understand about this place, but all of this is thrown back in my face'.[493] In August 1611 Velasco was in her sights when she explained to Calderón how necessary it was to have in England ambassadors of considerable courage, with it being even more important that they should know when to use it.[494] What really niggled her was Velasco's support for a marriage between James's daughter, Elizabeth, and a prince of Savoy, who had Habsburg blood running through his veins. Madrid was in favour of at least discussing the idea, as it would be a means of masking James's inevitable frustration when he discovered that Philip III's eldest daughter was to marry the French king and not the Prince of Wales. Whether an English–Savoy marriage was ever likely to happen does not matter, but Velasco made the classic junior diplomat's mistake of confusing a delaying tactic with an intention. Luisa relayed back to Spain that he was saying the Savoyard prince could marry the Princess Elizabeth because the Pope would grant the groom a dispensation to attend Protestant services, just as James's wife was allowed to do. If the same could be attained for English Catholics, Velasco went on, that would end the persecution. Luisa's sarcastic comment was: 'So great is his charity!'[495]

Towards the end of 1611 her relations with Velasco had deteriorated beyond repair and the decision was made to spend more time away from her house next to the embassy. Her health was worse than it had been when she left Valladolid. In search of cleaner air, she turned her mind to Zúñiga's suggestion about a house in Spitalfields.

16

Oran

UNMARRIED and with few friends, George Abbot was installed as archbishop of Canterbury at the age of 48. His contempt for Roman Catholics bordered on the obsessional though he would have no truck with Puritan friends who dared to disagree with him. Popularity did not matter to him, and although the great Gothic cross at Cheapside drew many admiring glances from London's ordinary citizens, Abbot campaigned unsuccessfully for its demolition on the joyless grounds that it encouraged the idolatry prohibited by God's law. Embittered by years of university politics, he was adept at playing on people's fears and the French king's assassination presented him with the perfect opportunity to press for greater persecution of the recusant community. Luisa heartily disliked him, making the curious remark that his face was disfigured 'like an aubergine'. Perhaps Abbot had liver spots on his face, and she may have had in mind the Spanish practice of chopping aubergines into round slices, to reveal the black pips against ovals of white flesh. Another explanation is that he was red-faced, possessing all the signs of being choleric.[496]

The archbishop had a peculiar dislike of monasticism and especially of female monastics. Clashing with his strict Calvinist belief that faith alone guaranteed a place in heaven without need of good works or intercessory prayer, conventual life also cut across Abbot's simplistic views about social order. The Elizabethan Jesuit John Gerard told two stories which reveal his blinkered outlook. Gerard used to travel round England disguised as a gentleman (and sometimes with a young Michael Walpole in tow if he needed a manservant to complete his disguise). He encountered the disapproving Abbot while playing cards in a country house. Discussion turned to a demented Puritan who had jumped off a steeple in London with a note to God asking to be saved. Abbot argued that it may not have been a sin because he could have repented at the very last moment. Gerard thought this unlikely while the wretched man was on the way down, or as he more elegantly phrased it, *inter pontem et fontem*. The debate ended when Abbot insisted it was not for gentlemen to discuss matters reserved for theologians.[497]

Abbot crowed about the efficiency of his archiepiscopal spy network. When Pedro de Zúñiga returned to England, he would boast that the envoy 'should not speak with no man nor tread a step, but he would know of it'.[498] In February 1611 he began to feed James titbits about the growing danger posed by his Catholic subjects and the king was incensed to discover that Luisa had dined with Roberts and Somers on the eve of their execution. Summoned before the king's councillors in Star Chamber, Stephen Houghton was charged with turning Newgate into 'rather a chapel for superstitious service than a prison or gaol'. With chauvinist disdain Luisa was dismissed by others connected with Newgate as 'the old Spanish lady' or 'the old lady who is in the Spanish ambassador's house', and royal anger was further aroused by news that Velasco's domestic chaplain was visiting prisoners.[499] The king's fury provided cover for Abbot to order a raid on the house of Lady Vaux, a noted supporter of the Jesuits whose son, the young Lord Vaux, saw himself as a rival to Lord Montague for temporal leadership of England's recusants. The trees and plants in her elaborate garden were uprooted, perhaps out of spite but possibly in search of the bodies of Roberts and Somers as it was rumoured her son was also involved in digging up priests' graves.[500]

Making his first direct move against Luisa, the archbishop let it be known that, if she dared visit the remaining prisoners in Newgate, she would be arrested on the spot, but, as she did not have the strength to make the short journey there, the impulsive archbishop dispatched pursuivants to the Barbican to fetch her. He was breaking new ground. Bishops did not normally involve themselves with foreigners as they were more properly a matter for the Privy Council, and Velasco's advice was to make polite apologies but decline the offer to go with them. Refusing to open her door she shouted through a grille that she did not believe they had come from the archbishop, as he would hardly want to see the likes of her. She was convinced that living next door to the embassy was all that had deterred them from breaking down the door, and in the end 'they were merely a little insistent with the doorbell'. Abbott had to make do with drawing up another description of what she looked like.[501]

King James's ministers were determined to make an example of her. Robert Cecil commented later that summer that she was 'of late nearly looked after, and shall be dealt with as befits her merit and quality'.[502] Actually she was extremely unwell, and fear of what would happen to the relics if her illness were to carry her off prompted her to add a codicil to her will in which she entrusted all her papers—and anything else she had—to Michael Walpole. Towards the end of the year she told Espinosa that her suffering was worse than when he had sat at her bedside in Valladolid, and the physician to the recusant community, Dr Foster, became concerned because all she could eat was egg or vegetable stew. Even drinking gave her palpitations. She barely slept, but a particularly high temperature or a bloodletting might induce a slumber so profound that her doctors became sufficiently alarmed to throw water in her eyes, or twist her fingers and hands to the point of damaging them in order to wake her up. One of Velasco's chaplains, Bartolomé Tellez, said that at this time it was not clear whether she was talking Spanish or English in confession.[503]

Doctors at the time had little or no knowledge of germs, believing that illness was ordinarily transmitted by obnoxious gases, and Dr Foster was adamant that the foul air in her narrow little house would do for her. This was not the martyrdom she hankered after, so she acted on Zúñiga's suggestion to look for somewhere to live in Spitalfields, a good mile or two away from her old house. The Spital lay outside the city walls beyond Bishopsgate, near today's Liverpool Street Station. The Flemish and Venetian ambasadors had their residences there, and, though Luisa had little time for either of the men, each envoy had his own chapel. A recusant community had taken root in the area because it enjoyed the privileges of being within the liberty of Norton Folgate. When the medieval hospital of the Spital was dissolved, jurisdiction over the area reverted to the more distant authority of the canons of St Paul's Cathedral with the result that parochial administration was notoriously weak. At the end of Elizabeth's reign Lady Vaux's sister-in-law, Ann Vaux, had kept a house in Spital-fields that provided Henry Garnet with a base for many years, and later, during the Civil Wars, the area's legal privileges continued to provide shelter for the most extreme of Protestants. At the heart of the Spital was an open air pulpit, where the Corporation of London continued to gather every Easter to hear sermons from the greatest prelates in the land.

Luisa explained how her new home was to be found 'just where the countryside ends, and is the last house in this part of London, spacious and full of light, and with cleaner air than in other parts of London'.[504] It lay next to the garden of Antonio Foscarini, the Venetian ambassador and abutted a portion of his residence. A stone's throw away lived the Flemish ambassador, whose wife turned out to be a niece of Magdalena de San Jerónimo and who, in a remarkable coincidence, had once been little Luisa's maid, probably in the Des-calzas Reales.[505] Being in a semi-rural setting, the new house was mercifully free of the noise of traffic, a serious problem of living in the Barbican. In the summer of 1612, Luisa's brother, now in the service of Rodrigo Calderón, made the short journey from Flanders to put pressure on her to join his master's nunnery, and it was explained to him that her new home was easy to find. Just ask for the Venetian ambassador's residence, and 'the house made of bricks, with the little round tower, is ours'.

An archaeological survey undertaken in 1998 confirmed there were only two brick houses in Spitalfields at the time, and the excavation of one of these houses revealed a puzzling circular adjunct which the archaeological team conjectured might have served as a second, smaller, latrine to a larger one at the back. Luisa's description of her building as being made of brick and with a little tower visible for all to see now suggests the round extrusion was an external staircase for a tall house which indeed had relatively deep foundations. The combin-ation of archaelogical and literary evidence means that it has become possible to identify this house as Luisa's and to conclude that the much larger building next door was the Venetian ambassador's residence.

Part of a brand-new development built by William Wyld sometime around the end of the sixteenth century, Luisa's house stood in what is today the remodelled Spital Square, on the site of what is now a distinguished Italian restaurant.[506]

Idyllic though it sounded, the house came at a price. Fresh air cost money in London, especially when it came with a whiff of legal preference. She had to find money for the upkeep of two properties, which came to the not inconsiderable sum of £50.[507] In 1606 her first house cost her £10 in rent. Since then her community had grown to include half a dozen companions, not including her French manservant nor the additional women and priests who temporarily lodged with her.[508] Finding room to accommodate everyone made renting an additional house a necessity, whatever the cost. At least at the start 'the friends'—either wealthy recusants or more likely, the Jesuits—paid for the less expensive of the two houses, presumably the one in the Barbican, but she had to implore Joseph Creswell to ask her Spanish lady friends to come to her aid. At the same time she could not resist including another swipe at Velasco, who had duly passed on a donation from Calderón but had used it as an excuse not to help her himself. The new house had one disadvantage, however. Being on its own it could easily be surrounded, especially as neither the Flemish nor the Venetian missions brought with it the degree of diplomatic protection afforded by a Spanish embassy. She speculated that God wanted her to be 'exposed to the trials and tribulations which the Catholics endure'.[509]

Extraordinary steps were taken to make the new house secure. Innumerable locks were fitted and her companions were drilled in how to repel unwanted visitors. The alterations were described in great detail by her handyman and carpenter Richard Brough, a Londoner and an obdurate Puritan who had worked for her for some time. The house in Spitalfields was on three floors with the space inside much reduced by having a series of double doors to control access. The front door had a grille so that bread could be passed through without seeing the face or even the hands of the person on the other side, and water was channelled into the house directly from the garden, which was turned over to lettuce, onions, beans, and cabbage. The chapel was situated on an upper floor being 'so hidden from everyone that only those who searched very carefully were able to discover it'.[510] When Brough had a job to do there, he was often fed inside the house so as not to attract attention by his comings and goings.

She liked to think of the house as 'our Oran', tall and strong like Spain's great fortress on the North African coast, and the need to be constantly alert was instilled into her companions. One companion remembered her as being 'very carefuile and watchful ou're her house preuenting still the daingers that might hapen by these bad folkes the purciuants and other such like'.

Given the idiosyncratic nature of her spelling, the whole passage needs to be modernized:

She was very careful and watchful over her house, preventing still the dangers that might happen by these bad folks the pursuivants and other such like, as she had heard that in the Catholics' houses sometimes they would break in at the windows and walls of the house and when the doors had been opened to thrust themselves into the house by force; but she with her wisdom and sharp understanding did prevent their devilish desires which they had against her, for she was very careful to see that all parts of the house might be strong and secure, she spent much money in the same although many times in cause of her poverty it went very hard with her. As for the doors she was always careful to choose one of the house most careful, obedient, and punctual that would follow her directions in all things for to be the porter and to keep the keys of all the doors. When anyone had knocked at the door she must look out of the window to see whom it was, then to tell her that such a one was there; and this she would have always done. She would say, because if anything should happen, she would be one of the first that should know of it, she must never go to the door without calling one of the other maids with her for to shut the second door before she opens the first.

Controlling access was a priority, which explains why one of her bitterest complaints about Ann Garnet was that she was too chatty to be trusted as the doorkeeper. There were exercise drills concerning what to do if security was breached, and she told Cousin Isabel that during recreation 'we spend a few moments dealing with what we have to do if there is an incident or problem arising from this persecution, because the important thing is to be prepared and on top of everything'.[511]

The most immediate risk turned out to have nothing to do with politics. A problem of living in a relatively isolated area was robbery, and since Luisa was new to the district not everyone had realized there was nothing to steal but a few matresses. During the night thieves got in through the garden and it was doubtless the women's cries that alerted the Venetian ambassador's men to come to the rescue. As he knew Luisa possessed nothing of value, Ambassador Velasco jumped to the conclusion that the break-in was an attempt to murder her, and he ordered her back to the city, even opening up a passage from her house into the chapel to make life more comfortable for her, which probably explains why Luisa happened to be at the Barbican when Archbishop Abbot first sent for her.[512]

The new house continued to be a staging post for women who wanted to go overseas and become nuns. An entire family, Joyce and Judith Smith and their mother, was helped on one occasion. Joyce was sent on her way to Lisbon and the English convent there in 1611 or 1612, with the date being uncertain on account of the peculiar English habit of changing the date of the year, not in January, but on Lady Day in March. Joyce wrote thanking Luisa for all the items she had received, including money, two pairs of stockings, and other items of clothing. She also said how fearful she was for the family members left behind. The indication is that the letter was written from Brussels, in which case it would normally have made sense for Luisa to lodge her with Ana de Jesús at the Carmelite house. The next we hear of Joyce is from Vitoria in the Basque country, almost certainly because she was to stay with the family of Luisa's great benefactress, Ana María de Vergara, the rich widow of an official in the Spanish exchequer. The route Brussels–Vitoria had been well trodden by Luisa's protégées over the years, but on this occasion Joyce Smith may have had no need of Carmelite hospitality. When he left in August 1612, Velasco agreed to a request passed through Zúñiga to conduct an English girl as far as Vitoria.[513]

Luisa's connections with Joyce's family stretched back years. Joyce sent word that the community in Lisbon had promised to make her 'very welcome', which is unsurprising as her sister Elizabeth was already there and almost certainly had been one of the Englishwomen who had briefly stayed with Luisa in Valladolid, on their way to Portugal a decade earlier. When she heard more from her sister about Luisa's work in London, she wrote to acknowledge her 'meritorious proceedinges there in our miserable country'. Elizabeth thanked her:

first in harbouring me in your house with the rest of our company as we cam hether, who all do giue your ladyship most humble thanckes . . . but aboue them all your ladyshipe hath heaped benefits uppon me since, that is to say in labouring to bringe my mother from the most daungerus estate wherin she liueth and so lykwise you haue done to my sister Judith . . . but as concerning my sister Joyse your charity hath bene redoubled, in being a mother to her both for soule and body, delueringe her from the daungerus and perilous estate of soule wherin she was, and the preseruing her from falling by maintayninge her in your ladiships owne house so long a tyme and then to prouide for her safe conducting to this holly company, to whome she is very welcome.[514]

No amount of pastoral work could stop Luisa from interfering in Spain's internal politics. In the summer of 1612 the former ambassador Pedro de Zúñiga returned to England on a delicate mission to inform King James of the two Franco-Spanish marriages. It was a snub of the first order, and a purpose of the mission was to shield the recusant community from James's inevitable displeasure at playing second fiddle at a French wedding. To do this, he was not to rule out a marriage between Philip's other daughter and the Prince of Wales, 'but always on the understanding that he turn Catholic'.[515] Better still, he was to listen sympathetically if proposals were made to marry James's daughter to a scion of the junior branch of the Habsburg family in Italy, but again on the strict understanding that conversion would be required for the Pope to grant the necessary dispensation. Without Rome's blessing, the legitimacy of any children of the marriage would be doubtful.

Luisa made her way back to the Barbican to meet up with her old friend and sparring partner, don Pedro. The last thing she wanted was for him to call on her in her new home in Spitalfields. Though her neighbour the Flemish ambassador was angry at being left in the dark about the reasons for Zúñiga's being sent back to England, the real reason was that she did not want to draw attention to where she was now living and to the priests she sheltered there.[516] Archbishop Abbot was doing his utmost to make life as uncomfortable as possible for Catholics in London, especially for the newly returned Zúñiga. He muttered how the former ambassador had first been sent to England at the time of the Gunpowder Plot, putting it about that the envoy might have returned for some equally foul purpose.[517] His house was kept under surveillance and Luisa's great friend and supplier of whips, the Jesuit John Blakfan, was picked up as he was leaving there under cover of darkness. Such was the hostility to Zúñiga's return that when the ambassador was crossing Holborn Bridge in a carriage pulled by six mules, a man on horseback snatched his bejewelled hat off his head, and rode off at high speed, to the great amusement of the crowd.[518]

What Luisa was whispering into Zúñiga's ear about Velasco can be reconstructed from what she was telling anyone in Spain who would listen. An ancillary part of don Pedro's mission was to report back on the flood of complaints about his replacement. In October she flatly contradicted her cousin Isabel who had made the mistake of praising Velasco: 'Don Alonso is not the politician you say he is.'[519] At the end of the year she informed Calderón it would be a kindness to get him out of the country as quickly as possible, as 'you only have to look to see that the embassy is a complete ruin'.[520] By then Spain had suffered the 'great unluckiness [of being] forced to renounce their ambassador', as Sir Charles Cornwallis wrote when he looked back on events. Velasco had compromised the duke of Lerma by giving King James the impression that Madrid was actively looking for an Anglo-Spanish match. As might be expected, when Sir Charles brought up the subject of these alleged offers of marriage in a meeting with Spanish officials, the minister who 'suddenly and peremptorily denied' that Velasco had any such instruction was Rodrigo Calderón.[521] Luisa was probably as responsible as any one person for humiliating Velasco but to her credit she did ask Calderón to try to help the disgraced ambassador, though little seems to have come of this. By way of return, Velasco whined in a semi-encoded letter to his successor in London that Rodrigo Calderón was '*the most brazen villain ever raised up by God since he populated the world*'.[522]

Luisa was drawn into discussions over his replacement in a way that she found strangely disturbing. Her brother Alonso's decision to come to visit her in 1612 was part of his campaign to secure backing for his bid to be the next ambassador. Given his relative lack of success in the world, for him it would be a step up. He broached the subject in a letter from Flanders in October, and she replied at once to make plain she could not see how it would ever work to have 'the sister a pilgrim and the brother an ambassador'.[523] He had the gall to ask the Jesuit Anthony Hoskins to put pressure on his sister, even persuading the venerable Ana de Jesús to write. Luisa could not stomach the idea of Alonso stealing her thunder. She grudgingly admitted that, though the posting might be good for his career, as far as she was concerned 'I totally prefer and wish to follow my path here alone, not with a brother'.[524]

Her favoured method of dissuasion was to explain precisely what was entailed in being ambassador in what she regarded as one of Spain's most difficult postings. By her reckoning, the embassy cost 10,000 or 11,000 ducats or around £3,000 a year.[525] She composed a remarkable 'job description', and though she tried to be as objective as possible her political bias crept in. The English were arrogant and detested Spain but the real difficulty was in transacting business with a Privy Council that was riven by internal disputes between English and Scots. To be successful, the ambassador needed to be able to cut a dash, with a sword in one hand and a ready supply of money for bribes in the other. The representative of Spain would do well not to evince much interest in talk of peace, and anyone who knew Luisa would have realized what she meant when she said that the ambassador must be prepared to listen to the advice of others. Her brother would need to bring his own chancery staff, including someone to act as his agent at court who could speak reasonable English or very good French. The current agent was paid 1,500 ducats a year. He would also need an interpreter who was also fluent in either English or French, at a further cost of 300 ducats a year, and the secretary in charge of the cipher received 200 ducats, though fortunately their salaries were charged directly to Madrid.

The ambassador required six gentlemen of his own for his household, with four young boys between the ages of 14 and 16 years of age being enough to act as pages since they were not much called for in England. In addition to the domestic staff there had to be two doorkeepers and two coachmen. For the honour of Spain, between six and eight dishes had to be served at table, more if guests were present, with silverware of high quality. Two members of a religious order could staff the chapel, but a careful eye would have to be kept on them so they did not fritter away their time playing cards or wearing fashionable vestments. If he brought with him a secular priest, he could also act as a scribe, though on no account must his secretary be a priest as that would cause problems with Catholics and Protestants alike. Three salons, a gallery, and a bedroom needed furnishing with carpets and wall-hangings as there was hardly any difference between summer and winter. Finally, it was better for an ambassador to leave his wife and children behind. Not only was it ruinously expensive to have his family with him, it was also undignified.[526]

After so many years of self-doubt, Luisa had reached a stage when she felt complete assurance that she was doing the right thing. She imagined that God wanted her to live exposed and unshielded in Spitalfields as a prelude to the martyrdom she still craved. But this was still not an opinion shared by everyone. The son of her much-loved aunt, María Chacón, who had brought her up in Madrid after the death of her parents, had become cardinal-archbishop of Toledo, the senior prelate in Castile and the richest clergyman in Europe. He sent her money and blessed her endeavours, but in conformity with the principles of Tridentine Catholicism he asked her to consider whether it would not be more appropriate to consider a life that was 'more reserved and quiet'.[527] His letter arrived at a time when she was steadily recovering from her long illness and finding immense satisfaction in the multifarious tasks she was performing for the priests and lay Catholics of London. She continued to seek out relics. In December 1612 her French manservant was despatched to observe the execution of the priest John Almond, a Lancastrian who had operated under the name of Molineux and who taunted the bevy of Anglican bishops at his summary trial by ordering them back to their wives and children. The Frenchman's task was to position himself under the scaffold, and he had with him two brilliant-white clothes to capture any drops of blood that might fall, and to take note of where the torso was buried. As the executioner had only a dirty handkerchief, Lemeteliel provided one of his cloths to cover Almond's eyes, which, Luisa was certain, 'looked in a trice on God with no blindfold'. She organized a group of men to rescue what remained of his body but danger fell on the party from an unexpected quarter. They came across another group of relic hunters—possibly working at the behest of Lord Montague and the secular clergy—who might have fired on their fellow Catholics either out of ignorance or from being 'carried away by the rage that comes from too much devotion to the martyr'.[528]

Luisa was now well versed in organizing rescue parties, and by the cruellest of ironies she had been called upon earlier in the year to rescue the body parts of the monk who had had himself asked her to receive Roberts and Somer. William Scott, or Brother Mauro de Sahagún, was executed early on the Saturday morning of 30 May 1612, along with the priest Richard Newport, who had himself been converted to Catholicism twenty-two years earlier after the shock of witnessing a double martyrdom. Velasco was sulking in the country— probably Putney—when the sentences were announced and his frenzied efforts to save the priests and curry favour back home came too late.[529]

Another Benedictine, Mauro de Merino, asked Luisa to exhume the bodies, and once more Lemeteliel was sent to observe where they were buried. As with Roberts and Somers, their quartered bodies were buried in a wide ditch as deep as a man near the gallows. Identifying the priests' remains was not difficult as the bodies that remained intact belonged to the sixteen or more common criminals whose executions had been delayed so they could serve as cover for the priestly remains. The snag was that the operation was taking place in the height of summer. It did not get dark until ten o'clock and it started to clear four or five hours later. In the three days which elapsed after the execution, Luisa rounded up a dozen friends, mostly from the Spanish embassy. They may have been eager to volunteer as Scott had acted as a confessor in the embassy. They did not want payment. A relic would do. Ambassador Velasco's young son offered his help, and he was not alone in recalling how 'everyone was armed in case they were spotted by the guards who were posted there by the authorities'.[530]

The work was utterly repulsive. Another embassy man, Lucas Ximenez, remembered a particularly distasteful experience. He lifted up one of the criminal's bodies all by himself but it fell back on him, and handfuls of detritus splattered his face. His comfort was that Luisa had asked him to do a noble thing and that, although the bodies had been underground for some time, 'the smell coming off had not been bad but good'.[531]

The priests' remains were placed in pouches made up from Luisa's torn-up sheets and carried by horse to a spot underneath some bushes a mile away. A merchant friend walked up and down, trying not to attract too much attention as he tried to ensure the parcels were not discovered. If he had been arrested, it would not just have been his life or liberty that he would have lost; his family would have lost a fortune. Luisa was by now becoming anxious. She had expected news by four o'clock, but Lemeteliel did not return for another two hours, owing perhaps to a well-meaning if time-consuming decision to fill in the ditch out of respect for the remaining corpses. In any event, Luisa asked the Flemish ambassador's coachman to lend her his carriage but he was reluctant to travel all the way across the city, and instead she managed to hire a coach for the usual price of 20 *reales* or 10 shillings. The city's gates ought to have been closed for the night, and most likely the carriage skirted the city's medieval walls, cutting across Finsbury Fields, to reach Luisa.[532]

The house in Spitalfields was brimming with flowers. It was surrounded by fields and orchards but well-wishers had heard that Luisa was unwell again and had also brought her flowers. When Lemeteliel and the merchant carried in the precious pouches the six companions lined up to form a procession into the chapel, each holding two candles. The way up was strewn with flowers and floral wreaths. The bodies were deposited 'on the carpet in front of the altar, and covered with large piece of red material that was new, with lots of sweet-smelling flowers on top. On bended knee, we offered up a prayer.'[533]

Why was it so important to preserve the relics? Catholic teaching held that holy relics created an environment akin to religious 'hot spots', being places where heaven and earth intersected. Miracles would happen, especially if the relics were touched, and prayers that were offered up in their vicinity were far more likely to be heeded. The Council of Trent had given new impetus to the ancient tradition that churches and their altars should be sanctified by incorporating the remains of those who had suffered for their faith. So as to be able to invoke the new saints by name, it was essential that the body parts of each priest be properly identified, with the correct labels being put on the lead caskets which housed the relics. Before this could happen, however, Luisa had to remove any trace of mud or other kinds of debris. She gently wiped them down using dry cloths or her own spit to avoid corrupting them with too much moisture before finally coating them with unguents made from strong-smelling spices. It must have been the work of the devil, she quipped, that made so many of her Protestant friends ('hereges amigos') pay a visit that day, but they could not halt the preparation of the bodies and the process was completed by dawn the following day. Ambassador Velasco's wife and sister apparently took two leaden boxes with them when they returned to Spain. Whose relics they contained is not clear, but it seems that the most important relics of Scott and Newport were taken by the incoming ambassador's chaplain, Simon de Ariza, to the village of Gondomar in Galicia. Ariza was himself the proud owner of a handkerchief which William Scott had used to wipe away his perspiration at the moment he had been sentenced to death.[534] Luisa, on the other hand, was amused rather than angry when a Catholic tried to sell her what he claimed were the true relics of her guests.

Preserving bodies did not come cheap. She estimated the preservatives and the caskets set her back precisely £17.[535] It was, of course, a price well worth paying for a tangible link between those left on earth and saints assuredly in heaven, but Luisa was engaging in this highly perilous activity in a part of London where the long shadow of the Spanish embassy could not reach. Could her own martyrdom be far off?

17

The Siege of Spitalfields

L UISA had always known there would be no difficulty in laying
siege to her house in Spitalfields. During her final summer she
dangled before Rodrigo Calderón the prospect that she might
yet become 'his very own martyr' after he had warned her that living
out in the Spital was too exposed.[536] He must have learnt of her
poverty-stricken life outside London's city walls from her scandalized
brother. Though she had to meet the costs of two houses, pay her
medical bills, and find the money for preserving relics, she was not the
only subject of the king of Spain to find London expensive. Ambassador Velasco had piled up huge debts, and he had the gall to ask if she
could help him find the money to pay for his journey home. At least
he had never dared to suspend her royal pension, which was dutifully
paid until the time he left.[537] His replacement was a man more to
Luisa's liking, don Diego Sarmiento de Acuña, lord of Gondomar,
who possessed a degree of swagger so conspicuously lacking in his
predecessor.

When Gondomar's ship sailed towards Portsmouth harbour at the
end of July 1613 he refused to strike his colours. It made no difference
to be told that Philip II had lowered his flags when he had landed, half
a century before, on his way to marry Mary Tudor in Winchester
Cathedral. Still defiant, Gondomar sent a message to James who was
hunting nearby, asking him to be allowed to return to Spain, 'because
I was born of a good and honourable family, and I wish to emulate
them; all of which obliges me to die, as I will, to defend my honour
and duty, which is that these ships should enter and then return from
this kingdom in the state that they left Spain'. The letter came into the
king's hands as he was about to kill a stag. Buoyed up at the prospect
of ending the animal's life, he was in a mood to be captivated by the

new ambassador's bluster and he made an exception for his entry into the country. This was exactly how an ambassador of Spain should behave.

Gondomar was a client of Lerma's, and though the duke admired his abilities he found this modest Galician nobleman highly irritating. He was always pestering for advancement and he did his utmost to avoid taking up the posting to London, which he rightly regarded as beneath his dignity. As the splendidly named bishop of Monópoli later confided to Gondomar's confessor, the duke had made up his mind 'to throw [him] out of the court'.[538] To his credit, he plunged himself into his job as soon as he reached England, establishing a warm relationship with the king, who continued to be amused by his combination of audacity mixed with erudition. He deliberately made mistakes in his Latin so the king could correct him. You, he once told James, speak Latin like a king whereas I only speak it like an ambassador. Rightly has he earned a reputation as one of the most effective diplomats in the history of Spain. He was on especially good terms with Rodrigo Calderón, whom he knew from his time as the royal official appointed to watch over the government of Valladolid, precisely when Calderón was busy acquiring properties in the new capital. One of Gondomar's first acts as ambassador was to pass on a written instruction from King Philip that Luisa's pension was to be raised by 200 *reales* to 500 *reales* (or £12. 10 s.) per month, a payment backdated to March when the king had signed the order. It was a much-needed source of regular income, though it was still less than the cost of a couple of embalmings.[539]

It was an astute move on the new ambassador's part to get on the right side of Luisa, who by now could lay claim to being London's most celebrated Spanish resident. When Calderón asked her for an assessment of the new envoy she replied that she held Gondomar in high regard. First because he was an ardent Catholic and second because of the company he kept. Among the retainers he had brought with him was the Dominican Diego de la Fuente, who had earned a solid reputation as a teacher of theology in Valladolid and who quickly became close to Luisa.[540] The recusant community was in sore need of support from Spain's man in London. Archbishop

Abbot's persecution was intensifying, and a sign of the government's new-found rigour was that it was at last putting into place measures to see that its wishes were properly implemented. Earlier in the year it was reported that guards were patrolling the streets at night, presumably in order to intercept priests as they moved from safe-house to safe-house, but what made this degree of surveillance exceptional was that the city fathers were 'inspecting them in person to ensure they are doing the job'.[541]

The tribulations of the Vaux family continued to be a worry for Luisa. The king had decided to make an example of Edward, fourth Lord Vaux, who was imprisoned and fined mercilessly for refusing the oath of allegiance, which placed Luisa in a difficult position. His distraught mother prevailed upon her to intercede with the Spanish authorities to let him go to Madrid, and a promise was forthcoming that the 24-year-old would give up gambling and swearing. For once, Luisa decided not to get involved, coming to the conclusion that it was too sensitive an issue even for her and it was with some reluctance that she agreed to pass on messages to Madrid. When the reply came back that the attractions of life in the Spanish capital might be the moral ruin of him, she decided that, although she did not personally know the young baron, it would be a good idea if she were to exaggerate the dangers of living in Madrid. As she told her brother, she did not want 'to lose her credit by sending some Englishman over there'.[542]

Luisa was by now living in England only through the forbearance of King James. In September there was a troubling rumour that his ambassador in Madrid was putting pressure on Lerma to order her to leave.[543] She was vulnerable to any swing in the king's mood. That came when Francisco Suárez, a distinguished Jesuit theologian living in Portugal, one of the Spanish king's dominions since the 1580s, published a book entitled *Defensio Fidei Catholicae*, or to give it its full title in English, *A Defence of the Catholic Faith against the Errors of Anglicanism*. It took issue with a number of matters James held dear. It was bad enough that it supported the Jesuits' line on the inadmissibility of the Oath of Allegiance which James had personally helped compose, but what really infuriated him was the enunciation of a particularly Spanish point of view about the nature of civil power. Sovereignty was vested in the people; they were free to invest a king with that power—and that transfer might be irrevocable—but it did not follow that kings ruled directly by divine right. 'No king or monarch has or had the power to rule immediately from God or by divine institution, but only by the will and investiture of the people'. What was more, Suárez argued that there were circumstances in which the people could rise up against a tyrannical or godless king.[544]

This was a red rag to a bull. Both as a defensive reaction to the violent dethronement of his mother, as well as a necessary bulwark against the claims of more radical Protestants that the people should rule over church and state, James's philosophy of kingship centred on the assumption that he was God's lieutenant on earth. As far as he was concerned, the Society of Jesus was yet again attacking kings and kingship. His indignation was kept at boiling point because his new ambassador in Spain, John Digby, was apparently sending back the sheets of Suárez's book as they came off the presses, chapter by chapter.

James had made a fatal link between Luisa and the radical constitutionalism of the Jesuits. The monarch could hardly contain himself, and, in a major breach of protocol, he spoke directly to the main interpreter from the Spanish embassy, Francis Fowler, snarling at the embarrassed agent, 'look at Suárez's book over there by the window which would rob kings and princes of the loyalty of their subjects'.[545] James was prepared to strike out indiscriminately at Catholics, finally letting his archbishop off the leash. Suárez's book was later burnt at midday in front of St Paul's Cathedral but Abbot had already been allowed to accuse Luisa of having set up a nunnery under the king of England's nose.

Abbot was right, of course. Luisa thought of the women attached to the Order of the Sovereign Virgin as members of a religious house. She might feign amusement that people like the old woman of Highgate called her a nun but this was only because she did not wish to be compared with those religious who lived an enclosed life, turning their back on the world. Without a second thought she repeatedly referred to her community as a convent. Twice in 1611 she told

Joseph Creswell that 'our house is a miniature nunnery', and later when she needed money from the duchess of Rioseco, she again told him to tell the duchess 'that our house is like a nunnery'. The following year Calderón was informed, and not for the first time, that 'our house is truly a little convent'.[546]

Though Catholic houses were being raided all round her, Luisa's final summer in London passed off relatively peacefully. Michael Walpole had secreted himself in Gondomar's entourage and re-entered the country, using her house in Spitalfields as his base, while she found time to urge Calderón and his friends to take advantage of the parliamentary crisis in Dublin by offering military assistance to Irish Catholics. Meanwhile her admiration for the new ambassador grew by leaps and bounds, and she particularly liked doña Constanza, his second wife who was as pious as her husband. In the middle of September Gondomar learnt that Abbot was about to make his move against Luisa. Instructions had been given to the pursuivants that she was to be arrested wherever she was found, even at the Venetian ambassador's residence, so long as it was not in Gondomar's house. Luisa had just returned to the Barbican but around 10 October she asked the ambassador for permission to return to Spitalfields, 'so that my companions I left there waiting for me don't get afraid'.[547] Gondomar felt unable to stop her but he insisted 'that she left publicly in our carriages, sitting on doña Constanza's right, with me accompanying them, to the great delight, they tell me, of the Catholics'.[548] For contrary reasons, ambassador and missionary made common cause to force the archbishop to play his hand: Gondomar, because he wanted any excuse to hasten his return to Spain, and Luisa, because only by remaining could she keep her sights on higher glory.

Many wolves for few sheep is Muñoz's description of the pre-dawn raid on the house in Spitalfields.[549] As far as we can tell, Luisa had five companions living with her when the house was surrounded. One died shortly after the raid and another, who acted as cook, managed to avoid capture, perhaps by staying behind to look after her sick friend. One of those companions made a record of the events of St Luke's Day, Monday, 18 October 1613: 'the bishipe of canterbery being informed of her retired life sent the shrife and the recorder of london

w[i]th many ofther offisirs to apprehend her at her owne house'.[550]
Some fifty or more armed men used ladders to scale the garden walls
and surround the house before breaking down all the doors and finally
reaching the sleeping quarters.[551] A brutal raid, the Jesuit Richard
Blunt described the assault as being carried out 'with such suddenness,
breaking down doors & as the very fright thereof so amazed and
astonished one of her maids a gentleman's daughter of good worship,
as within a few hours after she died'.[552] A companion called Michisan
had been suffering from smallpox died the next day from the shock,
and Luisa's carpenter recalled making a coffin for someone he referred
to as Ann.[553] According to reports reaching Blakfan on the Continent, it had taken a full half-hour to smash in all the doors.[554] Carpenter Brough had done a good job.

There was a bell at the top of the house to be rung in an emer-
gency.[555] News reached Gondomar of what was happening while the
raid was still taking place, though the first person to come to Luisa's
aid was the Flemish ambassador Ferdinand de Boisschot, whose
residence was so close that he must have been woken up by the
commotion. Though de Boisschot was personally very kind, Luisa
had not previously given him much thought, regarding him as too
envious of the greater diplomatic importance of his Spanish counterpart. The other diplomatic neighbour to be disturbed was the Venetian ambassador. She had hitherto thought even less of him than de
Boisschot. The Italian was all smiles, she admitted, but this had not
stopped him from initially being reluctant to let her use a door that led
directly to his chapel, and in her hour of need he did little to help.

The attack brought out the best in the Flemish ambassador. In-
stantly recognizing a man inside the house as Michael Walpole, the
envoy had the presence of mind to bark at him as if he were his
servant, rebuking him for having no business being in the house,
which allowed the Jesuit to make his escape as a seemingly crestfallen
member of the ambassadorial household.[556] When the pursuivants
finally got to see what was inside, they were disappointed. Unaccus-
tomed to evangelical poverty, they were taken aback that its contents
amounted to little more than a few beds and some ragged clothes. No
chairs were to be found for the officials with them to sit on, and all

they came across was some sea-coal for the fire and two large water containers. Such was their disillusion that the pursuivants lost heart before they got into the chapel, the one room with any decoration, which allowed Gondomar to salvage Luisa's chalice and other ornaments, along with her papers.

Gondomar had reached Spitalfields just as Luisa was about to be taken to Lambeth Palace. He tried to insist on taking her back to the embassy, offering to produce her before the authorities whenever she was summoned but instead he was shown an order for her detention apparently signed by King James himself. He was granted one concession, however. Luisa and the three companions who accompanied her were permitted, under heavily armed escort, to use the coaches of the three ambassadors to make their way across the city but instead of being delivered to the Privy Council, as the ambassadors had been told, the carriages were directed over London Bridge to Archbishop Abbot at Lambeth Palace. According to Mary Ward, amazed bystanders cried out, 'English nuns, English nuns!'

Abbot had been scratching around for evidence for some time, boasting that he knew the name of the tailor who made their habits![557] He declared Luisa to be 'a Jesuitess, and so are all her disciples, apparelled in every respect as the Jesuits' women'.[558] In the interview at Lambeth Palace he confronted her about her monastic life. What time did they say matins? How many were in the nunnery? What rule did they follow? Calmly she replied, you are not my judge.[559] He thought she spoke English well.[560]

It was 'with the authority of an ambassador's wife' that doña Constanza insisted on staying with Luisa after he sent her to the Gatehouse, a prison controlled by the episcopacy.[561] She was joined by de Boisschot's wife, and the two diplomatic wives remained with Luisa for the three nights of her imprisonment, bringing in food and only going home to sleep. Brough the carpenter also managed to get in, despite the fact that he was not yet fully converted to Catholicism.[562] Luisa had been placed among the religious prisoners but her companions were thrown in with the common criminals. Meanwhile Gondomar was campaigning for her release, and early on the morning of 21 October the Privy Council sent him formal notification of the king's decision to release her on condition that she abandoned the country within seven days. Gondomar refused to agree to any such thing, though he suggested that, if the council preferred, they would both leave England that very night, a precipitous offer to abandon his post that would later earn him an official rebuke. Under the face-saving formula that she would abandon the country as soon as was convenient, Luisa was released that evening.[563] Gondomar's confessor, Diego de la Fuente, remembered how Luisa was taken back to the embassy in the Barbican in doña Constanza's coach, trailed by another eight or nine carriages belonging to the Catholic embassies and to Luisa's supporters in London. In an unparalleled act of defiance, the procession passed 'in front of the gates of the palace and along the most important public streets of London'.[564] The head of the secular clergy, George Birkhead, who had replaced Luisa's old sparring partner in the Clink as Archpriest, grudgingly conceded she had left prison 'with great triumph to the admiration of the Londoners'.[565]

Why had the attack on Luisa's house been so brusque? Her explanation was simple. James had suffered from another of his periodic losses of temper. In her opinion, 'the king's anger with Father Suárez's book has been extraordinary', and this alone was sufficient to explain why he made up his mind that someone had to pay. It amused her to think that the king had miscalculated if he had reasoned that Spain's ambassador lived too far away on the other side of London to pay any attention to a raid taking place in remote Spitalfields.[566] In fact, James had a long memory for grievances, and he angrily told Gondomar's first messenger that he knew all about how Luisa had dined in Newgate with two condemned priests on the eve of their execution.[567]

The storm unleashed by Suárez's book had indeed made Luisa vulnerable, yet this does not fully account for the fierceness of the raid. Another of London's Jesuits thought her house had been 'so violently searched as it is supposed for Martin', one of Walpole's pseudonyms. Under another of his aliases, he had just published a book which defended some of Bellarmine's earlier views and which prophetically attacked the current persecution of Catholics 'from which neither frailty of sex, nor band of matrimony, nor nobility of birth can exempt any'.[568] But there is another explanation for setting so many wolves on so few sheep.

The anniversary of the Gunpowder Plot was looming, and the fifth of November had already become a day to remember how religious fanatics had come close to blowing up king and parliament. Word quickly spread that bomb-making equipment and other weapons had been found buried beneath Luisa's house.[569] Groundless fears that another conspiracy was being hatched would also explain why the pursuivants were acutely disappointed at not finding any riches. The previous summer Abbot had wondered aloud if Zúñiga had returned to help plot another attempt on the king's life, letting slip that the envoy had rapidly dispensed the astronomical sum of £12,000 or £13,000 on his nefarious dealings. Did the pursuivants long to find an ambassador's pot of gold?

Luisa's second and final imprisonment lasted, like her first, only a matter of days, but on this occasion she was treated far less considerately with Abbot callously cutting her off from her surviving companions, and presumably she was not allowed to mourn the companion who had died. Her health never recovered. In the weeks after her release, a worsening chest infection put intolerable pressure on her heart, in addition to which her companions were still locked up. She might be a pampered guest of Ambassador Gondomar and his wife, able to follow the mass from her rooms, but her followers were confined to Newgate, where she knew that unsubtle pressure was being brought to bear on them to accept King James's oath.

Luisa's end was overshadowed by the realization that she would either die in her bed—a singular form of martyrdom—or else be obliged to abandon England, which pained her more. Her last surviving letter was addressed to her distant relative, the duke of Lerma. In the middle of November 1613 she explained to him that she had been drawn to England ever since she was a young girl. He needed to know she could not have survived so long if she had not been performing God's will, and she begged him *never* to listen to anyone who suggested she should go away from England. Her body may have been broken, but her acuity of mind had not deserted her, and she sensibly chose not to deny Abbot's two charges that she had founded a nunnery nor that she was responsible for numerous conversions. Instead she informed the duke that the false archbishop had not been able to prove either of the charges or anything relating to them.[570] She may have written this, her only known letter to the favourite, because the rumours had come back to haunt her that the English ambassador in Madrid was trying to obtain an order for her removal. Little did she know that King Philip and his council had decided the time had come for her to return to Flanders or Spain, where she was to be received with full honours.[571]

As her death approached, she penned a now-lost letter to John Blakfan in which she lamented being confined to bed and how she missed the company of her companions. Michael Walpole and the ambassador's confessor, Diego de la Fuente, remained at her bedside and together they read aloud the Passion of Christ. It would be pleasing to think that they each read in their own language to celebrate Luisa's journey from Spain to England. When the end came, de la Fuente administered the Last Rites.[572] As she lay dying, her French servant cried out, 'My lady, remember Diego Lemeteliel when you are in heaven', and her faithful carpenter, who recalled the Frenchman's words, found her final hours so moving that he began to think the time had come to accept Catholicism.[573] Her very last visitors were her English companions, who, at Gondomar's insistence, were briefly allowed 'out of prison to see her, where having declared signs of affection the one to the other, & she spoken some few words unto them, she gave up the ghost'.[574]

There was still one more service for her to perform for London's recusants. Her body was gently cleansed by her companions, as it was agreed that such a saintly body needed no embalming, and then the obvious decision was taken that her funeral would take place in the Spanish ambassador's chapel, in ten days' time. It was a unique opportunity for the Catholics of London to come together and celebrate something akin to a state occasion. It took on an international flavour. The French ambassador attended as did the agent of the duke of Savoy, along with the Venetian and Flemish envoys. Her emaciated body was placed on top of a sepulchre next to the high altar and flowers and the finest white candles were placed all around. The sermon was preached by Diego de la Fuente, and in Spanish, though one wonders if a translation was provided for the many English-speakers who attended, as, in addition to mourners from all the great Catholic mercantile nations,

there was also a great number of English Catholics who attended the honours with great devotion, full of admiration at seeing the ceremonies and listening to a sermon and a sung mass at such a large gathering of people, something which had not been seen in England for many years.

Despite the music, it was indubitably a sober affair. There was no wailing or gnashing of teeth as Spaniards avoided such lamentations because the Inquisition thought they smacked of Judaism and Islam.[575] Outside the pursuivants were gathering but they had probably gone home by the time the mourners emerged as Gondomar had cunningly decided to invite the congregation to stay on as his guests while his staff probably served up the traditional cabbage and pork soup of his native Galicia.[576]

'Verily I take her to be a martyr', wrote Blakfan when he learnt of her death. According to the Gregorian calendar, Luisa died on 2 January 1614, her forty-eighth birthday. The English calculated this as 22 December and the year was still 1613; but the date is not important. The question for her supporters was whether her life had been taken as a result of defending the Catholic faith, in which case she would have undoubtedly have achieved her lifelong ambition of martyrdom. If her last imprisonment had destroyed her health, that would also confirm a martyr's death, putting her on a par with ancient Roman martyrs like St Agatha, who was released from captivity shortly before she died. Putting aside the rumours that she was poisoned on Archbishop Abbot's instructions, the Jesuits unhesitatingly proclaimed another saint for England. All she had suffered since coming to London, and especially because 'her end was hastened by this affliction, maketh me of opinion', explained Blakfan, 'that she died as it were a martyr'.

Gondomar concurred. On the day of her death he informed Lerma that God had fulfilled her wish to die a martyr in England, and to support this Michael Walpole had promised to provide a short account of her life and death.[577] The ambassador treated her remains with all the solemnity due to someone who had already taken an honoured place in heaven. In addition to paying off debts of £40 that she had fastidiously listed for him on her deathbed, he paid about £15 to preserve her body in a wood-covered lead cask which was for the time being to be placed in a niche at the front of the embassy chapel. Her carpenter made the coffin and seeing her at peace was what made him finally decide to ask Michael Walpole to accept him into the Catholic faith.[578]

To modern eyes, Luisa's life seems one of abuse and unrelenting suffering. This is not how it appeared to her at her end, if, that is, we can rely on the accounts we have of her last moments. Her final thoughts are said to have turned to the debt of gratitude she felt she owed to Christ and to the Virgin. Looking back on what she achieved in a hostile and at times resentful world, there is little need to doubt that she felt she had been hallowed. What she is credited as saying seems entirely apt, mixing as they do the self-effacing with the theatrical. She died repeating the words, 'My Lord, My Lady', wanting to know how she could ever repay them for an extraordinary life.[579]

Afterword

LUISA remained controversial in death. Solemn services were hastily arranged to honour her at the English Colleges in Seville, where she was lauded in six languages, and in Valladolid, where her brother was able to be present.[580] He died a couple of years later, and it was claimed that, in his final moments, she miraculously appeared to him, telling him not to fear as she helped him make his final passage. Her sister-in-law took bittersweet consolation in the fact that she was fulfilling a prediction she had allegedly made to the effect that she would be her brother's helper in death as she would be able to do little for him during her lifetime.[581] The tributes paid to Luisa could not mask the fact that a sordid squabble was waiting to break out over who was entitled to control of her body. Rodrigo Calderón assumed it would go to his convent, and he offered to provide her companions with a home; the English priests at her foundation in Louvain felt she belonged with them, just as some of the capital's recusants wanted her mortal remains to stay in her adopted country. Ambassador Gondomar vaingloriously hatched a plan to accompany the body in triumph back to Spain, but that would depend on his being relieved of his posting to London, something which could not come too soon for him. The suspicion is that the ambassador used possession of her remains to persuade Calderón to expend whatever influence he had left to secure him a better diplomatic posting, possibly in France or Rome. Meanwhile, Luisa's friend of old, Mariana de San José, re-entered the stage, as prioress of the splendid new royal convent of the Incarnation in Madrid that had been endowed by King Philip III's late wife. Gondomar offered to give her convent a portrait that had been made of Luisa while her body lay in his chapel. Finally, well over eighteen months after her death in the late summer of 1615, her remains were taken in her lead coffin aboard a ship, felicitously named the *María Luisa*, by the ambassador's chaplain and the still-faithful Lemeteliel. As it sailed towards the Spanish coast a storm blew up causing water to enter, and stories were soon rife that Luisa was continuing her struggle not to return to Spain. In spite of this near-disaster her body was eventually received with full civic and religious honours in San Sebastian before being transported inland to Valladolid, where it was greeted, amongst others, by Michael Walpole and Magdalena de San Jerónimo. Her coffin was taken to Calderón's nunnery but she lay there only briefly, poignantly in the same niche as her brother. Doubtless egged on by Luisa's more steadfast friend, Mariana de San José, King Philip stepped in to claim her remains for the royal nunnery of the Incarnation. When it arrived in the convent next to his palace in Madrid, the casket was opened, only to discover that sea water had seeped in. The smell was unbearable but her body was uncorrupted—miraculously so, was the claim—and it was still supple and intact, until, that is, her companion from the calle de Toledo, Isabel de la Cruz, was given leave to cut off a finger.[582] The coffin was temporarily placed in the convent's reliquary room, where it was to await a final decision on her sanctity.

Ten years later, in 1625, the slow process began in Spain to have her officially recognized as a saint. The voluminous documentation was forwarded to Rome but her cause was not formally taken up by the papacy. This was probably only because of rules introduced by Pope Urban VIII and which culminated, a few years later in 1634, in a decree which made it hard for new saints to be recognized unless a cult had been established for over a hundred years, though exceptions could be made for those who were evidently martyrs. Never quite fitting in, Luisa had contrived to die at a time when the administrative procedures were in flux and she was caught between two sets of rules. The impetus for the recognition of her alleged sanctity quickly withered. She was fondly recalled by the crypto-Catholics from England who visited Madrid in 1623 during the future Charles I's foolish mission to secure a Spanish bride, but the numbers of people who actually knew her inevitably lessened with the passage of time.

As far as we can tell, some if not all of her companions carried on the religious life she had taught them but they were hardly the type of women who could head up a campaign on behalf of their mistress. At the start of the last century, a half-hearted attempt was made to revive her cause at Rome but early twentieth-century Spain had more pressing concerns, and with the outbreak of the Spanish Civil War the question of who were martyrs for the Catholic faith took on a wholly new and highly politicized meaning.

The simple truth why recollection of her faded is perhaps no more than this: once her body had been removed from her adopted city of London, and then denied a permanent place of rest in Spain, it was impractical for an enduring cult to spring up around her. Memory was doomed to fade, irrespective of the fact that she had done things which no other woman had previously done.

To this day her coffin lies uncomfortably to one side of the reliquary room in Madrid's Convent of the Incarnation, where she remains barely remembered and still awaiting burial, after 400 years.

Appendix: Three Poems

From Luisa's fifty extant poems these three have been chosen because they appear prominently in the text. Her poems are especially difficult to put into English because of her habit of repeating words and ideas, a habit which does not easily conform to our poetical tradition; the necessary agreement of gender in Spanish means that passages that are relatively clear and straightforward have to be laboured when translated into English. My debts to the renditions by Elizabeth Rhodes and Margaret A. Rees will be obvious. Even though I have failed to do justice to the poetry, I hope these poems will allow Luisa to speak directly to us.

No. 4
On a Harsh Journey (1593)[583]

> On a harsh journey
> seeing with mortal sight
> a shepherdess was walking,
> her soul injured by love.
> With tears in her eyes
> she explained to herself
> 'Silva, if you ran away
> and abandoned where you lived,
> you know full well that the cause would be
> that strange beauty
> you noticed one day
> in He who robbed you of your soul
> and shot you with an arrow
> dipped in His love
> which took you to the edge,
> and in that instant you found yourself
> resolved to leave everything behind
> that was not of Him.

And the delicate care
enclosed within your breast;
burnt on the inside
like a blazing fire.

And in search of your shepherd
you went out onto the mountain
because you were sure
He lived in its fastness

Alone with only the love
that alone went with you,
you set foot in the wild land
thick with undergrowth,

And when you were deep inside
that immense solitude,
you grew accustomed
to hearing the great roaring of
beasts, and going at them
with unfettered freedom,
the flower of your youth
faded and disfigured,
your seductive figure lost
in loving pursuit,
gone your glittering charms
that pleased the vanities.

And between you and your sweet Love
the law was established
with a thousand solemn promises
and giving Him your word
to be His for ever
and His slave you shall be
and your future will be
to see yourself chained by Him,
having done with difficulties
and ready for more.
And now just one single thought
makes you so dejected,
with heart and face
heavy with sorrow.'

    This is what Silva says
and with great sighs,
rewarded with a pain
that consumes and does for her,
which caused it to seem to her

that her Shepherd had forgotten her,
and that everything she has said
counts for nothing,
for nothing can attain
what she feels obliged to.
And trying to pick herself up,
this was her remedy:
to forget herself
and to hide away in the harshest
and most rocky mountain
in search of Him whom she loves,
completely absorbed in Him
and to Him utterly sacrificed,
Silva places her trust in the one
in whom all her hope lies.

No. 31. *Mother, when I was little*

*which tells of when and how Our Lord won her soul and stole
her will for Himself, with what followed thereafter*[584]

Mother, when I was little
Love seized me;
with chains of gold
He left me captive.
I thought He was not serious
and He laughed at me
and said, 'Silva,
I am your Lord'.
I did not feel His fire
although it burnt me;
now I am older,
I feel it perfectly well,
for the jest and the game
turned out to be in earnest!

And now I belong to no one
but to Love,
who with powerful bonds
bound me
and His love knots are
so exquisite,

that by binding they release
and well do I know it.
With his 'S'and His nail
I am marked,
tokens of glory
with which He adorned me.
He turned His eyes on me,
and from them leapt
living, burning fire
that burnt Silva;
the fire burnt Silva,
soul and heart.

And I imagine
that His eyes are bows,
because He fired
an arrow from them.

He shot it at my soul
and hit the target;
I was left so wounded
that I am dying of love,
and the pain I feel
is a grievous pain.

Ease it, my Mother,
no one can, no,
for its only remedy
is my Lord;
only the hand can cure
that made the wound.

No. 43. '*Sweet Manacles, Coveted Noose*'

on the effects of a most enflamed love and desires for martyrdom

Sweet manacles, coveted noose
trials now gone, victorious hour,
delightful and glorious infamy,
holocaust burnt in a thousand flames:

tell me, Love, why has this fortunate fate
gone so far away from me,
and the pleasing and pleasureful chain
changed into harsh freedom for me?

Has it been, by chance, due to having wished
that the wound of my pierced soul,
with pain strong and beyond measure
    be neither helped nor cured
and that, with the feeling augmented and alight,
life be unbound to pure love?

Note on Sources

Of the printed sources available for Luisa's life, there is a confusing overlap between various, sometimes partial, editions. Her letters are available in Spanish in the scrupulous edition of her *Epistolario* by her first modern biographer, Camilo Abad; references to each letter are indicated in the text by the letter 'L' followed by the number Abad assigned to it. There is a relatively accurate copy of this text available online in the Biblioteca Virtual Miguel de Cervantes; though the numbering is sometimes out of kilter with Abad's edition, it has the advantage of an online word-searching facility. Additionally, seven of her letters have been sensitively translated by Elizabeth Rhodes in *This Tight Embrace*, her outstanding introduction to and selection from Luisa's writings. The collection of drafts which forms her spiritual autobiography is for the most part available in modernized Spanish in Luisa's *Escritos Autobiográficos*, though large sections of it have been published by Elizabeth Rhodes with English translation and excellent notes, again in *This Tight Embrace*. Because of the rarity of *EA*, I have tried wherever possible to cite the Spanish text from *This Tight Embrace*, citing Rhodes's transcription as 'Life Story'; I have provided my own translation though it will be evident that I have been heavily influenced and assisted by Rhodes's meticulous renditions; where the passage concerned is not included in Rhodes, I have cited *EA*. Luisa's vows are also printed in Spanish in *EA* and in Abad's *Una misionera española* but I have once more preferred to refer the reader to *This Tight Embrace*, citing them in my text as 'Vows' but making my own translation. I have also made my own translation of the rules for her companions, but, as 'Rule', I cite the version provided by Elizabeth Rhodes in her indispensable *This Tight Embrace*. Referred to as 'Poetry' and followed by a number, Luisa's poems are numbered as in her *Epistolario*.

Manuscript Sources

In the 1620s as much evidence as possible was gathered to press Luisa's claims to be formally recognized by the papacy as ultimately worthy of sainthood. For technical reasons her case was not pursued to the end on this occasion, but a vast amount of material has survived in the Convento de la Encarnación in Madrid. Not least on account of its size, this material has yet to be catalogued and I consulted it from boxes, folders, and envelopes of a bewildering variety of descriptions. At the collection's heart is a bound, handwritten volume almost 700 folios long containing the statements mostly by people who knew her in London or Spain. Though many of the answers are repetitious as well as formulaic, there is much that is highly personal. I refer to this volume as 'Proceso', with the name of the witness and the folio number. The formal deposition of her great friend and companion in Madrid, Inés de la Asunción, is contained in that volume but she also provided a preliminary sketch of her life with Luisa which I have simply called, 'Inés's Draft Submission'. Luisa's autobiographical sketches are to be found in this collection, and, as we have seen, have been skilfully put together by Elizabeth Rhodes as Luisa's 'Life Story'. The best version of Michael Walpole's Spanish life (the 'Vita') is also to be found there, with a copy in the English College in Valladolid. (Incidentally, the Latin versions of her life are also to be found in Valladolid, in the English College, and the Biblioteca de Santa Cruz: the Latin lives, in particular, are worthy of further study.) Many original letters, addressed usually to Luisa, are also preserved in the collection from the Encarnación, notably those from the Smith family. Finally, two of her English companions have left vivid memoirs of Luisa's life in England, and one of these I cite as by the 'Unnamed Companion', whereas the other is headed 'poyntes of my lady Dona luisa noted of her life in england'.

Dating

I keep the date according to which country Luisa was living in at the time, which effectively means that in Spain I have used the new-style Gregorian Calendar whereas for England I have made all dates conform to the older Julian Calendar; however, when giving the date of a document in the notes I have retained the date which the author wrote down. It will be noted that by the Gregorian Calendar, to which she always adhered, she died in 1614 but by the Julian Calendar the year was 1613.

Abbreviations

ACSAV	Archivo del Colegio de San Albano, Valladolid
AGR	Archives Générales du Royaume
AGS	Archivo General de Simancas
APC 1613–1614	*Acts of the Privy Council of England: 1613–1614*, ed. J. R. Dasent (London, 1890–1964), vol. iii (1921)
ARSI	Archivum Romanum Societatis Iesu, Rome
BL	British Library
BNE	Biblioteca Nacional de España
CRS	*Catholic Record Society*
Docs. Inéditos	D. Sarmiento de Acuña, *Correspondencia Oficial de Don Diego Sarmiento de Acuña, conde de Gondomar*, ed. A. Ballesteros Beretta (*Documentos Inéditos para la Historia de España*, series ed. Jacobo Stuart Fitz-James y Falcó, duke of Alba), iii (Madrid, 1944)
EA	Luisa de Carvajal y Mendoza, *Escritos Autobiográficos*, introduction and notes by C. M. Abad (Barcelona, 1966)
Encarnación	Convento de la Encarnación, Madrid
Epistolario	Luisa de Carvajal y Mendoza, *Epistolario y Poesias: Colección formada por don Jesús Gonzalez Marañon*, ed. C. M. Abad (Biblioteca de Autores Españoles, 179; Madrid, 1965)
HMC Downshire	*Report on the Manuscripts of the Marquess of Downshire: Papers of Sir William Trumbull*, Historical Manuscripts Commission (75) (1924–), vols. iii (1938) and v (1940), ed. A. B. Hinds et al.
L	Letter, in Luisa de Carvajal y Mendoza, *Epistolario*
'Life Story'	'Life Story', in Rhodes, *This Tight Embrace*
Misionera	Camilo M. Abad, *Una misionera españoles en la Inglaterra del Siglo XVII: Doña Luisa de Carvajal y Mendoza (1566–1614)* (Santander, 1966)
Muñoz	Luis Muñoz, *Vida y virtudes de la Venerable virgen doña Luisa de Carvajal y Mendoza* (1631; re-edited Madrid, 1897)
ODNB	*Oxford Dictionary of National Biography*, ed. H. C. G. Matthew and B. Harrison (Oxford, 2004)
PRO	Public Record Office, now the National Archives, Kew

RBM	Real Biblioteca, Madrid
Rees, *Writings*	M. A. Rees, *The Writings of doña Luisa de Carajal y Mendoza, Catholic Missionary to James I's London* (Lewiston, NY and Lampeter, 2003)
'Rule'	'Rule', in Rhodes, *This Tight Embrace*
SRP	*Stuart Royal Proclamations*, ed. James F. Larkin and Paul L. Hughes (Oxford: Clarendon Press, 1973–)
This Tight Embrace	Elizabeth Rhodes, *This Tight Embrace: Luisa de Carvajal y Mendoza (1566–1614)* (Milwaukee, 2000)
'Vows'	'Vows', in Rhodes, *This Tight Embrace*
Walpole, 'Vida'	'La Vida de Doña Luysa de Carbajal y Mendoça', by Michael Walpole, original in the Encarnación with copy in ACSAV

Notes

1. The best account of Luisa's parentage is in M. N. Pinillos Iglesias, *Hilando Oro* (Madrid, 2001), to be supplemented by Helen Nader (ed.), *Power and Gender in Renaissance Spain: Eight Women of the Mendoza Family* (Urbana and Chicago, 2004), and A. Fernández Hoyos, *El obispo don Gutierre de Vargas, un madrileño del Renacimiento* (Caja de Madrid: Madrid, 1994).
2. 'Life Story', 50.
3. Baptismal record, *Misionera*, app. 1, p. 371.
4. 'Life Story', 46.
5. Rhodes, *This Tight Embrace*, p. x and *passim*; see also Christine M. Cloud's 2006 doctoral thesis from Ohio State University, 'Embodied Authority in the Spiritual Autobiographies of Four Early Modern Women from Spain and Mexico', of which ch. 5 is a thought-provoking study of Luisa's autobiographical writings worthy of publication. Unlike Rhodes, she views Luisa's memoirs as 'a reflection of... lived bodily experiences' (p. 270) just as much as an attempt to portray herself as worthy of martyrdom.
6. L108, p. 291.
7. ACSAV, MS series II, lib. 8, no. 27.
8. 'Life Story', 50.
9. Along with the marchioness of Ladrada, Chacón was a member of Queen Ana's household and had been in charge of the royal children since 1570; see J. M. Millán (ed.), *La Monarquía de Felipe II: La Casa del Rey* (2 vols., Madrid, 2005), ii. 691 and L. Cabrera de Cordova, *Historia de Felipe Segundo*, ed. J. M. Millán and C. J. de Carlos Morales (4 vols., Salamanca, 1998), ii. 602.
10. See Hugo Rahner, *St Ignatius Loyola: Letters to Women* (London, 1960), 56 ff.
11. Ruth Betegón Díez, *Isabel Clara Eugenia, Infanta de España y soberana de Flandes* (Barcelona, 2004), 33.
12. For her arrival in the convent, see 'Life Story', 52.
13. Abad, in *Epistolario*, 18, suggests this was the Infante Diego's entry to Toledo but he only became heir after Fernando's death in 1578, when Luisa had already left Madrid.
14. 'Life Story', 58, 60, and esp. 61 n. 25.
15. See *Misionera*, app. 11, at p. 396.
16. 'Life Story', 64.

17. L1, p. 98.
18. 'No temáis, hija mía, que nadie os quitará de conmigo, porque no lo consentiré yo', 'Life Story', 56.
19. See Camilo María Abad, 'Un embajador español en la corte de Maximiliano II Don Francisco Hurtado de Mendoza (1570–1576)', *Miscelánea Comillas*, 43 (1965), 23–94.
20. An international scandal broke out after Luisa's death when an Italian writer mentioned the Jewish ancestry of one of the early members of the Society, Diego de Laínez, whom the Almazán family had been proud to claim as a relative; see Albert A. Sicroff, *Les Controverses des statut de 'pureté de sang' en Espagne du XVe au XVIIe siècle* (Paris, 1960), 285, 190–5.
21. *EA*, p. 150.
22. The ambassador's *relazione* is contained in an appendix to Luis Cabrera de Córdoba, *Felipe Segundo rey de España* (Madrid, 1877), iv. 511.
23. 'Life Story', 60.
24. Ibid. 82.
25. Ibid. 62.
26. Ibid. 68 and editor's note, p. 69, no. 35. For further discussion of alternatives to a Teresian view of female spirituality, see below, Ch. 12.
27. F. Bouza, 'Docto y devoto: La biblioteca del Marqués de Almazán y Conde de Monteagudo (Madrid, 1591)', in A. Kohler and F. Edelmayer (eds.), *Hispania-Austria: Die Katholischen Könige, Maximilian I. und die Anfänge der Casa de Austria in Spanien* (2 vols., Vienna and Munich, 1993 and 1999), ii. 247–310, at 273 and 282 (no. 35).
28. ACSAV, ser. II, libro 8, no. 2.
29. Extensively quoted in Pinillo Iglesias, *Hilando Oro*, 47.
30. 'Life Story', 70.
31. *Misionera*, 28.
32. George E. Ganss (ed.), *The Constitutions of the Society of Jesus* (St Louis, 1970), 80.
33. 'ejercitarme en modo bien extraordinario y dificultoso a mi natural humor, teniendo yo entonces catorce años de edad', 'Life Story', 80, 82.
34. Ibid. 82. There are several drafts concerning these events and, though fundamentally they do not differ, they are sensitively analysed in Elizabeth Rhodes, 'Luisa de Carvajal's Counter-Reformation Journey to Selfhood (1566–1614)', *Renaissance Quarterly*, 51 (1998), 887–911.
35. 'Life Story', 102, 104.
36. Ibid. 104. It is intriguing that Cloud, 'Embodied Authority', 297, 303, implies that Ayllón was her principal tormentor, and even E. A. Lehfeldt, in her outstanding book *Religious Women in Golden Age Spain: The Permeable Cloister* (Aldershot, 2005), at p. 208, says that Luisa 'embarked on a course of extreme penance and bodily mortification under the direction of both

[her uncle] and her governess, Isabel de la Cruz', whereas Isabel was one of her later companions.

37. Inés, 'Proceso', fo. 272.
38. 'heçedian a todos los limites de la rrazón', ibid., fo. 267^v.
39. *Actas de las Córtes de Castilla*, vol. i (Madrid, 1877), pp. 355–6, capítulo XLI, and M. H. Sánchez Ortega, *La mujer y la sexualidad en el antiguo regimen* (Madrid 1991), 39, 42.
40. Isabel, 'Proceso', fo. 299.
41. 'Life Story', 86; Bouza, 'La biblioteca del Marqués', 248 and n. 7. In the King James Bible, this is Psalm 34: 12.
42. M. B. Salón, *Oración panegírica* . . . (Valencia, 1616), parágrafo II, pp. 25–6.
43. *EA*, 147.
44. *EA*, 167.
45. 'Life Story', 62, 64.
46. 'que no hablase con su tia ni con las primas ni una palabra', Isabel, 'Proceso', fo. 299.
47. 'Life Story', 74.
48. Cruz's seminal article, 'Chains of Desire: Luisa de Carvajal y Mendoza's Poetics of Penance', is to be found in L. Charnon-Deutsch (ed.), *Estudios sobre escritoras hispánicas en honor de Georgina Sabat-Rivers* (Madrid, 1992), 97–112, at 105. Despite our differences of opinion, Cruz's work remains fundamental to any study of Luisa (and to Golden Age literature in general), and I unreservedly acknowledge that I have learnt much from her deeply insightful writings. For further differences of opinion, see below, Ch. 6.
49. 'Poetry', no. 3; cf. Rees, *Writings*, 119, which is a sensitive introduction to Luisa's poetry.
50. L76, to Lorenzo da Ponte, London, 14 Mar. 1607.
51. Brad S. Gregory, *Salvation at Stake: Christian Martyrdom in Early Modern Europe* (Cambridge, Mass., 1999), 10 and *passim*.
52. For Inés's description, see *Misionera*, app. 3, pp. 409–10.
53. 'metida entre tanta mortificación', 'Life Story', 92 and Rhodes's important comments.
54. 'Life Story', 66. Cf. Cloud, 'Embodied authority', 275–9, who claims that Luisa downplayed her beauty.
55. Inés, 'Proceso', fo. 272.
56. Discussed in *Misionera*, 50.
57. 'Life Story', 70.
58. *EA*, 172.
59. *EA*, 189.
60. Jesús Escobar, *The Plaza Mayor and the Shaping of Baroque Madrid* (Cambridge, 2004), 32.
61. Salón, *Oración panegírica*, parágrafo VII, fos. 139–42, at p. 141.

62. *EA*, 213.
63. *EA*, 210.
64. 'a bibir bida mas estrecha que la que la solia tener asta allí', Inés, 'Proceso', fo. 274.
65. Bouza, 'La biblioteca del Marqués', 250.
66. *EA*, 211.
67. 'con toda la fuerça posible', Walpole's 'Vita', ch. 17, and Inés's Draft Submission, fo. 15.
68. Inés, 'Proceso', fo. 275.
69. *EA*, 211.
70. ACSAV, series II, libro 8, no. 84; no more had been paid by the time she made her will in Dec. 1604, for which see *Misionera*, app. 5, p. 384. For her cousin's involvement, see Inés's Draft Submission, fo. 17.
71. 'a tener menos no fuera nada', Inés, 'Proceso', fo. 275.
72. Inés, 'Proceso', fo. 278^v, and Isabel's version, at fo. 299^v–300.
73. *Misionera*, app. 13, pp. 409–10.
74. 'estilo mundano', 'Vows', 108.
75. 'la madre de las brujas', Isabel, 'Proceso', fo. 305.
76. 'un estrecho monasterio', Muñoz, 114.
77. 'las lagrimas de ambre', Inés, 'Proceso', fo. 274.
78. 'mas para dar deboción q[ue] para comellos', Inés's Draft Submission, fo. 18^v.
79. *EA*, L1, p. 99.
80. 'tengo algo q[ue] açer hermanas', Ines's Draft Submission, fo. 19.
81. 'si leia romançe o latin', Inés's Draft Submission, fo. 20.
82. Stephen Haliczer, *Between Exaltation and Infamy: Female Mystics in the Golden Age of Spain* (Oxford, 2002), 260, and below Ch. 8.
83. *This Tight Embrace*, 10; the italics are mine.
84. Pinillos Iglesias, *Hilando Oro*, 65.
85. For a brilliant and witty introduction, see F. W. Hodcroft, '¿A mí un él?: Observations on *vos* and *el/ella* as Forms of Address in Peninsular Spanish', *Journal of Hispanic Research*, 2 (1993–4), 1–16. Mr Hodcroft has consistently been an inspiration.
86. 'como si fuera una trompeta muy sonora', Mariana de San José, 'Proceso', fo. 602.
87. 'en extremo pobres'; Aldonza, 'Proceso', fo. 576^{r-v}; for a slightly different version, see Inés, 'Proceso', fo. 279.
88. 'remedio edificacion y prouecho', Inés, 'Draft Submission', fo. 20^v.
89. Luisa to Isabel de Velasco, L1, 15 Sept. 1598.
90. Inés, 'Proceso', fo. 275^v; see also Da Ponte, 'Proceso', fo. 32.
91. See Olwen Hufton, 'Altruism and Reciprocity: The Early Jesuits and their Female Patrons', *Renaissance Studies*, 15 (2001), 328–53.
92. 'Vows', 108.

93. 'p[ar]a confundir erejes y sus eRores' [*sic*], Isabel de la Cruz, 'Proceso', fo. 306.
94. 'Vows', 112.
95. ACSAV, serie II, libro 8, doc. 36.
96. Ceráin, 'Proceso', fo. 111.
97. Inés, 'Proceso', fo. 278^v.
98. 'la salio a reçibir en el sombrero en la mano', Aldonza, 'Proceso', fo. 582.
99. 'un hombre tan grave y seuero que jamas le vio inclinado a Beatas ni a devoçiones de las que se usan entre algunas mujeres, antes las aborrecía'. Ibid., fo. 581^v.
100. See Albert J. Loomie, *Guy Fawkes in Spain: The 'Spanish Treason' in Spanish Documents* (*BIHR*, special suppl. 9, Nov. 1971), 10–11, 14.
101. *Misionera*, app. 3, pp. 409–10.
102. 'que pareçia milagro poderse sustentar', Aldonza, 'Proceso', fo. 577.
103. 'con harta rrisa y para ella no fué poca y deçiame algunas veçes riendosse aya dos años que estoy hecha un oprobrio del mundo y ando debajo de los pies de los caballaos y criados de mis parientes, y aún quieren cassarse conmigo', Inés's Draft Submission, fo. 22^v.
104. 'Vows', 112.
105. Ibid. 116, and for dating, p. 117 n. 95.
106. 'de no ofenderte venialmente, ni en modo alguno por más leve y peque- ñamente que fuese, aunque me haya de costar la vida, hallando en mí mucha mayor estimación en no disgustarte, que en tener vida', *EA*, 303.
107. 'Vows', 118; the documents relating to the vow of perfection have two dates, 1595 and 1598; the later date may be correct, as it is unlikely she would have been allowed to take two solemn vows (obedience and greater perfection) in quick succession.
108. Muñoz, 144.
109. 'más a propósito para mi', Luisa to Isabel de Velasco, L1, p. 99; 'ir a tomar el habito', Inés's Draft Submission, fos. 29^v–30.
110. Mariana de San José, 'Proceso', fo. 588; L1, p. 99.
111. *EA*, 215, which overrides Espinosa's suggestion that Sigüenza was respon- sible, 'Proceso', fo. 203^v.
112. 'sin pareçer y aprouación de el dicho Prouincial', Espinosa, 'Proceso', fo. 203^v.
113. *Misionera*, app. 3, p. 375.
114. *EA*, 215–16. For a different view, see Cloud, 'Embodied Authority', who argues that 'noticeably missing [in her writings] is the usual medieval and early modern female religious writer's seemingly obsessive need to present the Eucharist as a way in which to unite the female body with God's humanity', p. 292.

115. 'no la tenían por mujer de rrebalaciones sino de gran birtud y luz', Inés, 'Proceso', fo. 278^v.

116. Isabel, 'Proceso', fo. 304.

117. The story is brilliantly told by Richard L. Kagan, *Lucrecia's Dreams: Politics and Prophesy in Sixteenth-Century Spain* (Berkeley and Los Angeles, 1990).

118. *EA*, 220.

119. *EA*, 236.

120. *EA*, 286.

121. *EA*, 297.

122. 'como por donaire le dijo comulge v.md.', Isabel, 'Proceso', fo. 298, and Inés, fo. 276^v.

123. For an introduction to the complex relationship between Teresa's imagery and earlier works which Luisa and her contemporaries also had access to, see J. F. Chorpenning, 'The Pleasance, Paradise, and Heaven: Renaissance Cosmology and Imagery in the *Castillo Interior*', *Forum for Modern Language Studies*, 27 (1991), 138–47.

124. *EA*, 216.

125. 'realmente, tiene estilo derramado, y prolijo; repite una cosa muchas veces, para darse a entender, y con palabras demasiadas', De La Puente, *Vida y Escritos del V. P. Luis de la Puente de la Compañia de Jesús (1554–1624)*, ed. C. M. Abad (Comillas, 1957), 436.

126. *Epistolario*, poem no. 32, pp. 442–3.

127. *EA*, p. 212.

128. Ibid. Poem no. 4; see *Tight Embrace*, pp. 132–41, and app. 1 for a translation and Luisa's commentary. As for the purpose of the commentaries, Rhodes shrewdly points out 'they indicate that she imagined a public for her writings, since she herself obviously had little need for such elaboration', *Tight Embrace*, 130.

129. 'de afectos de amor encendidísimo y deseos de martirio', *Tight Embrace*, 180–2.

130. Isabel, 'Proceso', fo. 297^r.

131. No. 31, *Tight Embrace*, pp. 172–4.

132. 'un nuevo modo de vivir', Inés's Draft Submission, fo. 14^v ['nuevo' is interlineated and refers to when Luisa first lived apart in her uncle's house]; 'y para los otros cossa que no entendían', fos. 21^v–22.

133. Ceráin, 'Proceso', fo. 103.

134. H. Schroeder (ed.), *The Canons and Decrees of the Council of Trent* (Rockford, 1978), 220; for *Circa pastoralis*, see L. Lux-Sterrit, *Redefining Female Religious Life: French Ursulines and English Ladies in Seventeenth-Century Catholicism* (Aldershot, 2005), 1, 28, and Lehfeldt's *Religious Women in Golden Age Spain*, 175, 179, 185–7. These two books provide an outstanding introduction to the question of an active life for religious women.

135. *EA*, 224–5.

136. Ceráin, 'Proceso', fo. 111[v].

137. L2, pp. 100–1; though the chronology of Magdalena's life is unclear, a good introduction can be found in Lehfeldt, *Religious Women in Golden Age Spain*, 29–30, 208–11.

138. L1, pp. 97–8.

139. L2, p. 102.

140. L4, p. 107.

141. L5, p. 108.

142. L6, pp. 109–10.

143. See Magdalena Sánchez, *The Empress, the Queen, and the Nun: Women and Power at the Court of Philip III of Spain* (London and Baltimore, 1998).

144. L7, p. 112.

145. 'unos Místicos trampantojos', Ceráin, 'Proceso', fo. 114[v].

146. L8, p. 114.

147. Ceráin, 'Proceso', fos. 115[r–v].

148. L3, p. 104.

149. L10, p. 118.

150. L15, p. 129.

151. L21, pp. 139–40.

152. ACSAV, serie II, lib. 8, nos. 97 and 100 (misdated to the following year, in *Misionera*, 156).

153. Canonized in 1970; for what is known of Line's life, see *ODNB*.

154. Taken from St Matthew's Gospel and quoted in Jenny Wormald, 'Gunpowder, Treason, and Scots', *Journal of British Studies*, 24 (1985), 141–68, at 147.

155. Mendoza to Philip II, 4 Dec. 1581, *Colección de Documentos Inéditos para la Historia de España*, vol. 92, pp. 200–1 (Madrid, 1888); cf. Gregory, *Salvation at Stake*, 19–20.

156. Statement contained in a series of questions put to witnesses for her canonization; the list was printed as *Interrogatorio de pregvntas . . .* by Iuan de Doyega de Mendieta (of which a copy survives in the BNE, VE 184/31 and multiple copies in the Encarnación); also Cisneros, 'Proceso', fo. 232.

157. Inés, 'Proceso', fo. 268[r]. For Creswell's *Historia de la vida y martirio que padesció este año 1595 el P. Henrico Valpolo* (Madrid, 1596), see BNE R/39081, at fo. 1[r].

158. 'sabiendo auia venido algun p[adr]e de la conpañia o saçerdote de alguno de los colegios i[n]gleses luego su confesor se los llebaua como sabia era cosa de q[ue] gustaba y estaba largos Ratos hablando en las cosas de ingalaterra y en las grandes persecuçiones q[ue] los catolicos padeçian y diçe esta testigo q[ue] quantas mas crueldades y Rigores la contaban pareçe era echar leña Al fuego de su coraçon', Isabel, 'Proceso', fo. 300.

159. L9, p. 117.
160. Rhodes, 'Vows', p. 118.
161. L11, p. 123; for the dangers encountered by the nuns, see Anne Hardman, *Life of the Venerable Anne of Jesus, Companion of St. Teresa of Avila, by a sister of Notre Dame de Namur* (London, 1932), 162–4.
162. Anne J. Cruz, 'Willing Desire: Luisa de Carvajal y Mendoza and Female Subjectivity', in Helen Nader (ed.), *Power and Gender in Renaissance Spain: Eight Women of the Mendoza Family* (Urbana, 2004), 177–93, at 178. As I have stated earlier, I am profoundly indebted to Professor Cruz's work even if we do not always concur.
163. 'sus "deseos de martirio" no surgieron cuando joven, ni fue Inglaterra su destino inicial', Anne J. Cruz, 'Luisa de Carvajal y Mendoza y su conexión jesuita', in *La mujer y su representación en las literaturas hispánicas*, being vol. ii of *Actas Irvine-92*, XI Congreso of the International Association of Hispanists (5 vols., Irvine, 1994), ed. Juan Villegas Morales, 97–104, at 97. For a rebuttal of the suggestion that she earlier preferred the Netherlands to England, see nn. 158 and 177.
164. Cruz, 'Willing Desire', 185. The italics are mine.
165. 'Por obvias razones', Cruz, 'Luisa de Carvajal y Mendoza y su conexión jesuita', 99–100.
166. Cruz, 'Willing Desire', 177, also 'Luisa de Carvajal y Mendoza y su conexión jesuita', 97.
167. *EA*, 189.
168. *This Tight Embrace*, 68. There is confusion about precisely when Caracena became a marquess, but for discussion of this point, I am indebted to Ciaran O'Scea, the genealogist Jesús Chacón, Ben Ehlers, and Rodrigo de Calderón's biographer, Santiago Martínez Hernández.
169. *This Tight Embrace*, 33.
170. The autobiographical memoirs in *EA* dealing with her time in the Low Countries are, in fact, extracts from conventional letters dated as from London; as far as I am aware, the 'latest' autobiographical sketch in *EA* concerns her illness of 1604–5, and though this sketch was very likely written in England linguistic similarities suggest it may have been related to letters composed in 1611 which recalled how sick she had been in Valladolid.
171. *EA*, 190.
172. Ibid.
173. Probably his *Sinner's Guide* of 1556, Ceráin, 'Proceso', fo. 105.
174. 'el cuerpo no podía todas veces seguir el paso del ánimo', Luisa to Creswell, L62, p. 186.
175. Duchess of Medina de Rioseco, 'Proceso', fo. 64^v.

176. L11, p. 121; Juan de Ceráin also heard the group had connections with Queen Elizabeth, though his recollection was that they stayed with Luisa for much longer, 'Proceso', fo. 109.

177. 'que la vecindad de Inglaterra y la vivienda de Flanders son más para envidiar que para evitar', 6 Dec. 1600, L4, p. 105.

178. L14, p. 127.

179. 'A relation of the solemnitie made in Spaine in the citie of Valiadolid the seauenth of September a 1600 for the receiuing of an Image of our Blessed Ladye defaced by the English heretikes...', fos. 51^v, 62^v. I am grateful to the Rector of the English College for permission to quote from this and other manuscripts.

180. L9, p. 116; L16, p. 132.

181. Stephen Haliczer said that almost half of the *c.*45 female mystics he studied for Golden Age Spain expressed a desire for martyrdom, but he added that this 'remained a mere fantasy for most women. The only woman to escape from these restrictions was the remarkable Luisa de Carvajal y Mendoza, who pursued martyrdom by undertaking open missionary work in England', *Between Exaltation and Infamy*, 260. Isabelle Poutrin, whose work includes biographical sketches of 113 religious women, refers to Luisa's journey as 'une entreprise exceptionnelle', *Le Voile et la Plume: Autobiographie et sainteté féminine dans l'Espagne moderne* (Madrid, 1995) 297. Merry E. Wiesner-Hanks's outstanding introduction to the period, *Early Modern Europe, 1450–1789* (Cambridge, 2006), says that 'requests to serve as missionaries were almost always denied' with Luisa being her sole example (p. 175). The subject of who and what constitute female missionaries needs further investigation, but a thought-provoking start is to be found in N. Z. Davies, *Women on the Margins: Three Seventeenth-Century Lives* (London, 1995), esp. 106–9 for references to seventeenth-century Canada. For a superb and readable overview of the present state of knowledge regarding institutional missionary work (and the history of early-modern female monasticism generally), see S. Evangelisti, *Nuns: A History of Convent Life 1450–1700* (Oxford, 2007), ch. 6, 'Expansion: Nuns across the Globe', 175–99.

182. Lewis Owen, in his *The State of the English Colledges in Forraine Parts London 1626* (*The English Experience: Its record in early printed books published in facsimile*, 19; Amsterdam, 1968), 64–5.

183. L16, p. 131.

184. Walpole, 'Vida', fos. 50^r–51.

185. 16 Nov. 1603, L20, p. 138.

186. Walpole 'Vida', fo. 51; for Abad's argument in favour of Michael Walpole's protagonism, see *Misionera*, 157.

187. De la Puente, *Obras escogidas del V. P. Luis de la Puente*, ed. C. M. Abad (Biblioteca de Autores Españoles, III; Madrid, 1958), Letter 23.

188. *The Spiritual Exercises of Saint Ignatius*, ed. and trans. A. Mottola (New York, 1964), 86.

189. 'Proceso', fos. 166^v, 181; 376^v.

190. Inés, 'Proceso', fo. 288^v.

191. See Javier Burrieza Sánchez, *Los milagros de la Corte: Marina de Escobar y Luisa de Carvajal en la Historia de Valladolid* (Valladolid, 2002) for a splendid evocation of Valladolid's religious life during its years as Philip III's capital.

192. Inés, 'Proceso', fo. 275^v.

193. 'aunque el no le diera por consejo que hiziera la mission no se atrebia a impedirsela', Espinosa, 'Proceso', fo. 207^v.

194. *This Tight Embrace*, 15–16, where it is argued 'the decision to go to England was Carvajal's', with the suggestion that Luisa consulted males only as a precautionary measure and her departure was prepared 'without telling anyone what she was planning to do because of the need to conceal the entire trip'.

195. See de la Puente, *Vida y Escritos*, 478; for her life, see Poutrin, *Le Voile et la Plume*.

196. *EA*, L22, p. 140; cf. Inés's Draft Submission, fo. 32.

197. Muñoz, 274; for Inés's version, see 'Proceso, fo. 283.

198. 'sobrenatural', Espinosa, 'Proceso', fo. 211.

199. *EA*, 234.

200. L27, pp. 143–4.

201. 'non difficilius esset, quam periculosius', 'Vida Latina', ACSAV, libro 2089, p. 141, a phrase not found in the Spanish life; ascribed to Geraldus Orano, the copy of this version of her life in the Biblioteca de Santa Cruz in Valladolid (MS 293) I believe to be a copy of the MS in ACSAV.

202. 'si era possible sentir otro dolor en esta vida que este', Da Ponte, 'Proceso', fo. 29^v.

203. 'que hera Juntamente su perior', Inés, 'Proceso', fo. 282^v.

204. The will and financial instructions are to be found in *Misionera*, apps. 5 and 6, pp. 381–6; 387–9.

205. Da Ponte, 'Proceso', fo. 30 and ACSAV, ser. ii, libro 8, fo. 80.

206. In 1625, it was estimated that 100 ducats a year would support one nun, almost double the figure a century earlier. In 1573 the Infanta Juana's bequest of an endowment income of 2,000 ducats a year to the future Imperial College was regarded as exceptional, Olwen Hufton, 'Altruism and Reciprocity: The Early Jesuits and their Female Patrons', *Renaissance Studies*, 15 (2001), 328–53, at 337.

207. Aldonza, 'Proceso', fo. 577.

208. L28, p. 144.

209. L30, p. 147.

210. 'el pecho bien ruin de catarro', *EA*, 225.

211. He was in Belgium at the beginning of 1604 or 1605 (the year is uncertain). In Jan. 1605 Luisa indicated when still in Valladolid that Richard Walpole was there but that Michael had not written to her, L29, p. 146.

212. BL, Cottonian MS Caligula E XI(i), at fo. 119^r, contained in a letter from Ambassador Sir Thomas Parry, dated Paris, 7 Dec. 1604 OS.

213. 'sexus, sed et lingua', fo. 48^r, Blakfan's Annals, ACSAV. Blakfan's account is confused chronologically, added to which he claims that the priest refused to wait for Luisa at San Sebastian. The full version of his Annals is being published by the English College and I have generously been shown an early version by Fr. Peter Harris, archivist of the English College.

214. Lewis Owen, in his *The State of the English Colledges in Forraine Parts London 1626 (The English Experience: Its record in early printed books published in facsimile*, 19; Amsterdam, 1968), 63–5, is reliable for mood rather than details (he calls her a widow, for instance), and though he highlights Walpole's role he does say that the name of the priest travelling with her was Evans.

215. Walpole, 'Vida', fos. 51–2.

216. 'la jornada mas estraordinaria que jamas se ha visto en una muger', 'Proceso', fo. 590^v.

217. Walpole, 'Vida', fo. 56.

218. Richard Walpole to Henry Garnet, 12 Apr. 1599, ACSAV, serie II, leg. I.

219. Cornwallis to Salisbury, Valladolid, 15 Sept. 1605, SP9/213, p. 120.

220. 'si a reuera Catholicis, politicis tamen, et qui ad fictos illos'. I intend to publish this letter with critical apparatus.

221. 'in praesentis calamitatis'.

222. AGS, E2512/63, also, Loomie, *Guy Fawkes in Spain*, 14–15; for Stanley and Creswell, see AGS, E2513 (unfoliated).

223. Creswell to James, 24 June 1605, AGS, E2512/48; to Philip, 10 July 1605, E624/205. For James and Henri, see Redworth, *The Prince and the Infanta: The Cultural Politics of the Spanish Match* (London, 2003), *passim*.

224. Taken from A. J. Loomie, *Spain and the Jacobean Catholics*, i. *1603–1612* (Catholic Record, no. 64, 1973), 66.

225. A. J. Loomie, *The Spanish Elizabethans: The English Exiles at the Court of Phillip II* (New York, 1963), 206–10.

226. L32. No names, of course, were written down.

227. *Life of the Venerable Anne of Jesus, Companion of St. Teresa of Avila, by a sister of Notre Dame de Namur* (London, 1932), 162–4.

228. ACSAV, ser. II, libro 8, doc. 102; in 1606, she recalled that from Spain to Flanders the journey would cost a party of seven 350 *reales*, little over half what she had in *escudos*, EA, L72, p. 201.

229. *EA*, 226.

230. L72, p. 201.

231. 'Cómo estáis?', ibid.; *Obras completas de la Beata Ana de San Bartolome*, ed. Julián Urkiza (Monumenta Historica Carmeli Teresiani; Rome, 1981), i. 457, autobiografía B.

232. 'que la conozco y quiero muy bien', *EA*, 226.

233. L9, p. 117.

234. Cited in Loomie, *Guy Fawkes in Spain*, p. 10.

235. 'porque me iba deteniendo mañosamente el Padre M[iguel] V[alpolo], hasta escribir a Roma', *EA*, 226–7. The importance of St Omer for English Catholic women is little understood but see M. C. E. Chambers, *The Life of Mary Ward (1585–1645)*, 2 vols. (London, 1882), i. 109 ff.

236. For his presence in Naples in Apr. 1605, see ARSI, Rome, MS Anglia 38 ii, fo. 175.

237. Foley, *Records of the English Province of the Society of Jesus* (7 vols., London, 1875–83), ii. 628. Most accounts do not distinguish between the two legs of her journey, i.e. to the Low Countries and then to England. I am grateful to Tom McCoog SJ for informing me of Blakfan's whereabouts and for Garnet's refusal. More generally Father McCoog has consistently been most generous with his time and expertise.

238. 'abrevió mi jornada', *EA*, 227.

239. L99, p. 269.

240. L76, p. 211.

241. *EA*, 227; *Misionera*, p. 178.

242. L37, p. 155.

243. L46, pp. 165–6.

244. *EA*, 228.

245. Lady Georgiana Fullerton's conjecture that the house was at Scotney Castle or Lady Montague's estate near Hastings does not match Garnet's movements or the stated proximity to London, *The Life of Luisa de Carvajal* (London, 1881), 177.

246. For Charles de Ligny's memoir, and Byrd's musical relationship with the Garnet, see Philip Brett, *The Byrd Edition*, vol. v/a, (London, 1989), p. ix. I am grateful to Dr John Milson of Christ Church, Oxford, for sharing his knowledge of the composer's life with me.

247. A. G. Petti, 'Richard Verstegan and Catholic Martyrologies of the Later Elizabethan Period', *Recusant History*, 5 (1959–60), 64–90.

248. 'mesoncillo pobre', *EA*, 228. A riverlet ran through Enfield Chase towards London, and though Ann Vaux and Henry Garnet spent time at Erith in 1605, it is unlikely that the river referred to was the Thames Estuary; see G. Anstruther, *Vaux of Harrowden, a Recusant Family* (Newport, Mon., 1953), 355.

249. 'delicada, enferma, y sin fuerças corporales y q[ue] no sabia la lengua de la tierra', from loose sheet in the Encarnación, being basis for Muñoz, 279.

250. L68, p. 192. She left England in early 1606 for the Low Countries, and Luisa recommended her to friends there.

251. L37, pp. 154–5; they mistook her 'por de su nación', i.e. for an English-woman, *pace This Tight Embrace*, 18.

252. See Nigel Goose and Lien Luu (eds.), *Immigrants in Tudor and Early Stuart England* (Brighton, 2005), esp. ch. 3 by Luu, 'Natural-born Versus Stranger-born Subjects: Aliens and their Status in Elizabethan London', 57–75.

253. King James VI and I, *Political Writings*, ed. J. Sommerville (Cambridge, 1994), 147.

254. For the hardening attitude to English Catholics, see M. Questier, *Catholicism and Community in Early Modern England: Politics, Aristocratic Patronage and Religion, c.1550–1640* (Cambridge, 2006), esp. 271–2.

255. Cited in P. Caraman, *Henry Garnet 1555–1606, and the Gunpowder Plot* (London, 1964), 325.

256. 'que los catholicos deste Reyno no heran perseguidos, sino q[ue] biuian sin vexaçiones', Zuñiga to Philip III, AGS, E2584–69, at fo. b.

257. Anstruther, *Vaux of Harrowden*, 266.

258. L37, p. 153.

259. *EA*, 228.

260. L99, pp. 269–70.

261. Luis Tobío Fernández, *Gondomar y Su Triunfo sobre Raleigh* (Santiago de Compostela, 1974), 259–60. The house was later known as Bridgewater House. Probably due to a misreading contained in *Recusant History*, 8 (1965–6), 211 n. 2, Loomie stated that the embassy was in Seething Lane, on the other side of the city, *Spain and the Jacobean Catholics*, 122.

262. 'Proceso', fos. 34, 84, 442^{v}.

263. AGS, E2512–49, fo. b. She later joined the Irish exiles in La Coruña in Galicia.

264. Joan de San Agustín, 'Proceso', fo. 44$^{\text{r–v}}$.

265. 'recibo *trasordinario* desahogo', L36, p. 152.

266. L38, p. 155.

267. 'extraña fuerza', L49, p. 171.

268. L137, p. 154.

269. Isabel de la Cruz, 'Proceso', fo. 309^{v}.

270. L40 and L41.

271. L74, p. 207 (Mar. 1607).

272. L37, p. 154; *SRP*, i. no. 62 (15 Jan. 1606).

273. ARSI, MS Anglia 37, fo. 111^{v}.

274. L98, p. 267.

275. L61, p. 184; see also below, p. 157.

276. L40, p. 160.

277. *EA*, 231.

278. L61, p. 184.

279. L72, p. 203.

280. L78, p. 217.

281. John Minsheu, *A dictionarie in Spanish and English, first published into the English tongue by Ric. Perciuale Gent. Now enlarged and amplified* . . . (London, 1599); Lewis Owen, *The Key of the Spanish Tongue* (London, 1605).

282. L130, p. 331.

283. Simon de Ariza, 'Proceso', fo. 399ᵛ.

284. L94, p. 246.

285. 'exercitando el oficio propio de varones', *Interrogatorio*, no. 40.

286. L51, p. 174.

287. L50, p. 172.

288. 'y antes de serlo, se arrepintió de lo hecho', L39, p. 158. She may have been referring to Humphrey Littleton, who was executed in Apr. 1606.

289. L46, p. 164.

290. L47, p. 168.

291. L51, pp. 173, 174.

292. Gregory, *Salvation at Stake*, 299, 309–10.

293. L69, p. 193.

294. L87, p. 229.

295. L92, p. 239; Philip Caraman, *John Gerard, The Autobiography of an Elizabethan* (London, 1951), 276.

296. King James, *Political Writings*, 152.

297. L39, p. 158.

298. L56, L60, L65.

299. L40, p. 159.

300. L68, p. 192.

301. L78, p. 215.

302. Brough, 'Proceso', fo. 391ᵛ.

303. L73, p. 205.

304. L76, p. 213.

305. L124, p. 322.

306. L67, p. 191.

307. L103, p. 282.

308. L110, p. 293.

309. L102, p. 282.

310. L71, p. 198.

311. Brough, 'Proceso', fo. 391ᵛ. His name appears elsewhere as 'Lemeteyer'.

312. 4,000 *reales*, which must be an annual calculation. L78, p. 215.

313. L130, p. 330.

314. L78, p. 215.
315. A shilling being 5 new pence, and half a crown (2.5 shillings) 12.5 new pence, L78, pp. 215–16.
316. L93, p. 240.
317. L124, pp. 320–1.
318. L110, p. 293 and L124, p. 322.
319. L69, p. 194.
320. L71, p. 197; *pace Misionera*, p. 224 and *This Tight Embrace*, 233, 241, 245, 249, I suggest that in letters which went to Flanders her references to a merchant called 'Otaviano' are to Father Baldwin.
321. L85, p. 226.
322. L88, p. 230.
323. Zúñiga, 'Proceso', fo. 84^v; L78, p. 215. *Pace This Tight Embrace*, 20, it had become a monthly payment by 1610, Velasco to Philip, 9.x.10, AGS, E2587, no. 138, but cf. L123, p. 318; also below, Ch. 17.
324. L53 and L60, p. 183.
325. L91, p. 235.
326. L86, p. 228.
327. L91, p. 235.
328. L160, p. 383.
329. L100, p. 276 and L103, p. 284.
330. 'Parece gran India Inglaterra, de espiritu', L152, p. 370; and L175, p. 411.
331. L46, p. 166 and L40, p. 160.
332. For the role of prisons in Catholic life, see Lisa McClain's useful overview, *Lest We Be Damned: Practical Innovation and Lived Experience among Catholics in Protestant England, 1559–1642* (London, 2004), 144–7.
333. L81, p. 222.
334. L69, p. 193.
335. L54, p. 177.
336. L46, p. 164.
337. L111, p. 295.
338. King James, *Political Writings*, 86–8, 116.
339. Loomie, *Spain and the Jacobean Catholics*, no. 24; see also Drury's own account, translated into French, written the night before his execution, in Archives du Royaume, Brussels, Papiers de l'État et de l'Audience MS 365, fos. 185–6; it is followed, fos. 186–7^v, by an account of his execution. Drury's memoir dramatically turns into the present tense when his account ends, early on the evening of the 24th; for obvious reasons of security, neither Luisa nor his other visitors are mentioned. A hostile but very full account of his agonizing over the oath is to be found in W. Oldys and T. Park (eds.), *The Harleian Miscellany: A Collection of Scarce, Curious, and*

Entertaining Pamphlets and Tracts, as well in Manuscript as in Print, vol. iii (1809), 38–47.

340. Dom Hugh Bowler (ed.), *London Sessions Records 1605–1685* (Catholic Record Society, no. 34, 1934), pp. 24–5 and app. B, p. 381.

341. Richard Blunt, 28 Jan. 1607, ARSI MS Anglia 37, fo. 109.

342. L78, p. 216; see also Muñoz, p. 401.

343. *EA*, L124, p. 322.

344. Richard Blunt, Apr. 1607, MS Anglia 37, ARSI, fo. 107^v.

345. 30 Apr. 1607 NS AGS, E2586–24, fo. a.

346. AGR, Papiers d'État et de l'Audience, MS 365, fo. 186$^{r–v}$.

347. Muñoz, p. 401; Drury's mother, Anne Boorman, therefore considerably outlived her husband, who died in 1591, *q.v.* 'Robert Drury, 1567–1607' in *ODNB*.

348. L74, p. 206.

349. L88, p. 230.

350. Questier, *Catholicism and Community in Early Modern England*, 322, 336–7, 243–4 takes apart the tensions between Gage and his relatives.

351. L81 and 88; see also *CRS*, 34, pp. 35–6.

352. L14, p. 127; L41, p. 161; L46, p. 165.

353. L59, p. 182; L82, p. 222.

354. L124, p. 323.

355. Loomie, *Spain and the Jacobean Catholics*, nos. 25 and 36.

356. L161, p. 383.

357. AGS, MS E2513, s.f., Council of State to Zúñiga, 17 Jan. 1608.

358. Their names are given as Juana, Fe, Susanna, *EA*, L98, pp. 267–8.

359. *APC 1613–1614*, pp. 519–20.

360. 'Rule', 198–219, also Abad, *Misionera*, app. 12, pp. 398–407. The first part of the Rule alludes to the second part, and although they assigned separate chapters in Walpole's life, they were conceived as a single text being written on identical paper.

361. Encarnación, 'Unnamed Companion'.

362. Julián de Ávila, cited in *Introducción a la lectura de Santa Teresa*, ed. Alberto Barrientos (2nd edn., Madrid, 2002), 595. This work is indispensable for understanding the complicated textual tradition of her writings. For the *Constitutions*, see E. Allison Peers, *The Complete Works of St Teresa of Jesus*, 3 vols. in one (London, 1978).

363. The requirement to say matins in the middle of the night was moderated in the Middle Ages.

364. Cf. 'Rule', 96, 218. She also advocated her childhood practice of wearing a hair shirt once a week and three times a week in Lent. For the pre-Teresian constitutions, see T. Álvarez (ed.), *Constituciones de las Carmelitas Descalzas 1562–1607* (*Monumenta Historica Carmeli Teresiani*, vol. 16; Rome 1995), p. 47 n.

365. 'Rule', 214.
366. In de la Puente, *Obras*, but also in Luisa's *Epistolario*, 453–4, at 454.
367. See the superb article by Alison Weber, 'Spiritual Administration: Gender and Discernment in the Carmelite Reform', *Sixteenth Century Journal*, 31 (2000), 123–146, at 123.
368. 'Proceso', fos. 546 and 548ᵛ, being a letter from Cardinal de Trejo, dated Rome 1627, where he talks of his veneration for Luisa and his conversations with María de la Guardia, then living in Rome. Abad mistakenly denies that the two women knew each other (*Misionera*, 320). In addition to Chamber's biography of Ward, the best modern life is H. Peters, *Mary Ward: A World in Contemplation*, trans. H. Butterworth (Leominster, 1994) and supplemented by Lux-Sterrit, *Redefining Female Religious Life*, though neither refer to the cardinal's evidence. For the cardinal's relationship with Ward, see M. Emmanuel Orchard (ed.), *Till God Will: Mary Ward through her writings* (London, 1985), 85 n. 13. At the time of Luisa's final arrest and possible expulsion, there was a baseless rumour she might head up Mary Ward's house for English gentlewomen in St Omer, William Trumbull to George Abbot, *HMC Downshire*, iv. 260.
369. L103, p. 284.
370. 'a M.is francis ynbie ayer una disciplina grosera de mi propria hechura / aora ymbio otras tres la mas grossera para Anna, la de hilo blanco para M.is Ann[e crossed out]. la de cuerdas para Juana, para Helena ymbiere la primera que hiziere', unsorted and undated letter, Blakfan to Luisa, Proceso. A sister of [H]Elena Dutton was living with Luisa in Oct. 1607, L88, p. 231. In L113, p. 300 there is a reference to the fact that only two priests support the 'reglas y medidas de perfeción que yo quiero' (4 June 1610).
371. E. Rhodes, 'Join the Jesuits, See the World: Early Modern Women in Spain and the Society of Jesus', in John W. O'Malley et al. (eds.), *The Jesuits II: Cultures, Sciences, and the Arts 1540–1773* (Toronto, 2006), 33–49, at 45.
372. 'los soldados doncellas', L152, p. 371; for Luisa's reference to nuns as soldiers, see Elena Levy-Navarro, 'The Religious Warrior: Luisa de Carvajal y Mendoza's Correspondence with Rodrigo de Calderón', in Jane Couchman and Ann Crabb (eds.), *Women's Letters Across Europe, 1400–1700: Form and Persuasion* (Aldershot, 2005), 263–73.
373. *Misionera*, app. 11, pp. 392–7, at 396, 392.
374. ARSI, Anglia 37, fo. 111ᵛ.
375. Proceso, 'Isabel', fo. 309ᵛ, and BNE, MS 18434, fo. 1ʳ⁻ᵛ.
376. Cornwallis to Salisbury, 18 June 1605, PRO, SP94/11ii, fos. 136–7 (with billet).

377. Cornwallis to Privy Council, 8 Sept. 1605, PRO, SP94/12, fos. 139–142^v.

378. PRO SP94/11ii, fos. 186–7.

379. The passage continues, 'but she died in bed in London at the respectable age of 52', Rhodes, 'Join the Jesuits, See the World', 33–49, at 45; Luisa died on her forty-eighth birthday,

380. L87, p. 231. Only a fraction of Luisa's books are mentioned here; for a full list, see the forthcoming edition of her letters.

381. 'gustan mucho dellos acá algunos que entienden la lengua', L130, p. 330.

382. L131, p. 333.

383. L130, p. 330; see Kathleen T. Spinnenweber's convincing arguments in 'The 1611 English Translation of St. Teresa's Autobiography: A Possible Carmelite-Jesuit Collaboration', *SKASE Journal of Translation and Interpretation* [online], 2 (2007), 1–12.

384. L131, p. 333.

385. See G. Redworth, 'Books Not to be Sold: The Cost of Printing in the Golden Age', *Bulletin of the Society for Renaissance Studies*, 23 (2005), 17–26, at 23.

386. L104, p. 286.

387. L113, p. 298.

388. L115, p. 304.

389. L111, p. 295; L90, p. 234.

390. L83, p. 225.

391. L130, p. 330.

392. Simón de Ariza, 'Proceso', fo. 399^v.

393. L130, pp. 330–1.

394. L143, p. 354.

395. L155, p. 374.

396. Encarnación, 'Copia de dos casos q[ue] escriuio doña luysa de carauajal en . . . al s[eñor] prov[eed]or de sev[ill]a', being taken from a lost letter dated 14 Sept. 1610.

397. L111, p. 295.

398. Muñoz, 361; see also, 'Proceso', Brough, fo. 387^v also L94, pp. 249–50.

399. 'Proceso', Brough, fos. 378–95^v, and also fo. 416^v.

400. L124, p. 322.

401. L99, p. 270; Elizabeth Rhodes puts it like this: in England Luisa 'suspended her performance of the submissive, self-effacing holy woman to greatly expand her repertoire of personae', *This Tight Embrace*, p. ix.

402. L124, p. 322.

403. For Parsons, see T. M. McCoog, *Robert Parsons and Claudio Acquaviva: Correspondence* (*Archivum Historicum Societatis Iesu*, 68; 1999), 79–182, at 95.

404. Encarnación, 'Unnamed Companion', which briefly describes Luisa's activities in London; for Cheapside, see John Bennell, 'Shop and Office

in Medieval and Tudor London', *London and Middlesex Archaeological Society*, 40 (1989), 189–206. I am grateful to Hazel Forsythe of the Museum of London for this and many other references.

405. L94, p. 246.

406. Encarnación, 'Unnamed Companion'.

407. L95 p. 251.

408. L98, p. 264.

409. Encarnación, 'Unnamed Companion'.

410. See *This Tight Embrace*, 271 n. 10. He had been knighted in 1603, A. B. Beaven, *The Aldermen of the City of London* (2 vols., London, 1908 and 1913), i. 208, 240.

411. L94, p. 247.

412. F. North to Holtby, 8 June 1608, ARSI, MS Anglia 37, fo. 129ᵛ.

413. L94, p. 248.

414. Beaven, *Aldermen of the City of London*; F. J. Froom, *A Site in Poultry* (London, 1950), 17.

415. L95, p. 255.

416. L94, p. 247.

417. Zúñiga to Philip III, July 1608 in Loomie, *Spain and the Jacobean Catholics*, nos. 34 and 35.

418. L124, p. 321.

419. L98, p. 266; for fears about Ireland, see the newsletter of 16 May 1608 in AGS, E2586/104.

420. See Juan de Ribera's letter, in Ch. 14.

421. L94, p. 245.

422. L96, pp. 2587–8.

423. For the role of saints, see William Christian, *Local Religion in Sixteenth Century Spain* (Princeton, 1981), esp. 60, 65.

424. 'mas galano que modesto', Múñoz, 350.

425. L96, p. 261.

426. 28 June 1608 (OS), in H. Foley, *Records of the English Province of the Society of Jesus* (7 vols., London, 1875–83), ii. 500–3, at 502.

427. L102, p. 279, and Walpole, 'Vida', fo. 60. Cf. *Misionera*, 224, suggesting that approval from Rome came earlier.

428. See Luisa's *Epistolario*, 453–4; for her reaction, see L101, p. 279.

429. Ribera to Creswell, 17 Sept. 1608, Encarnación, being Luisa's copies in which one version omits Zúñiga's comments. For the link between the archbishop and her uncle, see María Isabel Osorio, 'La biblioteca de Dn. Francisco Hurtado de Mendoza, marqués de Almazán', in F. R. Marsilla de Pascual and Lope Pascual Martínez, *Littera scripta in honorem prof. Lope Pascual Martínez* (Murcia, 2002), ii. 796 n. 13. For Ribera's rivalry with Caracena, see Benjamin Ehlers's outstanding study, *Between Christians*

and Moriscos: Juan de Ribera and Religious Reform in Valencia, 1568–1614 (Baltimore, 2006).

430. L73, p. 203.
431. BNE MS 10794 fos. 127–50, at pp. 133$^{r–v}$.
432. 'ese monstruo de esa mujer', L2, p. 100.
433. L56.
434. L47, p. 168.
435. L93, 23 Apr. 1608.
436. 5 Nov. 1608, L100, p. 277.
437. I owe this information to Dr Ciaran O'Scea of the European University Institute in Florence.
438. Ehlers, *Between Christians and Moriscos*, 145.
439. L99.
440. L108.
441. Encarnación, undated MS letter from Isabel with internal reference to L99.
442. L126, p. 326.
443. Isabel to Luisa, 1 Nov. 1610, in Luisa's *Epistolario*, at 459; see also Ehlers, *Between Christians and Moriscos*, 146–7.
444. PRO SP94/11 ii. fos. 341–2, at 342.
445. *EA*, L93, p. 245.
446. *This Tight Embrace*, 222.
447. *EA*, L106, p. 287.
448. See Sánchez, *The Empress, the Queen, and the Nun*, 33–4.
449. 'a n[uest]ro s[eño]r que nos saque, de esta uauilonia y nos lleue a uibir por quietud a n[uestr]o cassa porque aunque aqui se puede hazer algun Vien es con gran peligro y con grandes occasiones de caer en mil trauajos', BNE, MS 12859, fos. 115–116^v, Calderón to Luisa, 4 Sept. 1609, being a secretarial copy.
450. L127, at 327.
451. 'mala semilla', L137, at p. 343, and L138, p. 345.
452. See PRO 94/19, nos. 29 & 32.
453. Alonso de Velasco, 'Proceso', 361; see also Juan Pardo de Arenillas, 'Proceso', fo. 521^v, who mentions being sent at this time to persuade Luisa to leave England, presumably for Portaceli.
454. See Abad's comments, *Epistolario*, 78.
455. L142, p. 351.
456. 28 June 1608 (OS), in Foley, *Records*, ii. 503.
457. 'amigo y señor', L101, p. 277.
458. L111, p. 294.
459. L120; L130.
460. L107, p. 290.
461. L146, p. 357.
462. L107, p. 288.

463. L102, p. 279.

464. G. B. Harrison, *A Second Jacobean Journal* (London, 1958), 197.

465. AGS, E2513, s.f., Council to Felipe, 18 Apr. 1608.

466. L113, p. 297.

467. L115, p. 304.

468. L171, p. 402.

469. L113, p. 297.

470. L115, p. 303.

471. L113, p. 299.

472. Richard Blunt, 18 Oct. 1611, ARSI, MS Anglia 37, fo. 106.

473. L115, p. 304.

474. L120.

475. Loomie, *Spain and the Jacobean Catholics*, no. 45, Alonso de Velasco to Philip III, London 21 July 1610.

476. 'il Parocho di Londra', ARSI, MS Anglia 37, fo. 109^v.

477. L121, p. 312.

478. L121, p. 313.

479. L124, p. 324.

480. L124, p. 322.

481. L121, p. 312.

482. L125, p. 324.

483. L123, p. 318; ARSI, MS Anglia 37, fo. 109^v confirms the fraternal greetings sent by Roberts.

484. B. Camm, *A Benedictine Martyr in England, being the life of . . . John Roberts*, (London, 1888), is a useful conflation of several sources. Mr Ian Davies kindly gave me several references for this topic.

485. L125, p. 324. See also Scott's 'Martyrio', ARSI, MS Anglia 37; his contemporary account confirms Luisa's version but she is not mentioned to avoid jeopardising both her and the relics in her care.

486. For executions and Catholic devotion, see McClain, *Lest We Be Damned*, 72–8, 148–156, 168–9.

487. 'pedazo', L123, p. 319.

488. L137 and L140, p. 349.

489. L157, p. 377 and L137.

490. Loomie, *Spain and the Jacobean Catholics*, nos. 49 and 50. Velasco's friends claimed that Roberts did not want the ambassador to intervene.

491. Blunt, 10 Dec. 1610, ARSI, MS Anglia 37, fo. 110^v.

492. Luisa's *Epistolario*, 461.

493. L121, p. 314.

494. L127, p. 327.

495. 'Tanta es su caridad!', L160, p. 381.

496. 'como una berenjena, moreteado', L163, p. 388.

497. Caraman, *John Gerard*, 170. I am grateful to Professor Kenneth Fincham for sharing with me his unrivalled knowledge of George Abbot.

498. Intercept of Zúñiga to king of Spain (I have modernized the translation), 1 Aug. 1612, PRO SP94/19, no. 133, at fo. 134.

499. PRO/STAC8/16/17, and *Calendar of State Papers Domestic 1611–1618*, 10–11. An overview of the investigation is contained in Camm, *Benedictine Martyr in England*, 240–2.

500. L135, pp. 338–9.

501. L124, p. 321.

502. *HMC Downshire*, iii. 127.

503. L134, p. 337.

504. L130, p. 330.

505. RBM, MS II-2168, fo. 28.

506. 'la casa de ladrillo, con una torrecilla redonda, es la nuestra', L139, p. 347. This information has been provided by Nicholas Holder, who is writing the history of Spitalfields for the Museum of London Archaelogy Service (MOLAS).

507. 'la última de Londres en este barrio', L130, p. 330. See also F. H. W. Sheppard (ed.), *Survey of London*, vol. xxvii (1997), 'Spitalfields and Mile End New Town', 1–20, 39–51.

508. In Oct. 1613, Archbishop Abbot stated eight virgins had been living with her the year before, when two left for the continent, but were quickly replaced by two more, *HMC Downshire*, iv. 239.

509. L131, pp. 332–3.

510. 'era tan oculto a todos que con mucha dificultad le hallaron los que con cuydado le buscaran', Brough, 'Proceso', fo. 391.

511. L152, p. 371.

512. See 'Proceso', fos. 237^v, 361^{r-v}.

513. L149, p. 363.

514. See three unpublished letters in the Encarnación from Joyce and Elizabeth Smyth.

515. AGS, E2863/18 a–g, at a.

516. L150, p. 366.

517. See Ch. 17.

518. *Calendar of State Papers Venetian*, vol. xii. *1610–1613*, ed. H. R. Brown (London, 1905) 412, 406.

519. L151, p. 368. Despite his poor showing as an ambassador, in my *The Prince and the Infanta: The Cultural Politics of the Spanish Match* (London, 2003) I could at least have mentioned Velasco. He was an honourable and cultivated man if ill-suited to be an ambassador.

520. L162, p. 386.

521. Sir Charles Cornwallis, 'A Relation of the Carriage of the Marriages that should have been made between the Prince of England, and the Infanta Major, and also after with the younger Infanta of Spain', in W. Oldys and T. Park (eds.), *The Harleian Misc.*, iii (London, 1809), 397–408, at 402.

522. RBM, MS II-2173, '*el mas desollado vellaco*, que a criado dios, en la tierra desde que la poblo'.

523. L156, p. 374.

524. L161, p. 383.

525. L164, p. 390. A ducat was worth 11 *reales*, and in modern terms a *real* was worth 2 ½ pence.

526. L161; for an extensive paraphrase, see Rees, *Writings*, 99–101.

527. 'mas retirada y quieta', Bernardo de Rojas, 30 Apr. 1612, unpublished letter, Encarnación.

528. L163, pp. 388, 389.

529. For Newport's indictment, see Loomie, *Spain and the Jacobean Catholics*, 192–7.

530. 'ydo todos armados por si acaso fueran sentidos de las guardas que en aquellos lugares estauan puestos por el Magistrado', Velasco, 'Proceso', 362^v.

531. 'que no auia sido malo sin bueno el olor q[ue] le auia dado', Ximénez, 'Proceso', 58.

532. That their remains went to Spitalfields is indicated by the fact that it says they were brought '4 miles' from Tyburn ; her house in the Barbican was '2 miles' away the execution site, L138, p. 316 and L82, p. 223. The bodies of Roberts and Somers had almost certainly been brought to the Barbican, but their interception by the nightwatchmen assuredly made it wiser to use Spitalfields in future.

533. L151, p. 369.

534. Ariza, 'Proceso', fo. 410^v; also fo. 362^v.

535. L171, p. 402.

536. L170, p. 399.

537. *Docs. Inéditos*, iii. 273; for his financial difficulties, see AGS, MS E2589.

538. Cited in Carmen Manso Porto, *Don Diego Sarmiento de Acuña, conde de Gondomar (1567–1626): Erudito, mecenas y bibliófilo* (Santiago de Compostela, 1996), 19, and Tobío Fernández, *Gondomar y su triunfo sobre Raleigh*, 230–1; Lerma's liking for Gondomar is persistently exaggerated.

539. *Misionera*, app. 15, p. 411.

540. L175, p. 412.

541. Anonymous report, AGS, MS 2590/41, 20 Mar. 1613.

542. L171, p. 403.

543. L171, p. 402.

544. Francisco Suárez, *Defensio Fidei Catholicae*, ed. E. Elorduy y L. Pereña (Consejo Superior de Investigaciones Científicas) (Madrid, 1965).

545. *Docs. Inéditos*, iii. 151.

546. 'y nuestra casa es un chiquito monasterio', L123, p. 319; 'nuestra casa es como un monesterio', L131, p. 333; 'nuestra casa es verdaderamente un conventico', L137, p. 344. In Spanish 'monastery/*monesterio*' refers to a religious house for monks (*monjes*) *or* women (*monjas*).

547. L174, p. 410.

548. *Docs. Inéditos*, iii. 129.

549. Muñoz, 456.

550. Encarnación, 'Poyntes of my lady Dona luisa', with date confirmed in *HMC Downshire*, iv. 239.

551. One of the most vivid descriptions comes from Richard Brough, 'Proceso', fo. 390^v.

552. ARSI, MS Anglia 37, fo.109.

553. 'Proceso', Brough, fo. 391 recalled making a coffin for someone called Ann, and it is unclear if 'Michisan' is a mistake for 'Mistress Ann' or whether her full name was Ann Mitchison. The Ann who died was not Ann Garnet, as she outlived Luisa. For the reference to smallpox, see Mary Ward's account of the arrest in M. Fridl, *Englische Tugend-Schul ... von ... Maria Ward* (Augsburg, 1732), i. 150–2; for an English translation, see Chambers, *Mary Ward*, i. 330.

554. ARSI, MS Anglia 37, fos. 133, 109.

555. *HMC Downshire*, iv. 231.

556. Being the inference of the 'Vida', ch. 72, and of L176, p. 414, with the reference to Martin Varner presumably indicating M[ichael] V[alpolo].

557. RBM, MS 2168, fo. 32.

558. Abbot to William Trumbell, 29 Oct. 1613, *HMC Downshire*, iv. 239.

559. Muñoz, 459.

560. *HMC Downshire*, iv. 239.

561. *Docs. Inéditos,* iii. 155.

562. 'Proceso', Brough, 390^v.

563. Though praised for his defence of Luisa, the opportunity was taken severely to rebuke Gondomar for thinking he could return to Spain without permission, José García Oro, *Diego Sarmiento de Acuña, Conde de Gondomar y Embajador de España (1567–1626)* (Santiago de Compostela, 1997), 293.

564. 'por delante de las Puertas de el (sic) palacio, y por las calles mas publicas y principales f.148 de londres', 'Proceso', de la Fuente, 147^v–148.

565. George Birkhead to Thomas More, in M. Questier (ed.), *Newsletters from the Archpresbyterate of George Birkhead* (Camden Society, 5th ser., vol. 12;

Cambridge, 1998), 248; Birkhead adds that she had campaigned against them, p. 246.

566. L177, p. 415.

567. *Docs. Inéditos*, iii. 151.

568. See the introduction dedicated to James in *A treatise of antichrist concerning the defence of Cardinal Bellarmines Arguments, which invincibly demonstrate, that the pope is not antichrist*, by Michael Christopherson Priest (alias M. Walpole), also known as *A treatise of Antichrist . . . The First Part* (St Omer, 1613).

569. *Docs. Inéditos*, iii. 185; 'Vita', ch. 70.

570. L178.

571. AGS, E844, fos. 82–8, 112–14; her recall was commented on at her trial by the men from the embassy.

572. 'Proceso', de la Fuente, fo. 154.

573. 'Señora mia acuerdese de diego lemetediel quando este en el Çielo'; for the innumerable details of her death, see Abad, *Misionera*, 352–8, and Pinillos Iglesias, *Hilando Oro*, 210–12, with extensive quotations.

574. Blackfan to Rector of English College, Rome, 18 Jan. 1614, ARSI, Anglia 37, fos. 111^{r-v}.

575. For Spanish prejudices, see James S. Amelang, 'Mourning becomes Eclectic: Ritual Lament and the Problem of Continuity', *Past & Present*, 187 (2000), 3–31.

576. *Docs. Inéditos*, iii. 240–1; further details are supplied by Muñoz.

577. *Docs. Inéditos*, iii. 208, 240.

578. *Docs. Inéditos*, iii. 272–3, 'Proceso', Brough, fo. 391^{v}.

579. Muñoz, 474.

580. Accounts of her life and the obsequies in Seville were sent by the local Jesuits to their counterparts in Mexico, see *Misionera*, 421–2.

581. Muñoz, 480.

582. 'Proceso', Mariana de San José, fo. 609^{v}; the laying on of Luisa's finger was used in the convent to cure illnesses, and for Luisa's (frankly minor) miracles, see Muñoz, 518–25, and 522.

583. For the full version of Luisa's commentary (and another version of this poem), see *Tight Embrace*, 132–41. Muñoz's enumeration of her poems is generally accepted and was taken up by Abad.

584. The poem contains a reference to the mark branded on a slave.

Bibliography

Abad, Camilo M., *Una misionera española en la Inglaterra del Siglo XVII: Doña Luisa de Carvajal y Mendoza (1566–1614)* (Santander, 1966).

—— 'Un embajador español en la corte de Maximiliano II Don Francisco Hurtado de Mendoza (1570–1576)', *Miscelánea Comillas*, 43 (1965), 23–94.

—— Also *see* Carvajal y Mendoza, *Epistolario y Poesías*.

Actas de las Córtes de Castilla, vol. i (Madrid, 1877).

Acts of the Privy Council of England: 1613–1614, ed. J. R. Dasent (London, 1890–1964), vol. iii (1921).

Álvarez, T., (ed.), *Constituciones de las Carmelitas Descalzas 1562–1607* (*Monumenta Historica Carmeli Teresiani*, vol. 16; Rome, 1995).

Amelang, James S., 'Mourning becomes Eclectic: Ritual Lament and the Problem of Continuity', *Past & Present*, 187 (2000), 3–31.

Anstruther, Godfrey, *Vaux of Harrowden, a Recusant Family* (Newport, Mon., 1953).

Barrientos, Alberto, *Introducción a la lectura de Santa Teresa* (2nd edn., Madrid, 2002).

Beaven, A. B., *The Aldermen of the City of London* (2 vols., London 1908 and 1913).

Bennell, John, 'Shop and Office in Medieval and Tudor London', *London and Middlesex Archaeological Society*, 40 (1989), 189–206.

Betegón Díez, Ruth, *Isabel Clara Eugenia, Infanta de España y soberana de Flandes* (Barcelona, 2004).

Bouza, F., 'Docto y devoto: La biblioteca del Marqués de Almazán y Conde de Monteagudo (Madrid, 1591)', in A. Kohler and F. Edelmayer (eds.), *Hispania-Austria: Die Katholischen Könige, Maximilian I. und die Anfänge der Casa de Austria in Spanien* (2 vols., Vienna and Munich, 1993 and 1999), ii. 247–310.

Bowler, Hugh (ed.), *London Sessions Records 1605–1685* (Catholic Record Society 34, 1934).

Brett, Philip, *The Byrd Edition*, vol. v. (London, 1989).

Brown, H. R. (ed.), *Calendar of State Papers Venetian 1610–1613* (London, 1864–1947), vol. xii (1905).

Burrieza Sánchez, Javier, *Los milagros de la Corte: Marina de Escobar y Luisa de Carvajal en la Historia de Valladolid* (Valladolid, 2002).

Cabrera de Córdoba, Luis, *Felipe Segundo rey de España*, vol. iv (Madrid, 1877), with appendices.

—— *Historia de Felipe Segundo*, ed. J. M. Millán and C. J. de Carlos Morales (4 vols., Salamanca, 1998).

Calendar of State Papers, Domestic Series, of the reign of James I: preserved in the State Paper Department of Her Majesty's Public Record Office, ed. M.A.E. Green, ii *1611–1618* (London, 1858).

Camm, B., *A Benedictine Martyr in England, being the life of . . . John Roberts* (London, 1888).

Caraman, Philip, *Henry Garnet 1555–1606, and the Gunpowder Plot* (London, 1964).

—— *John Gerard, The Autobiography of an Elizabethan* (London, 1951).

Carvajal y Mendoza, Luisa de, *Epistolario y Poesías: Colección formada por don Jesús Gonzalez Marañon*, ed. C. M. Abad (Biblioteca de Autores Españoles, 179; Madrid, 1965).

—— *Escritos Autobiográficos*, introduction and notes by C. M. Abad (Barcelona, 1966).

Chambers, M. C. E., *The Life of Mary Ward (1585–1645)* (2 vols., London, 1882).

Chorpenning, J. F., 'The Pleasance, Paradise, and Heaven: Renaissance Cosmology and Imagery in the *Castillo Interior*', *Forum for Modern Language Studies*, 27 (1991), 138–47.

Christian, William, *Local Religion in Sixteenth Century Spain* (Princeton, 1981).

Cloud, Christine M., 'Embodied Authority in the Spiritual Autobiographies of Four Early Modern Women from Spain and Mexico' (doctoral thesis, Ohio State University, 2006).

Cornwallis, Sir Charles, 'A Relation of the Carriage of the Marriages that should have been made between the Prince of England, and the Infanta Major, and also after with the younger Infanta of Spain', in W. Oldys (ed.), *The Harleian Miscellany* (London, 1808–13), vol. iii (1809), 397–408.

Creswell, Joseph, *Historia de la vida y martirio que padesció este año 1595 el P. Henrico Valpolo* (Madrid, 1596).

Cruz, Anne J. 'Chains of Desire: Luisa de Carvajal y Mendoza's Poetics of Penance', in L. Charnon-Deutsch (ed.), *Estudios sobre escritoras hispánicas en honor de Georgina Sabat-Rivers* (Madrid, 1992), 97–112.

—— 'Luisa de Carvajal y Mendoza y su conexión jesuita', in *La mujer y su representación en las literaturas hispánicas*, being vol. ii of *Actas Irvine-92*, XI Congreso of the International Association of Hispanists (5 vols., Irvine, 1994), ed. Juan Villegas Morales, pp. 97–104.

—— 'Willing Desire: Luisa de Carvajal y Mendoza and Female Subjectivity', in Helen Nader (ed.), *Power and Gender in Renaissance Spain: Eight Women of the Mendoza Family*, ed. Helen Nader, Urbana, 2004), 177–93.

Davis, N. Z. *Women on the Margins: Three Seventeenth-Century Lives* (London, 1995).

De la Puente, Luis, *Vida y Escritos del V. P. Luis de la Puente de la Compañía de Jesús (1554–1624)*, ed. C. M. Abad (Comillas, 1957).

—— *Obras escogidas del V. P. Luis de la Puente*, ed. C. M. Abad (Biblioteca de Autores Españoles, 111; Madrid, 1958).

Report on the Manuscripts of the Marquess of Downshire: Papers of Sir William Trumbull, Historical Manuscripts Commission (75) (1924–), vols. iii. (1938) and iv. (1940), ed. A. B. Hinds et al.

Doyega de Mendieta, Iuan de, *Interrogatorio de pregvntas . . . de la vida, virtudes, santidad, y milagros de la sierua de Dios, y venerable señora, D. Lvisa de Carbajal y Mendoça* (Biblioteca Nacional de España, *signatura* VE 184/31).

Ehlers, Benjamin, *Between Christians and Moriscos: Juan de Ribera and Religious Reform in Valencia, 1568–1614* (Baltimore, 2006).

Escobar, Jesús, *The Plaza Mayor and the Shaping of Baroque Madrid* (Cambridge, 2004).

Evangelisti, S., *Nuns: A History of Convent Life 1450–1700* (Oxford, 2007).

Fernández Hoyos, A., *El obispo don Gutierre de Vargas, un madrileño del Renacimiento* (Caja de Madrid: Madrid, 1994).

Foley, H., *Records of the English Province of the Society of Jesus* (7 vols., London, 1875–83).

Fox, Gwyn, ' "The king disapproves . . . ": Luisa de Carvajal's London Mission, 1605–1614', in C. H. L. George and Julie Sutherland (eds.), *Heroes and Villains: The Creation and Propagation of an Image* (Durham, 2004), 33–43.

Fridl, M., *Englische Tugend-Schul . . . von . . . Maria Ward* (2 vols., Augsburg, 1732).

Froom, F. J. *A Site in Poultry* (London, 1950).

Fullerton, Georgiana Lady, *The Life of Luisa de Carvajal* (London, 1881).

Ganss, George E. (ed.), *The Constitutions of the Society of Jesus* (St Louis, 1970).

García Oro, José, *Diego Sarmiento de Acuña, Conde de Gondomar y Embajador de España (1567–1626)* (Santiago de Compostela, 1997).

Gondomar, count of. *see* Sarmiento de Acuña.

Goose, N., and Luu, L. (eds.), *Immigrants in Tudor and Early Stuart England* (Brighton, 2005).

Gregory, Brad S., *Salvation at Stake: Christian Martyrdom in Early Modern Europe* (Cambridge, Mass., 1999).

Haliczer, Stephen, *Between Exaltation and Infamy: Female Mystics in the Golden Age of Spain* (Oxford, 2002).

Hardman, Anne, *Life of the Venerable Anne of Jesus, Companion of St. Teresa of Avila, by a sister of Notre Dame de Namur* (London, 1932).

Harrison, G. B., *A Second Jacobean Journal* (London, 1958).

Hodcroft, F. W., '¿A mí un él?: Observations on *vos* and *el/ella* as Forms of Address in Peninsular Spanish', *Journal of Hispanic Research*, 2 (1993–4), 1–16.

Hufton, Olwen, 'Altruism and Reciprocity: The Early Jesuits and their Female Patrons', *Renaissance Studies*, 15 (2001), 328–53.

James VI and I, *Political Writings*, ed. J. Sommerville (Cambridge, 1994).

Kagan, Richard L., *Lucrecia's Dreams: Politics and Prophesy in Sixteenth-Century Spain* (Berkeley and Los Angeles, 1990).

Lehfeldt, E. A., *Religious Women in Golden Age Spain: The Permeable Cloister*, (Aldershot, 2005).

Levy-Navarro, Elena, 'The Religious Warrior: Luisa de Carvajal y Mendoza's Correspondence with Rodrigo de Calderón', in Jane Couchman and Ann Crabb (eds.), *Women's Letters Across Europe, 1400–1700: Form and Persuasion* (Aldershot, 2005), 263–73.

Loomie, A. J., *Guy Fawkes in Spain: The 'Spanish Treason' in Spanish Documents* (*Bulletin of the Institute of Historical Research*, special suppl. no. 9, Nov. 1971).

—— *Spain and the Jacobean Catholics*, i *1603–1612* (Catholic Record Society, no. 64, 1973).

—— *The Spanish Elizabethans: The English Exiles at the Court of Phillip II* (New York, 1963).

Lux-Sterrit, L., *Redefining Female Religious Life: French Ursulines and English Ladies in Seventeenth-Century Catholicism* (Aldershot, 2005).

McClain, Lisa, *Lest We Be Damned: Practical Innovation and Lived Experience among Catholics in Protestant England, 1559–1642* (London, 2004).

McCoog, Thomas M., *Robert Parsons and Claudio Acquaviva: Correspondence* (Archivum Historicum Societatis Iesu, 68; 1999), 79–182.

Manso Porto, Carmen, *Don Diego Sarmiento de Acuña, conde de Gondomar (1567–1626): Erudito, mecenas y bibliófilo* (Santiago de Compostela, 1996).

Mendoza, B. de, Letter to Philip II, 4 Dec. 1581, *Colección de Documentos Inéditos para la Historia de España*, ed. M. Fernández Navarrete, vol. 92 (Madrid, 1888).

Millán, J. M., (ed.), *La Monarquía de Felipe II: La Casa del Rey* (2 vols., Madrid 2005).

Minsheu, John, *A dictionarie in Spanish and English, first published into the English tongue by Ric. Perciuale Gent. Now enlarged and amplified . . .* (London, 1599).

Mottola, A., *The Spiritual Exercises of Saint Ignatius* (New York, 1964).

Muñoz, Luis, *Vida y virtudes de la Venerable virgen doña Luisa de Carvajal y Mendoza* (1631; re-edited Madrid, 1897).

Nader, Helen (ed.), *Power and Gender in Renaissance Spain: Eight Women of the Mendoza Family* (Urbana and Chicago, 2004).

Oldys, W., and Park, T. (eds.), *The Harleian Miscellany: A Collection of Scarce, Curious, and Entertaining Pamphlets and Tracts, as well in Manuscript as in Print*, iii (1809).

Orchard, M. Emmanuel (ed.), *Till God Will: Mary Ward through her Writings* (London, 1985).

Osorio, María Isabel, 'La biblioteca de Dn. Francisco Hurtado de Mendoza, marqués de Almazán', in F. R. Marsilla de Pascual and Lope Pascual Martínez (eds.), *Littera scripta in honorem prof. Lope Pascual Martínez* (Murcia, 2002), ii. 789–806.

Owen, Lewis *The Key of the Spanish Tongue* (London, 1605).

—— *The State of the English Colledges in Forraine Parts London 1626 (The English Experience: Its record in early printed books published in facsimile*, 19; Amsterdam, 1968).

Oxford Dictionary of National Biography, ed. H. C. G. Matthew and B. Harrison (Oxford, 2004).

Peers, E. Allison, *The Complete Works of St Teresa of Jesus* (3 vols. in one, London, 1978).

Peters, H., *Mary Ward: A World in Contemplation*, trans. H. Butterworth (Leominster, 1994).

Petti, A. G., 'Richard Verstegan and Catholic Martyrologies of the Later Elizabethan Period', *Recusant History*, 5 (1959–60), 64–90.

Pinillos Iglesias, M. N., *Hilando Oro: Vida de Luisa de Carvajal* (Madrid, 2001).

Poutrin, Isabelle, *Le Voile et la Plume: Autobiographie et sainteté féminine dans l'Espagne moderne* (Madrid, 1995).

Questier, Michael C., *Catholicism and Community in Early Modern England: Politics, Aristocratic Patronage and Religion, c.1550–1640* (Cambridge, 2006).

—— (ed.), *Newsletters from the Archpresbyterate of George Birkhead* (Camden Society, 5th ser., vol. 12; Cambridge, 1998).

Rahner, Hugo, *St Ignatius Loyola : Letters to Women* (London, 1960).

Redworth, Glyn, *The Prince and the Infanta: The Cultural Politics of the Spanish Match* (London, 2003).

—— 'Books Not to be Sold: The Cost of Printing in the Golden Age', *Bulletin of the Society for Renaissance Studies*, 23 (2005), 17–26.

Rees, M. A., *The Writings of doña Luisa de Carvajal y Mendoza, Catholic Missionary to James I's London* (Lewiston, NY and Lampeter, 2003).

—— 'The Gaze of God: Doña Luisa de Carvajal y Mendoza and the English Mission', in John Macklin and Margaret A. Rees (eds.), *Convivium: Celebratory Essays for Ronald Cueto* (Leeds, 1997), 97–114.

Rhodes, Elizabeth, 'Join the Jesuits, See the World: Early Modern Women in Spain and the Society of Jesus', in John W. O'Malley et al. (eds.), *The Jesuits II: Cultures, Sciences, and the Arts 1540–1773* (Toronto, 2006).

—— 'Luisa de Carvajal's Counter-Reformation Journey to Selfhood (1566–1614)', *Renaissance Quarterly*, 51 (1998), 887–911.

—— *This Tight Embrace: Luisa de Carvajal y Mendoza (1566–1614)*, (Milwaukee, 2000).

Salón, M. B., *Oración panegírica . . . de . . . doña Isabel de Velasco y Mendoza . . . con una breve relación de la muerte de doña Luysa de Carvajal* (Valencia, 1616).

Sánchez, Magdalena, *The Empress, the Queen, and the Nun: Women and Power at the Court of Philip III of Spain* (London and Baltimore, 1998).

Sánchez Ortega, M. H., *La mujer y la sexualidad en el antiguo regimen* (Madrid, 1991).

Sarmiento de Acuña, Diego, *Correspondencia Oficial de Don Diego Sarmiento de Acuña, conde de Gondomar*, ed. A. Ballesteros Beretta (*Documentos Inéditos para la Historia de España*, series ed. Jacobo Stuart Fitz-James y Falcó, duke of Alba) iii (Madrid, 1944).

Schroeder, H. (ed.), *The Canons and Decrees of the Council of Trent* (Rockford, 1978).

Sheppard, F. H. W. (ed.), *Survey of London*, vol. xxvii (1997), 'Spitalfields and Mile End New Town'.

Sicroff, Albert A., *Les Controverses des statut de "pureté de sang" en Espagne du xve au xviie siècle* (Paris, 1960).

Spinnenweber, Kathleen T., 'The 1611 English Translation of St. Teresa's Autobiography: A Possible Carmelite-Jesuit Collaboration', *SKASE Journal of Translation and Interpretation* [online] 2 (2007), 1–12.

Suárez, Francisco, *Defensio Fidei Catholicae*, ed. E. Elorduy y L. Pereña (Consejo Superior de Investigaciones Científicas) (Madrid, 1965).

Tobío Fernández, Luis, *Gondomar y su triunfo sobre Raleigh* (Santiago de Compostela, 1974).

Urkiza, Julián, *Obras completas de la Beata Ana de San Bartolomé* (Monumenta Historica Carmeli Teresiani; Rome, 1981).

Walpole, Michael, *A treatise of antichrist concerning the defence of Cardinal Bellarmines Arguments, which invincibly demonstrate, that the pope is not antichrist*, by Michael Christopherson Priest (alias M. Walpole: part 1, St Omer, 1613).

Weber, A, 'Spiritual Administration: Gender and Discernment in the Carmelite Reform', *Sixteenth Century Journal*, 31 (2000), 123–46.

Wiesner-Hanks, Merry E., *Early Modern Europe, 1450–1789* (Cambridge, 2006).

Wormald, Jenny, 'Gunpowder, Treason, and Scots', *Journal of British Studies*, 24 (1985), 141–68.

Index